This book is for you if...

1. You want to generate sales and plenty of them from your marketing.

2. You want to reduce the amount of money you're spending (or wasting) on marketing.

3. You want to unearth a treasure trove of powerful, effective and proven 'insider' marketing tips and techniques.

4. You want to reduce your marketing mistakes and increase your marketing successes.

5. You want access to page after page of easy to absorb, expert marketing commonsense, not textbook theory.

6. You want to learn and be inspired by real business case studies.

7. You don't have all the money in the world to spend on marketing but you are willing to invest some time.

8. You've read marketing books before that have either baffled you or left you unimpressed.

9. You want to grow your business consistently through delighting your customers and turning them into raving fans.

10. You just don't 'get' marketing. You need to be convinced as to its real value in growing your business.

A little about Dee Blick

Dee started her marketing career in 1985 as a graduate marketing trainee working for a global insurance company. She was promoted rapidly and within just three years was entrusted with planning and running direct mail, advertising and marketing campaigns for some of the UK's biggest brands. After taking a little time off to bring up her two boys, Dee started her own marketing consultancy in 2001, realising that the tips, tools and techniques that she had learned within a corporate setting could be applied to small businesses with incredible results, and on a shoestring budget. She now works with a diverse group of businesses, helping them to grow with her no-nonsense, practical and down to earth approach to marketing.

Dee has extensive experience in new product development and marketing strategy, and has a track record of creating and delivering exceptional campaigns. She is also frequently called upon for her marketing troubleshooting skills to ascertain why a business is failing in its marketing.

Dee has an exceptional talent for writing and has won seven national awards for writing press releases and adverts, each having generated the highest reader response in its respective publication. She is also an avid blogger, and a regular columnist for many printed publications. Her first book, Powerful Marketing on a Shoestring Budget for Small Businesses, is in Amazon UK's top five bestselling small business books and has received dozens of five-star reviews.

In 2009, Dee featured as a marketing entrepreneur on BBC's 'Beat the Boss' alongside the 'The Apprentice' star, Saira Khan; an experience that resulted in Dee becoming a popular and sought after public speaker. In response to many requests from her readers, Dee has recently launched a series of one day Marketing on a Shoestring boot camps for small businesses.

Dee is also a Fellow of the Chartered Institute of Marketing, the highest status that can be awarded by the world's largest marketing body.

The Ultimate Small Business Marketing Book

By Dee Blick

Published by Filament Publishing Ltd
16, Croydon Road, Waddon,
Croydon, Surrey, CR0 4PA UK
Telephone +44 (0)20 8688 2598
Fax +44 (0)20 7183 7186
info@filamentpublishing.com
www.filamentpublishing.com

Printed by Berforts Group - Stevenage and Hastings
Distributed by Gardners

ISBN 978-1-905493-77-7

For Malcolm, Steven, Mark and Mum with love

Contents

Foreword

If you're considering reading this book, I'm guessing that you are either thinking of starting a business and you need your marketing to generate new customers quickly, or you're already in business and you've realised it's time to get to grips with your marketing to increase sales and make more money. Perhaps you are struggling with how to gain more customers or how to increase the number of prospects that convert to customers. Maybe your focus is on generating more sales from your existing client base. Or perhaps you are looking for a bit of everything. Well I can reassure you that this book will show you step-by-step how to achieve all of this – in a series of jargon free, easy to understand chapters. Each chapter is underpinned with genuine small business case studies and includes tips that you can apply with confidence, knowing that they have worked time and time again in the real business world. It does not matter what you do, the principles and strategies in this book can be readily applied to your business.

To demonstrate that marketing is simple, inspiring and accessible has been my life's mission. I am a qualified and experienced marketer that has chosen to specialise in working with small businesses. I understand the challenges that small businesses face and the common mistakes that they make when trying to market their business. I hope that as you read each chapter of this book, you will feel that you are on the receiving end of a hefty dose of expert marketing and business commonsense. In my opinion, marketing commonsense is most definitely uncommon.

Many small businesses spend time searching for that one elusive marketing tool or tactic to somehow transform their business. In fact they should instead be focusing on being brilliant at the basics and marketing consistently. The many proven tips and powerful marketing tools shared in this book will help you to achieve incredible results for your business – more qualified prospects, more sales, more recommendations and more delighted customers.

It has taken me over a year to write this book and doing so has been a real joy. I hope that you enjoy reading it as much as I enjoyed writing it, that it inspires you to greater business success, and that you end up looking upon it as your trusted marketing companion.

Good luck. I wish you success and happiness in building your business. Please write to me and let me know how you get on.

Dee Blick FCIM, Chartered Marketer.

CHAPTER 1

INTRODUCING THE 90-MINUTE MARKETING MASTERCLASS

Whenever I ask business owners to tell me what they believe the word 'marketing' means, you can be sure that each response will vary. 'Marketing is all about advertising', I hear, or 'It's producing sales leaflets and brochures', 'It's supporting the sales force', 'Marketing is all about networking with the right people'. Whilst each one of these responses is true to some extent, they also illustrate the misunderstanding that surrounds the meaning of marketing. Let's start this first chapter on the right footing with one of the best definitions of marketing that I have come across in the last 26 years. It's from the late Peter Doyle, who was one of the world's leading consultants on marketing and strategy. In his book, Marketing Management & Strategy, he defines marketing thus:

> ***'Marketing is a philosophy of business that places the customer at the centre of the universe.'***

What I really like about this definition is that it clearly defines marketing as being 100% about the customer. Most small business owners are in business because they have seen the potential in striking out on their own with what they believe is a winning product or service. However, once their initial excitement has subsided, they will only be successful in growing their fledgling idea into a sustainable and profitable business if they are fully customer-focused. Using Doyle's definition, we can see that marketing should run through every part of a small business - sales, finance, business development, IT, administration and customer care. By inference therefore, each element of a small business should have the needs of the customer at its core, and all decisions should be taken with the customer firmly in mind.

'How will this proposed change impact on our customers? Will they welcome it or regard it as a negative move?'

This question should be explored in detail before any changes are made to the business. In this way, the changes that are implemented will enhance the customer's experience, or at least avoid having a negative impact on the relationship that your customers have with your business.

And what about the connection between marketing and sales? Again, many small business owners confuse the role of marketing with the role of selling, and this is something that we can clear up with another statement from Peter Doyle:

> ***'Selling tries to push the customer to buy what the business has. Marketing, on the other hand, tries to get the organisation to develop and offer what the customer will find is of real value. In this way marketing seeks to build long term, mutually beneficial partnerships between the organisation and its customers.'***

This chapter and the seven that follow have been written to provide you with many of the tools that you will need to build long term and mutually beneficial partnerships between your small business and your customers. Marketing experience is not necessary to put these tools, tips and suggestions into practice, and in doing so you will see some remarkable results from your efforts.

I have worked with a number of small business owners that mistakenly believed that they could not market their business successfully because they had neither the relevant qualifications nor selling experience. *This is not true*. If you remain determined to place the 'customer at the centre of the universe', and to build your business on the simple but powerful ambition to satisfy the needs of your customers, you have the foundations for success. This book provides you with the practical marketing know-how you need to grow your business.

The case studies that feature throughout are those of small businesses like yours. Hopefully this will help you to identify with them and be inspired by their success. These are businesses that have achieved success with little, if any, previous marketing experience.

Another misconception about marketing is that little can be achieved without spending vast sums of money. Let me briefly return to the theme of my first book, the philosophy of marketing on a shoestring budget, and explain how you can bring this into the heart of your business.

The Benefits of Marketing on a Shoestring

After working for many years with blue-chip companies and annual marketing budgets in excess of £1 million, I realised that the same marketing ideas and strategies that I followed could be applied with equal effect to small businesses. For example, let's take 'lumpy mail'. Lumpy mail is a term used to describe a mailshot that includes a promotional item or product sample. The inclusion of this item causes the envelope to appear lumpy and therefore more intriguing to the recipient. This greatly increases the likelihood of the envelope being opened and the message inside being read. Lumpy mail is equally effective whether you have a budget of £100 or £500,000, provided that the lumpy element of your mailshot is relevant to the recipient.

The five 90-minute Marketing Masterclasses covered in this chapter require very little, if any, financial expenditure. The biggest investment required is your time. You only need to make a commitment to allocate 90 uninterrupted minutes of your time to marketing activity once a week to begin to see the results of your efforts. Set aside an extra day each month and you will be significantly rewarded for your commitment.

'Marketing on a shoestring' is most definitely not 'Marketing as cheaply as possible'. Cutting costs with poor quality sales literature, for example, can damage your brand with both existing customers and prospects. Instead, marketing on a shoestring is about investing your time and effort (rather than hard-earned cash) into building a customer-centred business, and communicating all that is great about your business in a relevant, professional and compelling manner.

Reviewing your marketing activities and halting those activities that are no longer serving the needs of your business, for example, is something that can reduce your marketing spend rather than increase it. You may have been spending money advertising in a local publication and yet subsequently identify that the local market is not one that you need to reach. Alternatively you may identify a more cost-effective way of communicating with your local market. In either case, the advertising should be reviewed and curtailed. Continuing to do what you have always done simply because you are familiar with it and it seems like too much effort to change, is the antithesis of marketing on a shoestring.

There are a number of effective marketing practices that can be employed without the need to spend money. Another example is collaboration between all relevant parties to ensure that each marketing activity is given the best chance of success. Don't fall into the trap of thinking that marketing is the responsibility of your telemarketer, your salesperson or your administrator. Everyone in your small business is responsible at some level for marketing, and this is something that we explore further in Chapter 5. If you are the business owner, it's your responsibility to ensure that marketing is the seam that runs throughout every element of your business. If you appoint a telemarketer, don't simply give them a 30-minute introduction to your business before leaving them to their own devices and expecting them to achieve miracles. Work closely with them, inspire them with your vision, explain your customer-centred ethos and ensure that they have sufficient information to represent your business successfully.

And be consistent in your marketing. The small businesses that continue to grow and increase their profitability, even when surrounded by competitors, are those that make a commitment to marketing their business consistently. When sales are climbing, they don't stop marketing. They may change their direction from attracting more customers to focusing instead on further improving what they offer. They may decide to put their networking and advertising on ice, and instead build their profile and reputation through PR. But they maintain continuous marketing activity. The benefit of doing so is that when times are lean, and demand is falling as a result, the businesses that have maintained their marketing presence are less likely to feel the same icy chill being experienced by their competitors.

Had We but World Enough and Time

Time is elusive, I know. And it can be a challenge for a small business owner to find sufficient time to devote to marketing their business. But that time *must* be found if you are aiming for real, measurable growth in your business. Something that I'm regularly asked when speaking at small business events is how much time should be devoted to marketing. My answer is that there are two ways in which marketing time can be spent. The first, and perhaps the easiest to give, is the time that you spend when servicing your customers. If you are focusing on how you can make their experience enjoyable and beneficial each time, you are marketing your business successfully. But the inescapable fact is that you will also need to earmark time outside the day-to-day running of your business, and spend it proactively marketing your business.

As mentioned earlier, if you can start by finding one 90-minute slot each week, you are off to a good start. Each of the five Masterclasses that follow is designed to provide a real, concentrated boost to your marketing in key areas. You will also need to allow some time to implement the actions that arise from your investigations and ideas. I would suggest that you set aside approximately one day every month to implement your marketing actions and to write your marketing communications. If you use the tools detailed in subsequent chapters and study the practical examples provided, this will enable you to use your marketing time effectively.

So let's take a look at how we can place some very important areas of your business under the marketing spotlight.

Five 90-Minute Marketing Masterclasses – Simple Rules for Success

For your business to really benefit from these Masterclasses, please book 90 minutes in your diary once a week. Find a space in which there is no risk of being distracted by phone calls, e-mails or visitors. Be prepared to commit your thoughts into writing – a pad, flipchart, your laptop, notepad etc. The quality of your thinking is instrumental in getting the most from these sessions. However it is the quality of what you *record* from each session that leads thought into actions. Beside each recorded action, add a date by which it should be accomplished and the name of the person responsible for owning the action.

I have placed these Masterclasses in what I believe is the right order for you. Even if you have recently made some of the recommended changes, it won't do any harm to revisit your plans in the light of the tips and advice being shared.

1. The Product and Service Review Masterclass

You will find this Masterclass beneficial whether you are just starting out in business and still considering the products or services that you are going to offer, or are a well established business.

Most small businesses undersell themselves simply because they have given insufficient thought to their products or services and how they can be segmented to really connect with their potential buyers. Let me illustrate this with the example of a pet sitting business, Tranquil Pets, Homes & Gardens, a licensee of The Pets Homes and Gardens Company. The licensees, Julie and Sarah, wanted to offer dog walking services. They both love dogs, are experienced dog owners, and have many years experience working with dogs in kennels. Initially, they had planned to advertise their dog walking services in much the same way that most pet sitters do, i.e. a line of text, followed by the cost of the walk. By earmarking just 90 minutes for their product and service review, looking particularly at how they could segment their dog walking services, they arrived at the following list:

- Cross-country, energetic dog walks.
- Your dog's favourite walk, to his exact route.
- Short walks, either locally or at a favourite park or woods some miles away.

- Bespoke dog walks. Tell us how long or short you want each walk to be each time.
- Partnering up and walking with your dog's favourite doggy companion.
- Wellbeing dog walks for dogs recovering from an illness or on a weight loss programme.
- Early morning dog walks to suit commuters.

You can see that by going into this level of detail about the range of dog walking services that they can offer, Julie and Sarah will attract customers seeking a service tailored to their needs and those of their dog. The dog walking service is now more appealing because specific needs are being addressed.

Another licensee, Paradise Pets and Homes, came up with the simple but ingenious idea of sending a daily text message and accompanying picture to devoted pet owners when they were on holiday to show them that their beloved pet was being very well cared for. It's a simple, low cost service but it provides added value to the customer and it reinforces their decision to choose Paradise Pets and Homes over less customer-focused competitors.

Look upon what you offer your customers as a diamond; a whole, but with many facets. Don't be content with producing just one line of bland text about your products or services. Go into more detail, using the dog walking example as a guide.

Make a list of the services or products that you are going to offer or that you currently provide, allowing a gap under each one to add in the detail.

Let's look at how this same approach could work with a service provider, such as a marketing consultant looking to promote their expertise to small businesses. They could promote their marketing consultancy in hourly, half-day and full-day slots to small businesses. This is not a bad start but they could go one step further and promote their expertise as follows:

- 60 minute one-to-one marketing Masterclasses.
- Three hour intensive marketing seminars, focusing on one specific small business marketing need.
- One day marketing planning workshops.
- Four hour 'troubleshooting' marketing clinic.
- 60 minute marketing health check.
- 30 minute complimentary telephone marketing session.
- 45 minute follow-up marketing mentoring sessions.
- Bespoke marketing package - the number of hours and commitment that your business needs on an ongoing basis.

Similar to the example of Tranquil Pets, Homes & Gardens, the marketing consultant does not need to increase the range of services they provide to attract more customers. They just need to make their services more enticing and appealing to their target audience. For many professional service providers it can be a real challenge to stand out and many rely upon fairly generic descriptions of what they provide. This, unfortunately, only reinforces their similarity to other businesses.

Another example is that of K A Marklew Associates, a bookkeeping business keen to inspire their target audiences with the services they offer. They went through this exercise and without having to expand upon the range of services they provide to clients, they developed five 60-minute health checks as follows:

- A start-up business bookkeeping and accounting health check.
- A credit control health check.
- A Sage training health check.
- An accounting function health check.
- A bookkeeping health check.

These health checks were then offered without charge to targeted businesses. Those businesses that expressed an interest in one of these health checks were provided with a fact sheet explaining what the health check would cover and its many benefits. Because these health checks are seen as being much more inspirational and enlightening than the more common bookkeeping offerings, they have proved to be very successful in gaining new local clients and in building the reputation of the business with accountants.

So, the three key questions to ask yourself are:

1. **How can I segment what I offer** so that I can appeal to all my targeted customers? Use the previous examples as a guide.

2. **Are there any specific improvements** that I need to make to my products and services? Are there any that can be easily implemented and at little financial cost?

3. **Are there any products or services that I need to mothball** for the time being because they are not in demand? Don't promote something that nobody now needs just because it was popular once. Archive or remove it.

In the next three chapters we look at how to promote your products and services through on-line and off-line sales communications. By answering these three questions beforehand, it will help make your communications more powerful, exciting and most importantly, targeted.

2. The Target Audience Review Masterclass

More often than not, a small business in its initial months of trading grows through a combination of hard work and the power of recommendation. Recommendations often come from two sources - networking and existing customers. Growth, however, can be haphazard, punctuated by barren spells during which little business is coming in. This can be unsettling and can make business planning difficult. The results of this haphazard growth can lead to one of two things. One is that the business may unintentionally become a specialist in a particular sector. For example, if the business takes on a customer in one sector, it may find that recommendations on the strength of their work are made only to other businesses in that same sector. The second option is that the business owner tries to sell to everyone they encounter regardless of whether there is a clear need for their services or not. Both situations limit the potential growth of the business. If the icy chill of recession strikes at the heart of the sector you are servicing, you could find that your business is dramatically reduced almost overnight. By continuing to service customers to a high standard and delivering on your promises, it is likely that work will continue to come in. It is difficult, however, to build a business on this alone. You are not in control and you can't influence the volume of business that you will receive.

You need to develop proactive marketing campaigns in which the people that you want to communicate with, your target audience, are identified.

- **Write down in as much detail as possible** who you would like to target in the next 12 months. You could start off with a generic heading - Accountants, for example - but should then break this category down further by including more specific details, such as the size of accountancy practice, where the practice is based geographically and whether the accountants are Certified or Chartered. Is it important whether the practice is well established or has recently started up? The more specific the information, the more targeted you can become.

- **When considering who you want to target**, you must have in your mind at all times your compelling reasons for doing so. For example, has your research suggested that this particular audience has a deep underlying need for your services and should therefore be very receptive to what you have to offer?

- **Consider whether you need to divide your target audience** into groups based on their differing needs. Are you purely targeting customers to whom you will be selling directly, or are you also targeting influencers - groups that will recommend you to their members or customers? For example, AccountAssyst, an on-line credit management company, targets both end-users of their system (small businesses in sectors especially exposed to the risk of bad debt) and influencers, strategic partners that can recommend AccountAssyst to their members or clients. This includes trade associations, chambers of commerce, and accountants.

- **It's important that you define your target audience** into distinct groups because you will not treat each group in precisely the same way. Your marketing communications must be relevant and targeted if they are to receive a positive reception. This is covered extensively in the following chapters. Something as simple as individualising the introduction to a sales letter can be all that's needed to achieve the personal touch.

- **Have you considered the media when looking at influencers?** Trade magazines, local newspapers, community magazines, specialist publications and national newspapers can all play their part in promoting your services, not to mention the various newsletters and magazines produced by the influencers that you want to bring on board. Find out which publications are most read by each one of your target audiences, and when researching your influencers, review the marketing communications that they use to communicate with their customers or members. There could be opportunities for you to carry your message through these channels.

- **At some stage you may want to embark on a targeted PR campaign**. Your local library and the Internet will yield the information that you will be looking for, such as magazine groups and on-line publications etc.

- **Once you have created a small, detailed list of the different groups** that you want to target, you need to identify the various businesses that fall into each group. There are many sources from which you can obtain this data, one of which being the Royal Mail website, *www.royalmail.com.* This is an excellent and trusted website with many resources, including low-cost consumer and business-to-business mailing lists. You can even clean your own lists using their on-line tools. The website also has very useful information on direct mail, with tips on how to increase the response to your targeted mailshot campaigns. Another website that I can recommend for high quality business mailing lists is that of Marketscan Ltd, *www.marketscan.co.uk*

- **It will help immensely if you are able to identify** and then deal with the decision-maker for each of your target businesses. You should be able to find this information by making a quick call to the business itself, by searching the company website or even by asking the people with whom you network whether they have any information on the specific businesses that you are looking to contact. In a small business, the decision-maker is usually one person - the managing director. You are therefore able to focus your attention on that one person. However, the bigger the organisation, the more likely it is that several people will influence the decision to buy. In these cases, if you focus your attention on just one individual, you are less likely to get the sale. This is because that individual will be required to sell you to the other members of the decision-making team before a decision to do business with you can be reached, and they are unlikely to be as good at singing your praises as you are yourself. There may be several people in the decision-making unit including:

    - **The initiator** - this person will make the initial suggestion to buy. You could meet the initiator at a networking event.
    - **The influencer** - this person will advise on the buying decision.
    - **The decider** - this person decides whether to buy, how to buy and where to buy from.

- **The buyer** - this person will make the actual purchase. It could be someone from the Accounts Department who doesn't need to know anything about you, nor have any previous contact with you. They will simply act upon instruction.
- **The user(s)** - this is the person or people who will use the product. They may be from within the company or customers of the company. Their vote counts – both in any initial trials and subsequent purchase.

If you can gather as much information as possible about the decision-makers in your target businesses, you are off to a good start. It may not be easy or even possible to do so in all cases, and you may find that you need to gather a little more information each time you communicate with your prospective client. But keep it in mind at all times. **Your chances of success will greatly increase if you are marketing your business appropriately, and to the right people.**

It would also be an advantage if you can unravel the decision-making process at the same time as identifying the decision-maker(s). This will help you to understand *how* your target businesses arrive at their decision to buy.

In my experience, decision-making processes are either simple or long-winded, with nothing in between! They also vary from sector to sector. For example, Dyno-Pest, a pest control company, are required by some businesses to complete pre-qualification tenders before even being allowed to go through the tendering process, whereas for others it is simply a matter of meeting with the business owner, surveying their premises, submitting a survey with an itemisation of cost, and the process is complete. Some customers will have a documented decision-making process that they are happy to provide you with. Others may be a little more vague. Ask, don't assume.

Any information you gather is absolutely vital if you are to build a marketing campaign that is both tailored and relevant, and that delivers the right communications at the right time. Most businesses overlook this process. Don't do the same, and it will stand you in good stead.

Determine which groups you want to target first, and why. Start with those businesses that you believe will be most receptive to your message. And, when you start targeting these businesses, don't be tempted to tackle huge numbers all in one go. Bear in mind the supportive infrastructure that will need to be in place to handle the prospecting and the delivery process. How much new business can you handle at any one time? Also, it is a good idea to test your initial approach on a handful of prospects to start with. You could find that you need to make subtle improvements to your message in the light of the feedback from the first approach.

Finally, you need to marry what you offer with the needs of each of your targeted groups, being sure to focus on your ability to satisfy these needs and deliver value. In subsequent chapters, you'll find that this is an oft-repeated mantra. Don't assume that everyone has the same needs and resort to a one-size-fits-all approach.

3. The Marketing Audit Masterclass

The first question I ask a small business that I'm going to be working with is how have they been marketing their business to date. When listening to the answer, I am regularly surprised by the amount of money that has been spent on random and non-targeted marketing. Although many small business owners tell me that they work to a very strict marketing budget, it often turns out that they have in fact been spending thousands of pounds on marketing without being aware of it. For example, I was recently approached by a franchisee with a retail outlet specialising in selling office consumables. They had been established for 12 months and despite what they claimed was a streamlined marketing programme, were not generating anywhere near the volume of sales that was needed to cover their overheads, let alone make a profit. When we itemised their marketing activities, noting the cost and the generated sales, we discovered that without realising it, they had spent £20,000 within 12 months, most of it on advertising and business networking. When I asked the business owner why he had chosen to spend over 80% of his budget on advertising and to continue with this strategy despite the fact that the adverts were failing to deliver, he was unable to give a rational explanation. Because he had not invested any quality thinking and planning time beforehand, defining who he wanted to reach and the most effective ways of communicating with this target audience, he had gone down the familiar path of many small businesses, namely networking and advertising.

Another small business, specialising in recruiting staff into the Care sector, had spent thousands of pounds on a direct mail list of care home managers and had been bombarding the people on the list each month with a home-made, uninspiring newsletter. Although this had worked initially to some extent and they had recruited a handful of new clients, their unsophisticated and ill targeted direct mail techniques had long since failed to deliver any new clients. Despite this, they continued to mail the list in the same manner, every month, simply because they had no Plan B.

And this is a common problem. Often a small business owner will persist with the same marketing activity whether it is working or not, simply because they don't know what to replace it with. Sometimes they have become comfortable with one particular marketing arrangement. The thought of change can seem to be more hassle than it's worth.

A regular marketing audit is absolutely essential for your business. It is imperative that you look back over your marketing activities and communications, identifying what has worked, what hasn't worked and how much each activity and communication has cost.

Start by writing down a list of your marketing efforts in the last 12 months. Your list may include some of the following:

- Local advertising - in community magazines and local newspapers.
- National advertising - in trade magazines, consumer magazines, specialist titles and newspapers.
- PR - you may have been promoting your business yourself or used a PR specialist.
- Local or national exhibitions.
- Radio advertising.
- Direct mail.
- Conferences.
- E-mail marketing campaigns.
- Blogging, on-line articles.
- Your website - search engine optimisation, pay per click advertising.
- Telemarketing - you may have made the calls yourself or used another resource.
- Organising seminars or events.
- Joint marketing initiatives with partners, suppliers or customers.

- Business networking - attending a regular group and ad-hoc networking.
- On-line directories and on-line advertising schemes.
- Sales promotion campaigns for resellers or direct to your customers.
- Referral campaigns.

Next, make a list of the on-line and printed literature that you have created and the cost of producing each item.

Now you have your list, it's time to review what you have spent and the return you received by way of increased sales and new customers. It's not going to be an exact science because in the real world, there will be some costs that you can't account for and some activities that you have forgotten. And with PR, it's very difficult to account for the financial contribution that it has made to your business beyond raising your profile. You may also need to group some of your marketing activities together and look at the total cost. If you have been working to the principle of the Power of Three, (we cover this principle in Chapter 3), you're not going to be able to judge individual marketing activities on their own merits. Rather, you will need to combine the cost of each element and then measure how many new customers or increased sales you obtained as a consequence of the campaign.

At this stage it is worth considering what your expectations were for each marketing activity, each campaign. Did you establish any yardstick by which you could measure the success of the campaign? Perhaps you just hoped that it would work and that you would make a profit? Don't worry if you have been a little vague in your objectives until now. Your marketing audit is the perfect opportunity to move your marketing activities onto a more strategic and measurable footing. From now on, when you are considering spending time and money on a particular marketing activity, ask yourself the following three questions:

1. **Will this be effective in reaching my target audience and if so, how many of the audience will it reach?** Is it too many or not enough? Is it impossible to measure? For example, a telemarketing campaign aimed at named decision-makers can be very precise whereas an advert in a trade magazine can be targeted but there is no way of knowing how many of the target audience will actually read the advert. Sometimes you will need to rely on your own gut feeling to judge whether the potential return justifies the cost of the activity.

2. **What will be the impact on my target audience of this particular campaign?** Am I reaching the key people within the decision-making teams directly? One effective campaign, for example, would be one that uses a 'lumpy' direct mailshot containing a thoughtful and targeted message combined with a telephone call and a follow-up e-mail. Not only should this achieve a positive impact with the potential customer, but additionally you will have obtained the details of the key contact people as a result of the phone call.

3. **What is the total cost of each marketing activity and what return does each need to generate to be profitable?** If the objective is for the campaign to generate new customers, how many new customers will you need in order for the campaign to be deemed a success? If the objective of the campaign is to increase sales, what uplift in sales will declare this a success? Sometimes your focus will be on

generating new customers even though the initial sale may be low. This is because you realise that each customer has a potential lifetime value that way exceeds that initial sale. At other times, it's all about sales and increasing them. Be clear in what you are aiming to achieve.

The effect of asking these questions is that you will save money, often huge sums of it, and you will become more selective and discriminating in your choice of marketing activity. You may belong to a networking group and your marketing audit could reveal that although you benefited from new customers in the first few months of joining the group, this has recently tailed off quite significantly. You will then have a decision to make. You may decide not to renew your membership, or to look for another group. You may even decide to give networking a break and redirect your energies to other marketing activities. You won't know until you have done your sums, and this is all part of the audit exercise.

You can apply this approach to your marketing communications too. Look at what you have spent, the impact that these communications have had and the part that you believe they have played in generating new customers or new business. Those 5,000 flyers that you had printed because they were a bargain at the time may prove to have been pretty useless.

In the following chapters we will cover in detail how to create targeted, attractive and compelling communications on a shoestring budget. Begin, however, with a thorough audit and develop the habit of regularly measuring how your business is benefiting from your marketing expenditure.

4. The Pricing Strategy Review Masterclass, by Paul Hopwood

This Masterclass has kindly been provided by Paul Hopwood. Paul specialises in facilitating the development and implementation of strategic plans for successful businesses, with a particular niche in accountants and lawyers, using a blend of strategy and senior level mentoring and training. He started his own business in 2001 following a successful career as a Chartered Accountant, latterly as the south region tax partner with a top 10 UK accounting firm. Paul is one of the leading Mindshop facilitators in the UK. Find out more at *www.paulhopwoodconsulting.co.uk* and *www.web.mindshop.com*

As we know – if the price is set too high, we lose the sale. Set it too low and we leave money on the table. In other words, the customer will quickly provide us with feedback on whether we've chosen the right price for our product or service. So, what factors should we consider?

The following tips are meant to be practical and useful, based upon what I have seen work spectacularly well and what I have seen cause truly disastrous consequences. 'Will I know which is which?' I hear you ask. I'm sure that you will. Now, as I only have room for 10 tips, I've chosen my personal favourites as follows:

1. **No surprises. Always agree the price in advance** – this prevents subsequent relationship breakdowns caused by misunderstandings. Remember the vehicle service businesses getting this wrong in the past? The bill was always a shock when you picked up your car. Instant dissatisfaction and any compromise results in both parties losing out. I always agree my prices – if the prospect doesn't want to pay, I don't do the work. Test the temperature nice and early!

2. **Use price as a tool to vary demand for your product** and thus choose customers you want to win, retain and lose. Probably obvious and rather a general rule, but increasing price will tend to lower demand and reducing price should increase it. Most businesses don't want to attract everyone, so I usually recommend increasing the price just enough to attract 'B' grade customers, but deter 'C's. 'C's typically create too much effort compared to the reward, causing cross-subsidy of profit and focus away from the valuable 'A's and 'B's. Remember the Pareto (80:20 rule)

    - 20% of your customers generate 80% of your sales.
    - 20% of your products generate 80% of your sales.
    - 20% of your customers generate 80% of your profit.
    - 20% of your customers generate 80% of your hassle.

3. **Never agree a discount without reducing something** in the value proposition, unless you have a planned time-bound promotion. Controversial? Well, consider this: people subconsciously align the perceived value of goods and services with their cost.

4. **Arrive at your price from two angles**:

    a. Traditional 'cost plus' (materials, labour and possibly overhead plus a little profit for you of course) and

    b. What is the market likely to pay for your product or service, based upon competitor prices? Research the market, so you have some certainty on how to position your product or service. So many businesses simply don't bother to do this.

5. **Once you have done the research and carefully selected your price** – you must have the courage to believe in it. Don't be embarrassed by it. For example, I gained a different perspective on my day rate when I found out that the garage at which I had my car serviced was charging £125 per hour for the mechanic. Remember the perception issue in tip 3.

6. **Consider allocating a percentage of sales to give away to a good cause** – after all, you get your income from the community, so why not give something back? Be very selective and make sure you are benefiting the intended target. You win too of course, because you feed your self-worth and build your positive reputation.

7. **Check where your product or service is on its life-cycle** – if it's in the growth phase, it should be easy to grab sales as there's plenty to go around and the price is less important to the buyer. If the product is in decline, or has commoditised, then demand may be shrinking. Awareness and knowledge will make the right pricing decisions obvious.

8. **Don't copy everyone else – look at innovative ways to differentiate your offering** through your pricing policy. I don't just mean being the cheapest. Explore other ideas. Can you fix, be transparent, guarantee in some way, link price to value or even let the customer decide?

9. **Be reluctant to promote price as your key differentiator**, unless there is compelling evidence to believe that the customer prioritises price ahead of quality or service. Even if you believe they do:

- Check that your perception is the reality, not just an assumption. My experience is that pricing issues only tend to score about 7 out of 10 in importance. A focus group or survey should deliver the feedback you need.
- Remember that 'cheapest price' isn't the only option – you might get some traction from 'fixed price', 'transparent', 'flexible', 'value-based' or even 'most expensive'.

10. **Avoid common errors**:

    - Many businesses choose to be 'bottom feeders'. They select a poor target market that delivers rather predictable outcomes – lack of money, low margins, bad debts, disproportionate time spent on servicing customer demands and even broken promises.
    - 'Mates rates'. If you offer discounts, your customers will recommend hoards of additional customers wanting the same deal. This can lead to you being a 'busy fool' – working flat out or piling up stock, but not making any money.
    - 'Scope creep' – very common when selling services. Giving extras without agreeing an additional price at the time.
    - Simply being too cheap, often caused by a lack of research or a lack of confidence. There's nothing wrong in being 'Expensive, but really good value for money'. It's so much better than 'Good, but really expensive'. The 'but' eliminates everything that precedes it!

Pricing policy is a critical success factor for any business. I have found that adopting a more strategic approach to pricing can have a major impact on the trajectory of the whole business.

5. The Tactical Marketing Plan Masterclass

As mentioned earlier in the chapter, businesses that are successful in marketing themselves are often those that make an unwavering commitment to continuous marketing. Come rain or shine, they continue to fly the flag for their business, with both existing customers and prospective ones. But it can be a challenge to keep track of your marketing, to know what you should be doing each week and the order in which you should be targeting prospects and customers. What we have covered so far in these 90-minute Masterclasses are the key elements of a robust marketing strategy, namely the importance of auditing your marketing activities and communications, deciding who you want to reach and why, identifying the decision-makers and the decision-making processes, reviewing your price strategy, and segmenting your products or services to increase their appeal. In the next three chapters we go one step further and look at the importance of developing your positioning statement. We explore why it's important to look at the barriers to a sale and to understand the marketplace in which your target audiences operate. These considerations also form part of your marketing strategy. In my experience, it can be more straightforward for a small business owner to tackle their marketing strategy in manageable chunks than to try to accomplish it alone in a couple of days. This is why I have broken down the key elements of your marketing strategy into these Masterclasses. Hopefully this will allow you to get to grips with one element before moving onto the next.

With the first four Masterclasses now under your belt, it's time to get tactical - to plan over a period of three to four months at a time how you are going to communicate with your different target audiences, when you are going to communicate with them and what background activity will be necessary to draw these campaigns together. You are going to create your tactical marketing plan.

At the end of this chapter I have included an example of a tactical marketing plan to illustrate exactly how one should be composed. It is simple, yet so powerful!

In the first column you should list those groups of people that you are going to target. You identified these groups in Masterclass 2. Your communication plans for each group over the coming months should then be documented in the next three or four columns. It may be that in some months you are not planning to do anything, in which case make a note of this in the relevant column.

The purpose of your tactical marketing plan is to distil your marketing strategy into a clear and simple document, so enabling you to take control and keep track of your marketing activity. It ensures continuous marketing momentum and encourages marketing activities to take place at the right time. In effect, it acts as a guilty conscience should you be tempted to postpone a campaign because business is flowing in - especially if your plan is stuck on your office wall!

It also helps you to measure the responses from each group and to compare the responses between groups. Instead of waiting until the end of each campaign to see the results, you can get a very good impression of its success or otherwise by recording the responses as each element of the campaign is introduced.

Top Tips to Help Create Your Tactical Marketing Plan.

- **Make sure that you plan your monthly activity on a rolling programme of three to four months.** More often than not you are going to be communicating with your target audience in several ways over a period of time. It is unusual for people to decide to do business with you at the first asking. Blending three or four different types of communications over a period of time works very well. You may well have several different campaigns, all at different stages, recorded in your tactical marketing plan. The beauty of the plan is that you can see at a glance what you need to do and when. You will also think in terms of short campaigns rather than individual marketing activities. Rather than planning just one advert in a bid to reach a targeted group, you can plan a series of simple campaigns that combine many elements, creating a positive impact that increases with each communication. If this is not all recorded in a logical order on your tactical marketing plan, you may forget what needs to be done, and when.

- **As each element of a campaign is accomplished, simply make a note of it on the plan and record the responses.** At the very end of each campaign you will be recording the number of leads generated, the volume of sales, the number of new customers that your activity has yielded and how many lapsed customers you have reinstated.

- **Once you have scoped out your tactical marketing plan use it as a catalyst to plan the background work** necessary to ensure that those dates don't slip. Draw up a list of what needs to be done and by whom. Include the detail of any third parties you will be involving, such as your designer, copywriter, web developer, printer and so on. You can then brief these people on your requirements and your deadlines. It is amazing how efficient you will become when you have your tactical marketing plan to guide you.

- **Your tactical marketing plan is not a document that's set in stone, however.** You may want to change it in the light of responses and reactions that you did not anticipate. You may achieve all of your objectives with just one mailshot or you may decide to make some changes in the light of constructive feedback. You may be presented with another marketing opportunity that is better than the campaign that you planned. Your plan should change to reflect new ideas and information as each becomes available.

- **Keep your tactical marketing plan updated with the responses as they come in.** This helps you to judge whether the campaign is a success and whether your initial forecasts were accurate. And, of course, record the costs. This ensures that you are aware of the acquisition costs and enables you to plan future campaigns with confidence and clarity.

Each of my clients, even those that were initially a little sceptical that something so simple could be so effective, would have to agree that they have found the tactical marketing plan to be invaluable in growing their business. I hope that you do too.

To conclude this chapter, I would like to introduce you to...

The Most Powerful Marketing Tool... *Ever*

There is one simple but effective little tool that I use for every marketing campaign that I embark on, *with no exceptions*. I wholeheartedly recommend that you use this tool before you plan your own campaigns too. Feedback from many small business owners is that this tool has really opened up their eyes to the power of what marketing can achieve for them on a shoestring budget. It's called The Continuum of Behaviour.

The Continuum of Behaviour documents the decision-making process followed by a person before deciding to purchase your products or services. This process is followed whether they are existing or lapsed customers, cold prospects, warm prospects or influencers. The five steps of The Continuum of Behaviour, shown in the diagram below are: 'Awareness', 'Interest', 'Evaluation', 'Desire' and 'Action'.

The Continuum of Behaviour

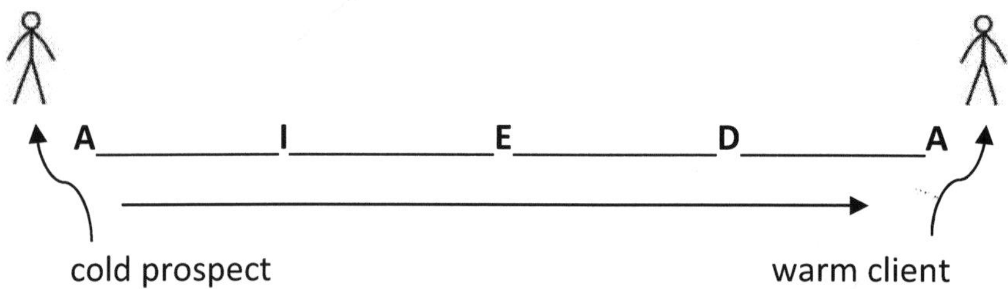

How Does The Continuum of Behaviour Work?

People rarely make the decision to do business with you at the very first asking. In fact, research has shown that in the Business to Business sector in particular, people need to be drip fed sufficient information about you and about what you offer before they will decide to buy. Usually, unless a business has an immediate need to buy your products or services and doesn't have the time to search for other providers, they will arrive at their decision to do business with you over a period of time. This could be days, weeks, months - even years in some cases. How much time it takes will usually depend upon the nature of the purchase, the amount of money being spent, whether any risk is attached to the purchase, and the number of people involved in the decision-making process. For example, a small business looking for a supplier of stationery and ink cartridges will reach that decision quite quickly. It could be that one mailshot including a special offer and a follow-up phone call is all it takes and the matter is concluded in days.

By contrast, a large organisation looking for an office refit will usually employ a tendering process that can stretch over several months. In most cases, if you try to accelerate a person along The Continuum of Behaviour from having no awareness of your business to being a fully paid-up customer with only one communication, you are unlikely to succeed. **You are asking for too much given the lack of a relationship and the lack of understanding of how the business arrives at the decision to buy.**

Think for a moment about your own decision-making process when purchasing products or services. Let's say you are looking to move from your existing bookkeeper and you meet a likely candidate at a networking event. It is doubtful that just the one encounter with this bookkeeper will be sufficient to persuade you to sign up for their services. A day or so later you receive a direct mailshot from a different bookkeeper introducing their services. Again, you may be impressed with the letter but are likely still to want to find out more before feeling sufficiently confident to take them on. Whilst we can assume that the networking event and the direct mailshot will both have successfully moved you into the 'Awareness' stage of The Continuum, and perhaps further into the 'Interest' stage, there is still a way to go before the 'Action' stage is reached. You require more information and you need to feel that you can trust them. Perhaps you will visit their websites or speak with other business owners that currently use their services. If you find this additional information encouraging, you move further along The Continuum into the 'Evaluation' stage.

At this point, you are evaluating the service on offer from these two new bookkeepers, and comparing it with that offered by your current bookkeeper. It is during the evaluation process that you will probably mull over whether their fees are reasonable and consider any added value that each of them could offer. You may want to meet each bookkeeper or discuss matters further over the phone. It is when you have decided which of the bookkeepers that you prefer that you will move from the 'Evaluation' stage into 'Desire'. Moving from the 'Desire' stage into 'Action' is usually determined by how immediate or otherwise is your need for their services. If you have no immediate need it may well be that the bookkeeper still has to galvanise you into action, perhaps by sending a letter of appointment or making a further telephone call.

It is the bookkeeper that understands The Continuum of Behaviour, and is therefore aware of the decision-making process of a potential client, that is best placed to influence that decision and become the preferred choice.

By employing The Continuum of Behaviour alongside your marketing campaigns, you will be able to determine exactly the communications that are required at each stage of the decision-making process. Many small business owners do not think in terms of campaigns and tactical marketing planning, instead pinning their hopes, for example, upon an isolated mailshot being sufficient to move a person from having absolutely no knowledge about their business, to wanting to buy. While this can happen on occasion, a blend of powerful, relevant and timely communications is more likely to do the trick.

Most of the time, planning your campaigns using The Continuum of Behaviour is straightforward. You know who you want to reach, and by referring back to your tactical marketing plan you can see which communications are needed at each stage of the decision-making process. However, I have also found that when introducing your services to a large organisation with a clearly defined decision-making process, it is crucial that you fully understand their 'communication protocol'. They may employ a tender or pitching procedure, for example, and so to move them from having an interest in what you offer to the 'Evaluation' stage you will need to have an understanding of how this works. There is no point in wasting your time by creating brilliant communications if they are not actually required. These organisations are usually very happy to explain their procedure.

Once you understand this procedure, map out the communications that will be needed at each stage of the decision-making process so that you do not overlook a vital stage.

Your Client Base and The Continuum of Behaviour

As mentioned earlier, you should also use The Continuum of Behaviour when planning marketing campaigns aimed at your existing clients. Unlike cold prospects, they are already aware of, and interested in, what you offer. But if you want them to increase their business with you - by spending more on what they're already buying or by purchasing additional products or services - The Continuum of Behaviour is the right tool to determine the communications required to navigate them from 'Interest' to 'Action'.

Always try to use The Continuum of Behaviour when you plan your three or four monthly tactical marketing campaigns. I am confident that you will see an increase in responses and sales. By standing in the shoes of a prospective or existing customer and determining the information they need before arriving at the decision to buy, you will be able to focus upon creating intelligent and relevant communications that meet their needs at each stage of the decision-making process.

Chapter Summary

1. Do not narrow your definition of marketing to random activities such as networking, advertising or direct mail. Marketing is about placing customers at the centre of your business universe.

2. You don't need marketing experience to be successful. You just need to be tenacious and consistent, allocating regular amounts of time to your marketing activities.

3. Marketing on a shoestring is not about marketing as cheaply as possible. It's about investing your time and effort into building great products and services, and communicating with flair, relevance and integrity.

4. Make sure that you allocate 90 minutes a week for an intensive marketing boost and one day a month to put this planning into action.

5. Think of your products and services as a diamond - with many facets. Be descriptive and thorough when communicating what you offer.

6. Carry out a periodic review of your products and services. What can you improve? What can be mothballed? When can you implement these changes?

7. Consider who you want to target and why. Don't dilute your message and waste time by attempting to target everyone.

8. Understand the decision-making process. Find out how many people are involved in the decision to buy and how they arrive at the decision.

9. Regularly audit your marketing activities. What are you spending? Are you reaching the right people in the right numbers? Is the cost reasonable? What are the results?

10. Always agree the price up front before starting any work. Aim to build value rather than being 'cheap as chips'.

11. Plan your marketing campaigns in three to four month sections.

12. Don't forget the behind-the-scenes planning. Who's doing what to ensure that these campaigns are successfully implemented without delay?

13. Make The Continuum of Behaviour integral to your marketing campaigns. Don't plan a campaign without it!

Example Tactical Marketing Plan – The S4B Tactical Marketing Plan

Target Audience	July	August	September	Results	Total Cost	Acquisition cost per client
50 local chartered accountants with two or more partners	Targeted mailshots	Telephone follow-up	Teaser Flyer	10 new clients with sales of £800 to date.	£150	£15
25 VIP local chartered accountants with two or more partners (high potential)	Targeted mailshot with 'fill your bag free ' offer	Telephone follow-up	Teaser flyer plus pen	Six new clients with sales of £500 to date	£90	£15
Three local charities	No activity	Initial phone call to ascertain interest	1 to 1 meetings	Two signed up. No sales as yet		
18 recruitment agencies in RH10 and RH11 postcodes	Initial phone call to establish key contacts	Teaser mailshot with free pen	Telephone follow-up call	Six new clients with sales of £700 to date	£60	£10
Hand-picked VIP warm prospects – 12 in total	No activity	Invitation to luncheon event	Hold luncheon event	Nine new clients with sales of £900 to date	£240	£27

Note – these figures are for illustration purposes only.

CHAPTER 2

HOW TO WRITE COMPELLING COPY THAT LEADS TO SALES

Powerful Copy Makes Money

Remember these four words as you read through the next three chapters. In these chapters, I demonstrate some tried and trusted copywriting techniques to melt the heart of the coldest of prospects, and provide some practical and simple advice on how to create thirteen different sales communications. At the end of these three chapters you will have a good understanding of the most effective methods of communicating with your existing customers and with those people yet to buy.

Forget any knock-backs you may have experienced in the past, and don't be shy about getting back in touch with those same people that have been resistant to your overtures so far. This time you will be revisiting them with a powerful, engaging and relevant message. Sometimes you have to go through the ignominy of rejection before success strikes. This is certainly my experience and of course it makes the success that follows all the sweeter.

It's a good idea to have your pen and pad to hand as you read through each chapter. I guarantee that inspiration will strike as you begin to think more about those people that you would like to target. Don't lose those emerging ideas; they are a valuable currency that will lead to your next copywriting triumph.

'Why should I bother with the written word when face-to-face communication is more effective?'

I was asked this question at a recent networking event. I'm sure that most businesses would like to be in the enviable position of being able to meet every single potential client face-to-face, in a world where time was no object and each person signed up there and then. But in reality we simply do not have the time nor the opportunity to be in front of every person to whom we are trying to sell. And even if that was possible, face to face contact doesn't automatically guarantee that the person will buy there and then.

Re-visit The Continuum of Behaviour

The written word plays an increasingly important part in moving a prospect along The Continuum of Behaviour. A written communication, such as a sales letter, can move a cold prospect from being unaware of your business to being interested in what you have to offer. Similarly, after a face-to-face meeting with a warm prospect, a follow-up written communication, such as a summary of your discussion, can move that prospect further along The Continuum again towards becoming a new customer.

Written communications can kick start the sales communication process, they can maintain a relationship in between scheduled meetings and can even act as the catalyst that guarantees the sale. And this is the case regardless of what you do for a living.

Learn from Drayton Bird

Before we embark on our copywriting journey together, I'd like to tell you about another journey that began 27 years ago, when I was a young marketing rookie attending my first direct marketing conference. I attended a seminar presented by a man called Drayton Bird. I had read about Drayton in various marketing magazines. I was aware of his association with advertising legend, David Ogilvy, and knew of his reputation as one of the world's most influential and successful copywriters. During the seminar Drayton flashed up examples of adverts that he regarded as good, bad, horrendous and brilliant. He illustrated the 'brilliant' category with an advert that blew me away. It was a text only advert of approximately 100 words, placed in the classified section of a newspaper, and advertising a Bed & Breakfast in the Yorkshire Dales. In just one paragraph it managed to recount a beautiful story, providing rich and vivid descriptions of the stunning views from the bedroom windows and of the crackling log fire and warm home-baked scones that would greet weary hikers as they returned from an exhilarating and tiring day in the Dales. What Drayton taught me that day was that effective copywriting starts by really understanding your audience. Once we understand their needs we are then better able to progress to the stage of crafting our messages, messages that are simple, relevant, timely and engaging. A large budget is not necessary for an advert to hit the spot; it simply needs to appeal directly to its target audience and to be written in a charming manner. The inexpensive Bed & Breakfast advert was an example of charm in action. The person who had written this advert had clearly stood in the shoes of a hiker and looked at what was important to them when choosing a Bed & Breakfast. Warmth, great views and delicious home-cooked food would definitely appeal, and in a very small space the writer had captured just what was needed in order to make an impact.

In the next few pages we will look at how to receive the highest responses from your communications. Let's start by identifying the most common mistakes that people make when trying to promote their business through the written word. Hopefully, by being aware of the pitfalls beforehand, we're less likely to fall into them.

- **The product or service that is being promoted is simply not relevant to the person receiving the communication.** This is usually because insufficient thought or research has been devoted to understanding fully the needs of the target audience. Sometimes it's a combination of the two.

- **There is no clear message.** Instead, a jumble of different messages hit the reader, usually because too much information is being crammed into one communication. The result is often a bewildering maze of narration that serves only to confuse the reader.

- **The communication is a hurried afterthought.** The business owner has panicked because sales are slowing down. Worse still, they've got wind that a competitor is being active and getting results. Instead of taking a little time to research the needs of their target audience and communicating this understanding in, say, a well-written letter, newsletter or flyer, the business has fallen into a 'shoot-from-the-hip' copywriting mode. Within 30 minutes, a letter or a flyer has been hastily scrambled together and it's on its way to the recipient. The marketing activity box has been ticked, but that's about it.

- **The content of the communication is pitched at the wrong level.** It either assumes too much knowledge on the part of the recipient, or too little. Or, as is more often the case, it assumes that the recipient will immediately fall in love with the business purely because the business owner loves the business. Important elements such as addressing the potential barriers to a sale and explaining clearly what is on offer are overlooked because the business owner is simply boasting about how great the business is.

- **The communication looks unprofessional.** One glance tells you that it is homespun. A potentially powerful message is struggling for breath, buried in a DIY communication. I see this happening often with sales flyers and newsletters. The business owner thinks that a few magic tricks on their computer will conjure up the desired design, layout and print. Unfortunately, the recipient does not appreciate their efforts and the waste bin usually becomes the new home for this missive.

- **The communication is lacking in passion and enthusiasm.** It comes across as a technical summary containing a few 'About our Business' paragraphs that were probably written several years ago. That rich seam of passion that runs through every person within the business, and that is most definitely on show in meetings with potential clients, can be lacking in written communications. This could be because the task of copywriting has been assigned to a colleague with neither the time, skill nor the enthusiasm to do the job justice.

- **The communication is written from the perspective of the business.** It is crammed with references to 'we', 'our', and 'us', when in fact it should be full of references to 'you' and 'your'. I'm sure that you will have been on the receiving end of these irritating communications. Bursting, often boastfully, with an unrelenting stream of references about the business and their largesse. In fact the communication should be written conversationally, concentrating instead upon the many benefits on offer and with the aim of captivating the reader.

- **A powerful message is totally obscured by an abundance of spelling mistakes, incorrect punctuation and clumsy grammar.** The reader concentrates on the amusing sport of finding the next glaring error rather than absorbing the message, a message that could well be of interest were they not otherwise engaged.

- **The individuals within the business have allowed their own personal preferences to override their business judgement.** Something that I have seen on more than one occasion is the cartoon style communication sent to a cold prospect. It includes inappropriate language, maybe even swearwords, all wrapped up in an over-familiar style. This style may work down the pub and perhaps when networking informally with business peers, but in a written communication it is wholly inappropriate and could actually damage the reputation of the business.

- **The timing of the document is wrong, either too early or too late.** A good example of this being a budget summary sent by an accountant or financial advisor three weeks after the budget. The target audience would have been at their most responsive within 24 hours of the news breaking. Conversely, I received a sales flyer from a business on the first day in September promoting their Christmas range of cakes and sweets. Had they delayed sending the flyer by a month or so they could well have grabbed my attention, but encouraging me to buy Christmas gifts immediately after the summer holidays was not a successful move.

- **Not knowing when to stop, the sales message goes on and on and on.** Although the most brilliant copywriters may succeed in writing sales letters that stretch into several pages, for most people it's vital to get one or two concise messages over in quick time before running the risk of boring the reader.

- **The Continuum of Behaviour is overlooked.** A communication is sent out as a stand-alone piece of correspondence rather than as one element within a fully integrated communication campaign, a campaign in which the right communications are utilised at the right stage of the decision-making process.

- **The importance of undertaking some market research before putting pen to paper is overlooked.** I'm not talking about engaging a market research agency, just laying some basic groundwork. For example, you can review what your competitors are currently up to, consider what's happening in the current marketplace that could impact on your sales message, talk to existing clients and find out what really matters to them. Creatively, the message could be brilliant, well written and attention grabbing, but if it's the wrong one it won't make people want to buy. If this groundwork is overlooked, the whole exercise becomes very much hit and miss.

So, now we know the big mistakes, it's time to put them to one side and make a mental note never to repeat them. Let's concentrate instead on how to write powerful and winning copy that delivers results every time.

Understand and Define Who You Want to Target

At this stage, if you have not yet studied the target audience Masterclass in Chapter 1, it is a good idea to read it now. It is impossible to create successful communications without knowing who is going to read them, what their needs are for what you offer and what is really important to them when making their decision to buy. You should always write to your readers, not to yourself. So using Chapter 1 to guide you, build a detailed picture of the people you are going to target. They should be foremost in your mind when you are writing. Think about what makes you buy a product or service, especially one that is a sizeable investment. Top of your list is likely to be the fact that you believe that the product or service is an ideal match for your personal needs.

By way of example let's consider Direct Route, a business that offers professional 'business to business' debt collection services. Although it's acknowledged that most businesses have a need for debt collection services, there are some sectors in which the need is greater - businesses that sell promotional gifts, and printers for example. These businesses tend to come at the bottom of a debtor's paying priorities because their services are not imperative to the daily functioning of the business and it's relatively straightforward to find another. Before Direct Route begins its sales communication process, they segment their cold prospects into sectors, and then further still into size, usually based on the number of employees and turnover. This avoids a small business with one or two employees receiving exactly the same sales communication as a global brand looking to outsource their entire debt collection process.

You must bring this level of detail to the groups that you want to target with your communications. In doing so, you will begin to write communications that demonstrate your understanding of the sector in which the business operates, and also of the needs that they have for what you offer. It also provides an opportunity to use sector specific examples as case studies within your communications. For example, Direct Route only use small business case studies to support the sales letters being sent to small businesses. These same case studies would not be appropriate in letters to global brands.

Understand and Document the Barriers to a Sale

In order to write copy that delivers sales you need to understand and address the barriers that can prevent a person buying from you. You can shout from the rooftops about your fantastic business but if you're not identifying and addressing those barriers, you won't be making the sale. It's important to identify the barriers for each of the groups that you are targeting, i.e. cold prospects, lapsed clients, VIP clients, and so on. Go further still - if you are grouping your cold prospects by sector, identify whether each sector has specific barriers. In my experience, the barriers to a sale will vary from group to group and from sector to sector. For example, a few years ago I worked with a franchisor who wanted to introduce business coaching to his franchisees. The biggest barrier to the sale was that the franchisees did not understand how their business would benefit from this coaching. They were labouring under the misconception that business coaching was only applicable to senior executives in big corporations.

Our initial marketing messages focused on communicating the tangible benefits that business coaching could offer a small business owner. We explained what business coaching was all about and provided a list of other small businesses that had previously benefited from business coaching. We encouraged the franchisees to talk to some of the businesses on that list to help them better understand the advantages that business coaching could bring.

Recognising the barriers enabled us to focus our communications specifically to address those concerns uppermost in the minds of the franchisees. By doing so we were able to move beyond any initial scepticism and ultimately the majority of franchisees attended the complimentary coaching session on offer before deciding whether their own business would benefit from a full course.

For another client, the higher than average price for his service was the potential barrier. He was in competition with businesses that offered an inferior service but at a much cheaper price. The marketing messages, therefore, needed to drive home the quality of the service being provided, compared with that on offer from the competitors, and importantly, just how this superior service significantly benefited the clients. We needed to tackle the potential barrier of the higher price head-on. Had we tried to ignore it, the positive messages delivered in our communications would have stumbled over this issue. Ignoring something does not mean it will go away!

How to Identify the Barriers to a Sale

- **Spend a little time on the Internet researching the groups you aim to target.** This will enable you to understand more about the marketplace in which your target audiences operate, and so help unearth barriers as well as opportunities.

- **Pick up the phone** - ask the people that you are looking to target to articulate their reservations or objections when it comes to buying your products or services. What would it take for them to switch from their current supplier? I find that this is a great way of better understanding just what is important to the people I want to communicate with. Not only will you be helped in identifying those barriers to a sale, you may also obtain information to help you formulate a winning sales message. In Chapter 4 there are plenty of tips on how to create and conduct a survey.

- **Again, stand in the shoes of the people that you're looking to target.** Using your business acumen, commonsense and knowledge of the sector, imagine what they are likely to see as the main sales barriers. Consider actually meeting up with some of your target audience. One of my clients was targeting local architects and was keen to know their thoughts on his product. We therefore organised a couple of informal lunches to which we invited many representatives of this sector. This provided the architects with an opportunity to network with their peers over something to eat, while at the same time enabling my client and I to speak directly with the exact people that we were trying to sell to. The information provided at those lunches was invaluable when it came to writing our sales literature.

You should find this an illuminating exercise. Documenting your findings and the information that you gather should help you in creating your all-important sales messages.

And it really does work. I was recently asked to write a punchy sales letter inviting a group of local food suppliers to a networking event in Sussex. The purpose of the event was to launch the Horsham and District Food & Drink Festival, a month-long event during which local food suppliers extend special offers, food tastings and other activities designed to increase their profile and sales. We wanted to demonstrate to the food suppliers the simple and low cost ways in which they could promote their businesses and so gain most value from the festival.

Our market research unearthed three key barriers:

1. **Most of the invited audience were not used to networking** and so to them, standing in a room chatting with their peers was a daunting prospect. As an inveterate business networker, this had not occurred to me.

2. **Because most of the invited audience were retailers, they couldn't simply shut their shop** or visitor attraction to attend a networking event. The timing of the event was therefore crucial. Too early and many would be unable to turn up, too late and they would most likely be too tired to turn up!

3. **Some were sceptical about the marketing of the event**, assuming that they would need to contribute money towards an expensive advertising campaign.

Armed with this knowledge, I used the back of the sales letter to address the key objections in a simple question and answer format. The letter was then followed up with a personal telephone call, another opportunity to allay any fears or objections and to emphasise the benefits of attending. Finally an e-mail was sent confirming the benefits of attending the evening and emphasising the later than usual start time. Over 80% of the people that had confirmed their attendance actually turned up on the evening. This exceeded our expectations. Had I omitted to perform my research before I put pen to paper, I know that my message would have lacked relevance and would most likely have been ignored.

What Problems are you Solving, What Needs are you Satisfying?

People buy from you if at some level you are solving their problems and satisfying their needs. It doesn't matter whether you sell services or products, the same principle applies. In order to write razor sharp, targeted copy, that delivers the right message to the right recipient at the right time, you need to demonstrate a clear understanding of the buyer's needs and problems.

I am often asked by a perplexed business owner to appraise leaflets, brochures and newsletters that have generated a very poor response or no response at all. In some cases, professional copywriters and designers have been employed and the writing and presentation itself is very good. But what screams out from the text is that there is no understanding of what really matters to the buyer or of how their needs can be satisfied by the business trying to woo them.

So in a similar way to listing the barriers to a sale, you need to document the underlying needs for each group that you are targeting and how you can fulfil them with what you offer. Re-visit your product or service, analysing the benefits you offer. In the small detail you may unearth some real gems.

A Word of Warning

There is nothing to be gained from deluding yourself that you are capable of satisfying every single need if in fact this is not the case. It's better to perform an honest stocktake of what you offer and acknowledge the areas in which you over-deliver and where you don't deliver at all.

And if you are concerned that you must find your unique selling point, put this to one side for the time being. Don't worry if what you are offering is not unique. Scrabbling around trying to invent a unique selling point can be onerous, time-consuming and can even set you off on the wrong route. I have heard business people at networking events laying claim to a unique selling point that is anything but, simply because they presume that what they are offering is unique, or they have been told that the route to business success is paved with unique selling points. It is not. You don’t have to be unique to be successful.

Take a Peek at Your Competitors

It is always a good idea to take a look at what your closest competitors are doing, without being obsessive about the detail. There is undoubtedly plenty of room in the marketplace for good businesses that, on the face of it, are offering the same products or services. More often than not, when there is little to choose between small businesses, it's the strength of the selling message, combined with great marketing communications and a robust approach to sales that enables one business to perform better than another. Take a look at your closest competitors. The likelihood is that you know most of them already. What can you learn from them? What are you doing that is better? What are you doing that is different? Are you aiming at the same buyers? What is their pricing structure? How do they market themselves?

Answers to these questions can often help inspire your communications and with the Internet at your disposal, research should be relatively straightforward, whether in fact you have a unique selling point, or not.

Let me reassure you with this quotation from Joel Raphaelson of the advertising agency, Ogilvy and Mather. It neatly puts paid to the myth that you have to be unique to be successful.

> ***'In the past, just about every advertiser has assumed that in order to sell his products he has to convince consumers that his product is superior to his competitors. This may not be necessary. It may be sufficient to convince consumers that your product is positively good. If the consumer feels certain that your product is good and feels uncertain about your competitors, he will buy yours. If you and your competitors all make excellent products, don't try to imply that your product is better. Just say what's good about your product - and do a clearer, more honest, more informative job of saying it.'***

Although what Joel is saying relates to advertising and how to write great advertising copy, you can apply this within the broader context of all sales communications.

What you will usually find when you audit your buyers' needs and compare your own offering with that of your competitors is that there are some areas in which you excel and others in which there is room for improvement. And that's okay. This will either galvanise you into improving what you offer or it will make you focus your energies on targeting only those groups whose needs you mostly meet. You may even do both.

Develop your Positioning Statement

As a young marketer, one of the first things drummed into me by my elders was that before I put pen to paper and started writing all manner of sales communications, I had to create a positioning statement for the business that I was looking to promote. A positioning statement is simply a succinct, clear and unambiguous description of what you offer. It comprises of a series of bullet points. You may also have heard it referred to as a 'benefit statement'. You are well on the way to creating your positioning statement having identified the barriers to a sale and understanding how your products or services best fit the needs of the people you want to target.

Look at the landscape through the eyes of the people that buy from you. If you really want your sales messages to resonate, include the specific benefits relevant to those target groups in your overall positioning statement. For example, if we look again at business coaching for franchisees, a key message was that the coach had many years' experience working with small businesses, and some working specifically with franchisees. If targeting senior executives in blue chip organisations, these facts would not be relevant. Executives would be more interested in the life coach's experience with other executives and how they had specifically helped these executives to progress. The qualifications and accreditations of the business coach, however, would be important to highlight to all target groups. In this case therefore, the business coach would note in his positioning statement that his sales message to the franchisees should include his previous experience working with small businesses, whereas when communicating with the senior executives he would concentrate instead upon the experience he gained with blue chip organisations. The complimentary session, his qualifications and accreditations would be appropriate to all.

In effect, your positioning statement is your copywriting anchor. It prevents you from floundering when tasked with producing written material to promote your business. Rather than desperately searching for inspiration, the answers will be in your positioning statement.

Make sure that you review it regularly to avoid falling into the trap of writing communications based on old and weary data!

In summary, therefore, by creating a positioning statement:

- You'll never struggle again for what to write.
- You'll have a good understanding of what really matters to your distinct target audiences. The triggers that make them say 'yes' and the barriers that can make them say 'no'.
- There will be a reduced risk of including irrelevant brilliance in your sales messages.

What Could Influence your Sales Message?

People will rarely make the decision to buy your products or services in isolation. Their decision will be based on a number of factors including:

- How your messages are presented.
- Your overall branding, including how your business looks on paper and on-line, and how you and any employees inspire and impress.
- Their budget.
- How you demonstrate that you offer real value.
- Any knowledge of or existing relationships with competitors.
- How high on their agenda is their need for your services.

For each of the groups that you are targeting, it will help to consider what is happening in their wider world that could have an impact on their ability and desire to do business with you.

For example, when the recession struck, Techmobility, a company that adapts vehicles for disabled motorists, became exposed to a downturn in sales of new motor vehicles which threatened to undermine their growing business.

Yet the company actually managed to grow their business in a year in which motor dealership car sales fell by 13%. Subtle changes were made to the sales messages, further emphasising how a motor dealership could save time and money by using Techmobility rather than relying on a competitor. Because Techmobility's engineers operate from mobile workshops they can adapt a customer's vehicle at the motor dealership itself. Many competitors are unable to offer this mobile service. The renewed focus of the marketing communications was on the mobile workshop service and the fact that a salesman can therefore remain on the forecourts selling, rather than being required to bring the car to the adaptation company's premises.

At a time when every car sale was vital to car dealerships, this benefit proved to be especially attractive.

Your message will carry so much more weight if you can prove that you understand what is happening in the marketplace in which your targeted prospects operate. Better still, if you can align this understanding with what you are offering within the framework of your sales communications you will be placed head and shoulders above competitors that are simply trotting out the same old weary sales statements. Let prospects and customers know that you understand what is happening in their world and how you are best placed to serve their changing needs.

Don't be put off from marketing your services to a sector that is experiencing challenging times. If you can demonstrate that your business is poised to help them through turbulent times, you can still make those sales. Unless a business is in dire straits, it will usually continue buying those products and services that are essential to its lifeblood. Once you've done some research to find out if there is still ample potential in this market, it is down to you to demonstrate that you are their best option.

Style and Presentation

So far, we have been looking at the importance of building a detailed picture of what you offer and matching this to what people need. This practical research will help define your powerful sales messages and this should in turn lead to sales. You will also benefit from this knowledge when you are networking and in face-to-face presentations with clients and prospects. When you stand up at a networking event to deliver your 60-second presentation, often referred to as your elevator pitch, you will not be scrabbling around for the words to inspire people. When you present to a potential client, you'll have a list of compelling and relevant benefits at your fingertips. And of course, you'll be better able to handle any questions having done your homework.

Whilst your method of communication may change, your messages will remain consistent, and as we discover in Chapter 5, consistency is at the heart of building a successful brand.

Armed with this information, it's time to get down to writing for response. In the two chapters that follow, I explain how you can create 13 communications to promote your business, including the all-important sales letter which warrants a chapter of its own. Each communication has been used by many different types of businesses to great effect.

However before you begin your sales letter, compile your survey, create your voucher or brainstorm your questions and answers, there are some copywriting guidelines to follow:

Use 'you' and 'your' more than 'we', 'us' or 'I'.

You'll arouse interest if you talk to the person as though they were in front of you. Many business sales communications are full of statements similar to this:

> *'We have 50 years' combined experience and we believe that we deliver more for our customers than any other company.'*

Whereas it would be better to say:

> *'The team looking after you have over 50 years' combined experience in delivering results for businesses like yours.'*

Using the word 'we' can be positive, but it can still be improved, for example:

> *'Raring2Go! Worthing is a quarterly family targeted publication delivered to over 12,000 families in the Worthing area. We pride ourselves on the attentive service that we give to all our advertisers and consequently our advertisers can receive some amazing responses from their adverts. In fact, one local restaurant owner recently received over 50 new customers from their restaurant feature. We have a selection of special offers for new advertisers and are always happy to discuss the benefits of additional editorial to increase responses dramatically. We also offer a range of different advert sizes to suit any budget.'*

could be changed to:

> *'If you'd like your business to be marketed regularly to over 12,000 families in the Worthing area, you need to be talking to Raring2Go! Worthing, your family targeted publication. You'll benefit from an attentive service and, if the experience of other advertisers is anything to go by, you'll also enjoy an exceptional response rate to your adverts. One of our advertisers recently gained 50 new customers from their restaurant feature. What would 50 new customers mean for your business? As a new advertiser you'll benefit from special offers plus the option of additional editorial to boost that number of responses even further. And you can choose from a range of advert sizes to suit your budget.'*

Great sales communications should focus on being personal but should never come across as being insincere. To reinforce this point, look at the two examples promoting the marketing and web design company, LWS Creative.

It's all about us:

> *'We are a web, design and marketing consultancy based in West Sussex. We work with both local and national clients, of varying size. Our services deliver impact but not a huge bill. The breadth of services we provide include logo and letterhead design and creating websites on a shoestring budget. We also provide bespoke websites for blue chip companies. We are often approached by potential clients looking to compare our services with the service that they are receiving from their current agency. We work with businesses that are growing and want to improve their branding, and also with those wanting to*

trade in their current home spun website for something more powerful and professional. Please give LWS Creative a call to have a chat about how we could help your business.'

It's all about you:

'If you are looking for design, web or marketing services that really deliver but you don't want to pay over the odds, then LWS Creative is the right team for you.

Based in West Sussex, our clients are both local and national, both large and small. You may be a start-up business in need of a logo, letterhead and a 'get me up and running quickly' website, or a multi-million pound brand looking for an all-singing, all-dancing bespoke website. Perhaps you are interested in comparing the service and quality of your current agency with what we could offer instead. Maybe you're experiencing the pains and pleasures of growing your business and it's time to improve your branding and to trade in your current home spun website for something more powerful and professional. Let's chat today about where we can take your business.'

If you want to create impact you must make the reader feel as though you are talking to them personally. Do this and you will form a bond, maintaining their interest sufficiently for them to receive your sales message.

Write as though you are having a conversation with just one reader. I have used the word 'conversation' deliberately. This is because the best writers create the impression of holding a friendly, informative and focused dialogue with the reader. They are simply using printed words as the channel through which they initiate a conversation.

They tell a story in a chatty style, while being careful to avoid jargon and not to cross the line into being unprofessional.

For instance, you could say:

> *'Please contact us to arrange a meeting which will last approximately 30 minutes. We can meet at your place of work or at our office.'*

But it's much better to say instead:

> *'Don't hesitate to get in touch if you'd welcome an informal, 30-minute meeting at a time and at a venue that suits you.'*

Warming to this theme you could say:

> *'Each one of our superbly positioned bedrooms boasts magnificent views of the Yorkshire Dales.'*

But it's much better to say instead:

> *'Gaze out of your bedroom window and be greeted by a breathtaking view of the Yorkshire Dales.'*

Use Words that Convey Passion, Warmth and Inspiration.

One of the problems with using e-mail on a regular basis is that normal courtesy and politeness can be overlooked and messages treated as being purely functional. As a result, e-mail messages can sometimes be open to misinterpretation, with bluntness often being seen as rudeness. There is a risk that we can carry through this style into our sales communications. You can enliven an otherwise stark paragraph of text with some warm, engaging and descriptive words.

For example, you could say:

> *'We have had many responses to our survey and look forward to receiving your answers too. Don't forget, you will receive a drinks mug filled with jelly beans if you respond within the next seven days.'*

And in all fairness, that's not too bad. But if you want to get responses, you have to deliver more than just mediocre. Look what happens when a few subtle improvements are made to this message.

> *'Many people have responded to our survey so far. But not you! We'd love your opinion too. And don't forget, you will receive a funky drinks mug filled to the brim with jelly beans if you respond within the next seven days.'*

The improved wording helped one of my clients achieve a response rate of 22% from a notoriously unresponsive audience. This was particularly pleasing as the average response rates for all types of surveys range from 5% to 12%. Warm, engaging and friendly copy does make a positive difference to your responses and sales.

One tip is to start by making a list of the words that you can use to add some extra sparkle and impact to your messages. Keep adding to this list as new words occur to you. Also, consider whether there are any buzzwords in the marketplace in which your target audiences operate that will grab their attention and demonstrate your understanding of their business. Familiarise yourself with the on-line and off-line publications that are read by your target audiences. When you have the specific details of the businesses or individuals that you are targeting, visit some of their websites for additional inspiration. This will help you pick up an abundance of relevant words, phrases and terminology. Try to avoid reusing the same words over and over again, simply because you can't think of any alternatives. I see this happening frequently with food and drink copy. The words scrumptious, delicious and moist are often repeated throughout a sales communication. Similarly, I wonder if it is because the same person is writing all hotel descriptions that I keep reading the words 'boasting, spacious, charming and contemporary...'. There's nothing wrong with these words, but when they are being repeated several times throughout a sales communication, they lose their lustre and impact.

Have a thesaurus to hand to help you find alternative words and expressions.

To get you started, here's a selection of my favourite words and phrases that can be appropriate for virtually any business in any sector.

Fantastic	Superior	Brand-new
Overwhelming	Compelling	Competitive
Genuine	Experienced	Proven Track Record
Meticulous	Shoestring	Improve
Incredible	One-Off	Effective
Superb	Time Bound	Exquisite
Exceptional Quality	First-Class	Complimentary
Unbelievable	Irresistible	No charge
Passionate	Long Serving	Risk-free
Measurable value	Award-Winning	Exceptional
You	Qualified	Quality assured
Your	Accredited	Free

Limited Offer	Vibrant	Dedicated
Enhanced	Trusted	Guaranteed
Pioneering	Value Added	Ground breaking

Tell a Story

This topic is also covered in Chapter 5 but it's important enough to warrant a mention here. Winning communications contain a compelling sales message within the wider context of a story. You can see this demonstrated on the television programme, 'Dragon's Den', during which would-be entrepreneurs pitch their ideas to the 'Dragon' investors. Those that succeed in arousing the interest of the Dragons often do so by spending a little time telling their own story – their working background, what had sparked their original idea and how they had gone about bringing the idea into fruition. When it comes to writing communications, try to follow this principle. For example, if you are mailing a survey to your customers, tell them why you are doing so and the improvements that you are considering based on their replies. Most people like to know this information because it enables them to see the purpose of completing the survey. What is the story that led to the communication you are writing now? If you can condense it into a few words, share this within the communication itself.

By way of example, here is an introduction to one of my blog posts. Notice how I arouse the reader's interest in my message by wrapping it within a story:

> 'Last week on holiday, I read an article that almost ended up in the swimming pool. Face down. I should have known from the introductory paragraph that it was going to challenge me. The forcibly put assertion of the writer was that *'traditional marketing such as direct mail and advertising is dead. The*

> *only way forwards is social media, on-line advertising and blogs.'* Nonsense I tell you, nonsense! We have to identify the communication channels that we can effectively use to reach our potential buyers. This may or may not include social networking, direct mail, on-line advertising and so on. Even then, one particular channel, although effective, may not in itself be the only route to riches.'

Make sure that you place your compelling message within your credible story. Stories arouse interest. They were our original currency and source of entertainment when we were young. Commit to reviving this art in your marketing communications.

Use a Blend of Short and Long Sentences

The variety will maintain the interest of the reader. Here are three examples:

> *'In this workshop you'll learn how to write direct mail that generates responses and press releases that get published. How does that sound?'*

> *'You are a tough nut to crack. Although we have had over 2,000 responses to our special offer, we've not heard from you. Why is that?'*

> *'Many marketing practitioners claim that you need extensive marketing experience to grow your business. You don't.'*

By following a paragraph or a long sentence with a sentence of just a few words you can make the reader stop and think about what you are saying. This also works well if the short sentence is separated from the previous paragraph, as illustrated in this example:

'"Shop local and support your local businesses, shops and producers" is now the rallying cry the length and breadth of the United Kingdom. We're being encouraged to shop local for many reasons. Not least to reduce the impact on the environment and to benefit the local economy.

It's all good stuff isn't it?'

Ask Questions

You know that sinking feeling when you are on the end of a one-sided conversation, when you are being talked at? Well, sometimes reading sales literature can feel the same. One way to make sure that your communications don't fall into this category is to ask the reader a question or two as they read through your text. It's a technique to make the reader think about what you are presenting to them and to reinforce your selling proposition. How does it work? Well, let's look at some more examples:

You could say:

'Our website services offer you real value for money.'

'We can turn you into an accomplished public speaker capable of holding your audience spellbound.'

'It's a good idea to work out how much you spend on print each year.'

'You will benefit from a complimentary 60-minute marketing MOT.'

but why not reword those statements into questions instead?

> *'When did you last get real value for money from your web developer?'*

> *'How would it feel to be an accomplished public speaker, holding your audience spellbound?'*

> *'Are you spending too much on print each year?'*

> *'What questions would you like answered in your complimentary 60-minute marketing MOT?'*

The easiest way to include a question in your text is to review the copy that you have written and identify those statements that can be turned into questions.

Be Prepared for When Inspiration Strikes

You will find that when you start to gather your thoughts about writing sales literature, ideas will strike at the most unexpected times. You can be at a networking event and a comment from the speaker will give you an idea. Or maybe you're in a supermarket wrestling with your shopping and a great thought will pop into your head. Brilliant! It shows that you are subconsciously becoming tuned into generating ideas. Be equipped with a small pad and a pen or an appropriate piece of electrical gadgetry upon which to record these ideas when they strike. From great ideas, compelling copy is born. And the more ideas you capture, the more creative your writing will be.

When you actually start writing, you must be prepared to check and re-check your work. Evaluate it against the tips in this chapter and the two that follow. Your first draft will contain the essence of what you want to say, but it will then need shaping. Some words you will replace, certain paragraphs you will restructure or shorten and there will be entire areas that you will delete as part of your review. This is perfectly normal and is the hallmark of a conscientious writer. Once you get into the swing of writing and editing, it will seem quite natural. However, if this does not appeal to you, either because you are pressed for time or you find it difficult to edit your own work, all is not lost.

A good freelance editor, especially one with experience in your sector, can turn your carefully thought out ideas and the most basic draft of your sales literature into something very special. And editorial services are very reasonably priced. Use the Internet to search for possible candidates. They don't need to be based in your local area but I would advise that you take a look at examples of their work and appraise their experience. You want to be confident that they are capable of fully grasping what you offer and the purpose of the sales communication you are asking them to edit. You can't expect an editor to second-guess your needs so the more information you can give them the better.

If you have thoroughly prepared the ground work by evaluating your target audience and defining their needs, and have developed a credible and thorough positioning statement, there should be plenty for an editor to work with. If you are paying for an editing service you will get the maximum value from it by providing a thorough briefing.

I hope that you feel inspired by what you have learned so far.

Chapter Summary

1. Always use The Continuum of Behaviour.

2. Study, and then avoid the 13 main copywriting mistakes.

3. Ensure you are clear about the people you want to target.

4. Make sure that you know who you want to communicate with. Go back to Chapter 1 if you are in any doubt.

5. Make sure that you understand the barriers to a sale for each group.

6. List the problems that you are solving, the needs that you are satisfying.

7. Your claim to uniqueness must be genuine, not wishful thinking.

8. Develop your positioning statement, your copywriting anchor.

9. Research the marketplace of your target audiences.

10. Use the words 'you' and 'your' in preference to 'we' and 'us'.

11. Write as though you're having a conversation with the reader.

12. Use words that inspire and that convey enthusiasm and warmth.

13. Tell a story to build the reader's interest in your proposition.

14. Use a blend of long and short sentences.

15. Can you make the reader think by asking them questions?

16. Be prepared to capture your ideas at all times.

17. If you're not comfortable editing your work, use a freelance editor.

CHAPTER 3

HOW TO WRITE SUCCESSFUL SALES LETTERS

'The truth is not that people receive too many sales letters, but that they receive too many irrelevant ones. When people say they hate junk mail, this is what they really mean. They don't like receiving things that don't interest them. On the other hand there is ample evidence that the reverse is true. Any letter which talks to the right person about the right subject at the right time, and appeals to that person's self-interest, will succeed. And it does not have to be clever to do so. Of course, if it is also ingenious it may well succeed even more. But that touch of originality is far less important than being relevant to the reader.'

Drayton Bird, 'How to Write Sales Letters That Sell'

This is good to read if you're interested in writing sales letters but have a niggling doubt in your mind that this sort of correspondence comes under the banner of junk mail. Especially in a world in which everything seems to be happening on-line.

Hopefully by the end of this chapter I will have persuaded you that the old-fashioned sales letter is, in fact, a very powerful tool to have in your marketing toolkit. And you'll be able to write a cracking one.

I think it is safe to say that sales letters work without exception, regardless of what business you are in. Whether you manufacture widgets, make exquisite fruitcakes, build websites or coach executives - you can successfully promote your business with a sales letter. If you run an on-line business, don't think that the only way to communicate with your audience is on-line. Some of the biggest on-line businesses, including eBay and Amazon, target prospects and customers with paper and print based marketing. Adopt a wider view of your business and how you market it to prospects and customers.

What's So Special About a Sales Letter?

It's an intimate communication. The recipient holds your letter, hopefully reads it from beginning to end and thinks about your message as they do so. Research has uncovered the positive but hardly startling fact that physical material is more real to the brain. It has a meaning and place. It's better connected to memory than digital communication. A well-written and engaging sales letter can have a positive emotional impact on the recipient, one that is far more enduring than a digital communication.

Your sales letter can have real impact if accompanied by a natty free gift or a sample of your products or services. In an era when we are so reliant upon e-mail, your sales letter provides an opportunity to engage and inspire your audience, and encourage them to find out more about you. On-line sales messages often struggle to be anything other than impersonal, with many being automatically routed to spam folders to save the recipient from even opening them. A sales letter will always be picked up from the doormat, will always be opened if correctly targeted, and, if well-written and relevant, has a very high chance of being read.

The Challenge

When targeting cold prospects with a sales letter, you are writing to someone that doesn't know you from Adam. Whereas you have many reasons for wanting to convert them into customers, they, on the other hand, are unlikely to share your enthusiasm for this to happen. Their lives are not incomplete because they have yet to come across your products or services.

So you face the difficult, but not impossible challenge of inspiring them through the content of your sales letter to find out more about you. You face a lesser challenge when communicating with your existing customers but still need to motivate them sufficiently to buy more.

This chapter is all about writing effective sales letters, and the tips that follow are based on 26 years' experience of doing just that. I also include 13 very different sales letters I have written over the last two years for a diverse range of organisations. Each letter has made it into this chapter because it was very successful in achieving its objectives. I hope they help you to write your next winning sales letter.

Spend Time Researching and Planning

At one of my direct mail workshops recently, a delegate was emphatic that sales letters did not work for his business. He was a florist and had brought a sample of his most recent sales letter for my evaluation. Although the letter was good, it fell down in many areas. There was no clear call to action and it included so many different selling messages that it was confusing. He had paid no attention to what would motivate his target audience to buy their floral arrangements from him as opposed to one of his many local competitors.

Don't write your sales letter in isolation concerning yourself only with presenting an attractive and well laid out document. It must contain substance and be relevant to the readers. Spend time identifying and understanding your audience and supplement this with some competitor research. Although we have covered the importance of research in the previous chapter I would like to reinforce some of those points, relating them specifically to your sales letter.

These six tips will help get you started.

1. **Consider who you want to communicate with.** Before you can think about writing a sales letter, you need to identify the groups of people that you want to communicate with. As discussed in Chapter 1, this can be a broad or narrow spectrum that includes:

   - Cold prospects - people that you are yet to do business with.
   - Warm prospects - people that have expressed an interest in what you offer but are yet to buy.
   - Lapsed clients - people with whom you have had a buying relationship in the past but this has now ceased.
   - Existing clients - you may want to segment your existing clients even further depending on what they buy from you, when they buy and their value to your business.
   - Influencers - people who can recommend you to potential new customers, i.e. trade associations, buying groups, membership organisations and consultants etc.

You must be clear about who is going to receive your sales letters because you're not going to write the same letter to each group. The message may be the same, but each letter will need to be tweaked to reflect the differing needs of each target audience.

2. **Once you are clear about which audiences you aim to target, stand in their shoes and appraise your business through their eyes.** (Something covered in Chapter 2.) If you are not writing from your customer's point of view, your sales letter will fall at the first hurdle. Prospects and customers are not interested in what you want; they are

after answers and solutions to their needs. Try to discover what your prospects or customers already know about your products or services. If you're not sure, pick up the phone and speak to a handful. Explain that you want to find out more about their needs and what influences them to buy the products or services that you supply. If you don't have accurate answers to these questions, your sales letter may offer too much or too little information and be focused in the wrong direction.

3. **Find out what's happening in the marketplace in which your prospects and customers operate**. People are influenced in their purchasing decisions by their own prosperity and the underlying trends within their marketplace. So if times are tough, your sales letter should demonstrate your understanding of this. You may need to focus on showing the recipients how you deliver value for money, for example.

4. **Carry out some competitor research.** This is not as onerous as it may initially appear. Your sales letter should demonstrate that you understand your reader and their needs and that what you are offering will meet these needs. In all likelihood, the people that you are targeting will also have some knowledge of what your competitors offer, even if it's a bit sketchy. However, as covered in Chapter 2, shy away from using the word unique. Your letter will not be lacking if you don't pepper it with unsubstantiated superlatives. Instead, acquaint yourself with a handful of competitors before writing your letter. Visit their websites, engage in a spot of mystery shopping and compare your respective offerings. Are your products cheaper, faster, easier? Are they more reliable? Are they

the best performing, recommended by experts? Do they offer the best value? Have you won awards or been accredited for your services? Do you offer unconditional guarantees? Do you hold the highest possible qualifications in your sector? Have you amassed experience that's hard to find elsewhere? If the only tangible outcome of this exercise is to make you realise that you are offering an excellent product or service, it will have been a success.

5. **Evaluate your most popular benefits.** Re-visit the positioning statement described in Chapter 2. You're not going to cover all of the benefits within your positioning statement. Which are the main benefits that you want to include in your sales letter? If you can focus on three key benefits, this should usually provide more than enough content for you to write a great sales letter.

   Many business people when writing sales letters overlook the importance of focusing on benefits. They prefer instead to grab the attention of the reader with gimmicks, such as an exaggerated limited edition offer or a once in a lifetime opportunity and so on. The fact is, however, that without seducing the reader with the many relevant benefits that you are offering, you are very unlikely to move them from their current inertia.

6. **Will a genuine offer trigger activity?** Open up any newspaper and you'll see all manner of adverts accompanied by an incentive to reply or buy. One example is the offer of a free pen for requesting a life insurance quote, and free retail vouchers if the quote is taken up. An offer is something extra, something over and above the product or service that you're promoting in your sales letter. It's

designed to prompt the reader to act immediately before they forget or are distracted by another business. For an offer of this kind to work, it must be appropriate and appealing to the readers. They will be unimpressed by an empty gesture and won't thank you for wasting their time. And don't believe that every sales letter you send must include an offer for it to work. In some cases an offer may not be appropriate or financially possible. You may struggle to think of an offer that's relevant. Simply focus instead on writing a brilliant sales letter and it should have an impact, with or without an offer.

If you are unsure about the idea of including offers with your letters, start by taking a look at those offers included in the sales letters at the end of this chapter. They illustrate how offers can work for many types of businesses with widely varying sales messages and calls to action.

When including an offer, consider imposing a close date and a limit on the number of people that can benefit. By way of illustration:

> *'To take advantage of a complimentary 60-minute one-to-one coaching session you must respond to this letter by 1st December. This genuine offer is only available for the first 25 people to respond.'*

This encourages people to respond promptly and enables you to limit your financial outlay. You may also want the person to yield some information in order to qualify for your offer and this is a good way to screen out the freebie hunters.

> *'Please ensure that you complete the enclosed questionnaire to qualify for this genuine offer.'*

Writing That Sales Letter

You are now at the stage where you know who you are targeting, you've done some competitor research and you're confident about the appeal and the relevance of your offering. You have undertaken informal research with your target audiences and have a clear grasp of their needs. You have a small but perfectly formed list of benefits appropriate for each group and you have decided whether to include an offer or not. You're feeling confident that the groundwork has been thorough. Right, let's get writing!

The Basics - The Small and Inexpensive Things that Count

- **Always use good quality paper** - a minimum of 120 grams. Your letter is going to be felt and studied. Do you really want your reader to judge your business based on a cheap and flimsy piece of paper? You may want to consider a textured finish to emphasise the tangibility of your letter. It must look and feel crisp and attractive.

- **Attach your business card with a paperclip**. If your letter does end up in the bin, your business card may well be held back.

- **Hand-sign each letter** with a legible signature using a decent quality pen.

- **Your signature should be followed by two short lines of text** - your name accompanied by any qualifications and your title. Beneath my own signature, I print,

Dee Blick, FCIM Chartered Marketer,
Managing Director
The Marketing Gym Ltd

This conveys a professional image and shows that you are making a personal effort to contact the reader rather than outsourcing the task to a telemarketing company or delegating to a member of staff.

The Layout

If you have a powerful opening statement, use the space referred to in direct marketing circles as 'The Johnson Box'. This is the area that sits in between the space designated for the reader's address details and the opening salutation. There's usually room for two to three lines of text. Only use this space if you have something of importance to say. In some of the letters at the end of this chapter you will see how this space can be used.

- In your early days of letter writing, I would advise that you avoid extending your letter beyond one side of A4. Focus instead on delivering your message on just that one page, a very good discipline in itself.

- After your introductory paragraph in which you outline your reasons for writing to the reader, highlight your key benefits in three or four bullet points. This will virtually guarantee they will be read, especially if each bullet does not extend beyond a few lines of text.

- Your bullet points should be followed by a few paragraphs of text in which you highlight certain phrases and key points using **bold text** and *italics*. Readers will gravitate towards these highlighted areas but only if you are sparing in their application.

- Always try to include a postscript (P.S.). I often include a postscript to highlight a particular benefit or to reiterate any offer and I vary it depending on the reader. For example, you'll see in some of the letters that I use the space earmarked for a postscript to include genuine customer testimonial and to reveal the results of a market research survey. This can work really well because it's unusual to use the space in this manner. You can guarantee that it will be read.

- Become your own severest critic. It's tempting to write a first draft of your sales letter and then to leave it at that. Don't succumb. Generally it takes me three or more drafts before I am happy with the final wording. If you are not happy with editing your own work then paying a professional editor will cost very little but could ensure that your letter jumps from being good to brilliant.

The Style

We have covered the need to make your marketing communications friendly and engaging in the previous chapter and it is worth remembering this advice when you are ready to start writing. Your letter should be an intimate communication. It must be interesting, informative and charming. You are having a conversation, albeit one-sided, with the reader and attempting to paint a picture of your products and services that is so attractive, so tuned in to their needs, that they contact you to learn more. Avoid using jargon unless you are sure that your target audience will be receptive to it. Write in a friendly, conversational manner.

Adding the 'X' Factor

- Whenever possible, underpin your benefit statements with facts and figures linked to your performance, your service, your products and your levels of customer satisfaction.

  '90% of our customers renew their service contract with us each year compared to the industry average of just 60%.'

  '9/10 trade stockists recommend our product as the best for their customers.'

  'Why do three of the leading trade journals endorse our products?'

  'Be a confident public speaker with just three short sessions.'

- Include genuine testimonial from happy customers. If it's not possible to include their full name, ask for permission to use their initials. Don't write the testimonial yourself – this is something that we cover in more detail in the next chapter.

- Make it easy for the reader to contact you. Offer your telephone and fax number, e-mail address, and website address. Don't assume that everyone is comfortable using e-mail. They won't be. Don't put off a potential customer by offering just one communication channel simply because it's the most convenient one for you.

Turn the Page...There's Potential in that Space

If you really want to add some sparkle to your sales letter, don't overlook the fantastic selling opportunity that's presented on the other side of the page. Earlier I mentioned that your sales letter should be no more than one side of A4. However, as you become a more confident writer there are many ways in which you can use the back of the sales letter to communicate other messages in a different format. And of course, it allows you a second bite at the cherry. Most people will read your letter then turn over the page to check for anything else. Greet them with another message.

So, what could you consider writing on the back of your sales letter? How about:

- Your genuine unedited testimonial - three or four delighted customers raving about you.
- Frequently asked questions and answers - the top 3, 5, 6, 7, 10 questions that new customers ask before doing business with you.
- A couple of case studies of existing clients that match the profile of the readers you are targeting.
- A quiz or competition.
- Your latest press release.
- More information on your special offer.

Full Colour, or Black and White?

It's easy to assume that your letter needs to contain a riot of colour and imagery for it to achieve the impact necessary to motivate readers to respond. It doesn't. You are sending a well-written sales letter, not a brochure or a sales leaflet. If you can focus on writing a compelling and relevant message and presenting it in a professional and attractive way, you won't need gimmicks to make an impression. One thing worth considering, however, is lumpy mail.

Lumpy Mail

There are times when your letter needs a helping hand; a guarantee that before the recipient opens up the envelope their curiosity is aroused, and upon opening it they are greeted by something that puts a smile on their face.

Adding a small gift to your sales letter that ties in with the subject matter, is relevant to your brand and is likely to be well received by the recipient, can have quite an impact. The enclosed item could be something that reflects a popular element of your service and promotes your one big selling message, or could simply be a sample of your product. Popular examples include a pen, a coaster, a mouse mat branded with your company details. If the purpose of your letter is to motivate people to attend your exhibition stand or seminar, and you will be giving away some goodies at the event, why not enclose the packaging from one of the gifts? You could then add a postscript to your letter explaining that to pick up the gift itself, the recipient needs to visit your stand at the event. It is surprising the effort that people will make to receive something free and many high-value relationships have begun with a simple sales letter and a little gift.

Examples of How Lumpy Mail Can Have an Impact

- The rather snazzy gift tag from some equally snazzy drink mugs was attached by paperclip to a sales letter, and this letter was then sent to a selected group of lapsed clients. It explained that if they booked and attended a meeting with the sales person they would receive two of the mugs filled with organic chocolates. There was a 55% response to this campaign, and from these meetings the salesmen gained over £40,000 of new orders. This was from the same audience that had previously resisted their e-marketing overtures. The letter is included later in this chapter.

A similar approach was taken to motivate the attendees at a seminar to visit a client's exhibition stand. This time the gift tag belonged to a jumbo bar of organic chocolate. By the end of the day there were no more chocolate bars left to hand out! This letter is also included later.

- A tea bag was attached to a sales letter in which the recipients (hard-working and busy tradesmen) were encouraged to put their feet up at the end of the day, and have a cuppa whilst reading the letter.

- A selection of retro sweets including Love Hearts, Parma Violets and Black Jacks were enclosed with a letter to promote telemarketing services to social media businesses. The message was that traditional marketing still delivers and is unlikely to ever go out of fashion.

- The old favourites never fail. By enclosing a good quality pen with a client's annual customer survey, it helped generate a response rate of 22%, with many of those responding commenting that the pen was a nice touch.

- A client of mine recently commissioned some independent market research and discovered that 9/10 stockists preferred my client's product to that of the nearest competitor. Within days a sales letter was issued containing a coaster branded with the headline result of this research. This helped generate a 20% increase in sales of this product.

As you will see from the sample letters that follow, lumpy mail has many commercial advantages and is well worth considering even if you decide for budgetary reasons to limit the lumpy mail approach to VIP clients and prospects only.

Stand and Deliver! Your Envelope

So far we have been looking at sales letters and how to write a cracking one. It's time now to look at the envelope that will house your sales letter. It would be a pity indeed to create a good looking, professional sales letter, to add a natty little gift, and then to fall down at the final hurdle by enclosing it in a tatty envelope.

- Make sure that you use an envelope that matches the quality of your letterhead paper. The last thing you want is for the envelope to scream 'flyer' or 'junk mail'.

- Handwrite the envelope if your handwriting is neat and legible. This will arouse curiosity and guarantee that your letter is opened. Try this out on a handful of VIPs.

- Using a stamp rather than a frank mark will also attract attention. Make sure that you pay the correct postage though, especially if the enclosed gift makes it a package, as you will not win many friends if the recipient has to pay the additional postage fee.

- A printed label can give the impression that the envelope contains junk mail. Best to be avoided if possible.

- A brown envelope is not as appealing as a white or cream one, but ultimately it is the quality of the envelope that counts. Your envelope can be in any number of colours if it matches your corporate identity. However, in my experience a good quality plain envelope, meticulously hand addressed and posted with a stamp can achieve the right impression on the smallest of budgets.

- Should you put a message on your envelope or not? It can be a risky strategy not least because it's straying into junk mail territory. If in doubt, it is probably best not to.

- Make sure that you have the correct name, salutation and, if relevant, job title of the person that you are mailing. With a surname like Blick, I can be on the receiving end of many creative interpretations. And the majority do not put me in a positive frame of mind to read the enclosed letter!

- If you really want to go the extra mile, consider hand delivering some of your sales letters. This is more appropriate, of course, if the people that you want to target are close by. Make sure that you write the words 'By Hand' in the top right-hand corner of your envelope. I was in a meeting recently when the MD received such a letter. Her curiosity was aroused to the extent that she actually brought the meeting to a close so that she could read the letter. If you are delivering by hand, it is advisable to handwrite the envelopes.

The Power of Three

In the ideal world, you would send one lovingly-created, well targeted sales letter to your prospects and customers, and the sales would simply flow in. Whilst this may happen occasionally, it's unlikely to do so in the quantities you are aiming for. As illustrated by The Continuum of Behaviour, most of us need to be communicated with in stages if we are to be persuaded to part with our money – whether business or personal funds. As a young copywriter I was taught about 'The Power of Three' - the concept that if you want to clinch a sale, especially from a cold prospect, you need to target them with three separate communications. This doesn't just mean sending out three letters. If you vary the method of communication whilst sticking to the same marketing message you're more likely to get a positive result. So, how could the concept of 'The Power of Three' work when a sales letter is one element in your communication process? Here are three suggestions:

Campaign No.1

1. Introductory telephone call to ascertain the initial interest of the prospect or customer.

2. Targeted sales letter using lumpy mail.

3. Follow-up telephone call to evaluate the likelihood of a sale.

Campaign No.2

1. A teaser message sent to your prospects and customers. This could be a very short letter or one of the creative communications covered in the next chapter. The communication can be printed or sent on-line. Your teaser message is just that - it's revealing a smidgen of what will follow. It will usually include an offer and a note to the recipient that they will be receiving further details in a few days.

2. Targeted sales letter using lumpy mail.

3. Follow-up telephone call to evaluate the likelihood of a sale.

Campaign No.3

1. A concise questionnaire sent out with an incentive designed to attract those early bird responders. All you are looking for at this stage are responses to your questions as opposed to a strong signal to buy.

2. Follow-up telephone call to discuss the responses and ascertain interest levels.

3. Follow-up sales letter using lumpy mail.

The ideal time lag between each communication is three to five working days. You want to maintain the momentum and don't want the person to forget about you, yet you also want to avoid battering the recipient with your messages over a very short period of time.

These are good campaigns if you are able to allocate sufficient time to make follow-up telephone calls. The telephone still plays a vital role in moving both prospects and customers along The Continuum of Behaviour. If you are time-pressed, why not use this communication process for your VIP prospects and clients only, the ones that you really want to bring on board? The results that you achieve from making these telephone calls should indicate whether it would be beneficial to make follow-up calls to the remainder of your target audience too.

When the On-line World Complements your Sales Letters

If you want to increase the impact of 'The Power of Three' further, it's a good idea to ensure that your website and your blog are complementing the messages in your sales letters. Before you embark on your sales letter campaigns, make sure that your website is well stocked with up to date content and latest news. Your blog, if you have one, should include content that will appeal to the people you are targeting. You may have built a successful off-line campaign but one of the first places that your prospects will visit if they are interested in finding out more about you, is your website and your blog. Don't let your good work unravel because your website news is woefully out of date and your blog has seen better days.

13 Successful Sales Letters

Over the next few pages I include some of the most successful sales letters I have written. They cover a diverse range of businesses. In most cases, a follow-up telephone call was made to the targeted recipients within 5 days of the letter hitting the doormats. As you study each letter, try to relate it to your own business. How can you benefit from the techniques that I have used? You will see that although the products and services differ greatly, each letter is written in a friendly conversational style with an absence of jargon.

The Document Shredding Business – Letter 1

The purpose of this letter was to introduce S4B's secure document shredding and recycling services to local accountants. It was accompanied by the Managing Director's business card and a four-page prospectus outlining the services S4B provides. Note the use of the Johnson Box and the judicious use of bold text and italics. The three bullet points are used to highlight the main benefits.

This was a very successful letter – 25% of the list responded immediately, buying S4B's services even before the scheduled follow up phone call had been made.

The Recruitment Business – Letter 2

The purpose of this letter was to introduce YourRecruit's on-line recruitment and advertising services to targeted cold prospects. It was accompanied by the recruitment consultant's business card and a small bar of high quality chocolate to add an element of intrigue to the envelope. You can see the Johnson Box in action again with a quirky line to grab attention. This is a concise letter that was reinforced by using the space on the reverse to share a genuine case study to add credibility. This is especially important when launching a new service.

The Printer – Letter 3

The purpose of this letter was to entice lapsed clients and warm prospects to contact the printing business, Quentin Press, and arrange a meeting.

The gift tag from the Pantone mugs was included with the letter. A four-page newsletter accompanied this letter which included the offer of two free Pantone shade mugs filled with organic chocolates for each person that booked a meeting. Note the short and snappy bullet points and the use of the words, 'you' and 'your'. The letter signs off by reinforcing the offer of the free mugs. It worked exceptionally well in bringing in thousands of pounds worth of print business. The many previous e-mail campaigns had failed to bring in any business at all.

The Linseed Farmer – Letter 4

The purpose of this letter was to persuade lapsed clients to consider buying linseed again from the business, High Barn Oils. Timed to coincide with the launch of the brand-new website and accompanied by a free seven-day supply of linseed pods, the call to action was simply to visit the new website. Note that although the letter promotes ordering on-line, the option of ordering by telephone is still available.

The Training Company (Part 1) – Letter 5

The purpose of this letter was to encourage a targeted group of women in the public sector to attend a one-day training conference. It was a tough task because budgets were tight and it was notoriously difficult to prise people away from their desks. Accompanying the letter was a gift tag from a bar of organic chocolate. Note the use of the Johnson Box to grab attention and how the reason for the gift tag has been explained in the postscript. The three main bullet points were used to describe the prestigious speakers and the five workshops were highlighted with simple one line bullet points. Note also the powerful words used throughout this letter - stunning, animated, stimulating, delicious, outstanding, inspirational, pivotal etc.

The Vehicle Adaptation Specialist – Letter 6

Techmobility is a vehicle adaptation business that operates in a competitive marketplace. Telephone research with motor dealerships had revealed that most were firmly committed to their existing adaptation specialist and had no intention of moving, even though using Techmobility would be more convenient.

The sales letter sent out was inspired by the Doyle Dane Bernbach advertising campaign, 'Avis versus Hertz'. This campaign was rated by David Ogilvy as 'one of the most powerful campaigns in the history of advertising'.

Do you remember the iconic headline?

'When you're only No.2, you try harder. Or else.'

This campaign helped Avis to become the No.1 car hire firm, outperforming the previous market leader, Hertz. The Techmobility sales letter was aimed at dealerships whose loyalties were with another adaptation specialist. It did not attempt to hide this fact as you will see from the Johnson Box and the opening two lines. It's much better to be honest and to acknowledge the true situation than it is to make false claims. The second paragraph of the letter focuses on the benefits that the dealership will gain from using Techmobility at times when their service provider is unable to help them. The results so far have been excellent with many of these dealerships now using Techmobility as a backup.

The Promotional Gifts Specialist – Letter 7

The purpose of this letter was to motivate existing customers to place an order from the new 2011 gift catalogue which accompanied it. A free high quality pen was also enclosed. You can see how the Johnson Box has again been used to highlight the special offer which is explained in more detail in the final paragraph. Rather than adding a postscript, a testimonial from an existing client was used instead. Some of the text was emboldened and placed in italics to give prominence to the special offers.

The Motor Accessories Specialist – Letter 8

The purpose of this letter, the first of two, was to encourage selected commercial vehicle Motor Factors not currently trading with Kalimex, a supplier of motor accessories, to request a free sample of a Kalimex product. This is a classic sales letter that encompasses most, if not all of the tips that have been shared in this chapter. Note that on this occasion the Johnson Box is populated with powerful testimonial from a leading trade magazine delivered to commercial vehicle workshops. The three bullet points are used to highlight the key benefits of the product that are most likely to encourage the stockist to open an account. The final paragraph describes the offer tied into a close date, whilst the space usually occupied by the postscript is used instead to share an important statistic. Finally the letter concludes by asking the reader to turn the page. The space on the back was taken up with questions and answers. This letter, and the one that follows it, led to over 100 new accounts being opened and minimum monthly sales of 1,000 units of K-Seal HD, the Kalimex product being promoted.

The Motor Accessories Specialist (Continued) – Letter 9

This letter was sent to the stockist when they requested a free sample of K-Seal HD. The Johnson Box is used to highlight the free product and the special offer, repeated again in the introductory paragraph. Asking questions encourages the reader to think about the message. The two bullet points cover the benefits that the stockist will gain from selling Kalimex products. The postscript is short but to the point. Sometimes a few words are more than enough.

The Training Company (Part 2) – Letter 10

The purpose of this letter was to introduce a brand-new project management workshop to delegates that had attended previous project management and leadership taster seminars run by Youthforce. All recipients had indicated in previous feedback that this type of workshop would be of interest to them. Competitor research had revealed that the project management training from Youthforce was clearer, easier to understand, and more practical than workshops run by leading competitors.

The letter is written to the individual in a very personal style, and the two calls to action are numbered in order to stand out that little bit more. We are effectively instructing the delegates to read the enclosed project management outline and pick up the phone. The postscript has been used to share a relevant and thought-provoking quotation.

The Debt Collection Specialist – Letter 11

The purpose of this letter was to encourage cold prospects to review their outstanding debts and to instruct Direct Route to collect them.

It was sent in the last week of November and accompanying the letter was a pen, a registration form and a sample of one of the demands that their debtor would receive. The Johnson Box is used to introduce the Christmas theme and the most powerful part of the letter, the testimonial from a delighted Direct Route customer, is saved until last so that it has the greatest impact. This was an extremely successful letter, resulting in 20 new clients.

A tweaked version of this letter was also sent to existing customers and was similarly successful, proving that your existing customers need to be reminded about you too!

The Artisan Baker – Letter 12

The purpose of this letter was to tempt customers that had previously bought one cake from Country Farm Cakes to buy another. Most of the sales from existing customers originally derived through the website, but this letter shows how an off-line communication can be effective in driving on-line sales. The tone of the letter is friendly and chatty but informative. It's giving the reader a glimpse into what has been happening in the bakery, the delicious cakes that are being baked and why they should place a further order. The special offer details are included in the penultimate paragraph.

You will see that customers are given the option of re-ordering through the website, by telephone or by post. Again, this letter uses many descriptive words to paint a seductive culinary picture of the cakes and to describe the passion for baking possessed by this family business. The testimonial at the foot of the letter from a master chef completes the message.

The Credit Management Specialist – Letter 13

The purpose of this letter was to introduce a brand-new on-line credit management service to the small business client base of local bookkeepers who had signed up to become strategic partners of AccountAssyst. It needed to communicate to the bookkeeper's client that this new on-line credit management service was unique, that it had been designed specifically for small businesses and that it was worthy of their closer inspection. The offer in the letter was a free trial of the system.

The information has been broken into bullet points and short paragraphs to make the letter easy to read. The layout was crucial in gaining the many positive responses from readers to a free trial. The sparing use of italics and emboldening text draws the eye to the parts of the letter that we wanted the reader to dwell on.

Letter 1

In business your reputation is everything. It helps you to stand head and shoulders above your competitors. Make sure it *never* falls into the wrong hands.

Dear Mr Walker,

I'd like to introduce our Gatwick-based business to you because we offer a service that is becoming increasingly popular with accountants. If you need to dispose of confidential documents, but don't want a scrap of this information falling into the wrong hands, you will welcome our secure document destruction service.

And, it won't cost you over the odds. In fact, we may even be able to *reduce* your document disposal costs whilst also reinforcing your reputation as an environmentally friendly business. Once we have shredded your documentation beyond recognition, it is then recycled into paper-based products. Take a look around your office now. How many unwanted client documents are taking up precious space? What information are you storing about your business that's no longer needed?

Why is S4B the secure document destruction company of choice for accountants?

- **We are a local business**. So we can offer you a regular or ad hoc collection service. Some accountants opt for our cabinet service and we collect their unwanted documentation every two weeks. Others prefer our ad hoc bag only service. Really it's down to you and your business need.
- **It's an incredibly cost-effective service**. The good news is that you can protect your business's reputation and do your bit for the environment without making a dent in your budget. *We may even be able to save you money...*
- **With ID fraud well and truly on the rise**, it's no longer an option for any business handling sensitive or confidential data to bury their head in the sand and hope that neither they nor their clients become victims.

Interested in finding out more?

Please get in touch. You can e-mail xxxxxxxx or call 01293 534966 to discuss the full facts and figures. And ask about our introductory discount which runs until August 31.

Yours sincerely,

Mike Potts

Managing Director

Letter 2

An on-line matchmaking service that is good for business and won't make you blush!

Dear Sarah,

If you're looking to recruit it can be a time-consuming and frustrating task, especially if your budget doesn't stretch to a full recruitment service.

You can of course try advertising in the local papers, but with more candidates than ever now searching for vacancies on-line, you may end up with nothing, or just a handful of candidates to choose from. You can advertise your vacancy on the Internet job boards. But this can be problematic too. Which ones should you use, how much will it cost you...does your advert have the right keywords to attract the right people and not the time wasters?

There is a much better solution....

Introducing your on-line recruitment matchmaker

YourRecruit has developed three powerful on-line recruitment services at a price that's less than the cost of advertising your vacancy in a newspaper or directly onto the Internet job boards. What's more…

- We help you to write your advert, making sure it has the right keyword density
- Within minutes we'll post your advert on the leading job boards
- If you don't want to search through a mountain of CVs, you can add our CV filtering service
- If you want us to, we can telephone interview your candidates for just £20 per interview

It's amazing value and it works. In the current marketplace there are more vacancies than there are high-calibre candidates to fill them. Choose YourRecruit's on-line recruitment matchmaking service to ensure that as many of the best candidates as possible find out about your vacancy. Go to www.yourrecruit.com or contact us for an informal chat on 0845 070 7873.

Yours sincerely

xxxxxxxxxxxxxxxx

Turn over to discover how one small business owner found the perfect match for her vacancy through YourAdPlus, one of our on-line recruitment services - just £345 including CV filtering.

This was on the back of the letter.

Once upon a time.... a true story

A new small business client wanted to recruit a tax advisor for her growing business. It was a position that she would usually try to fill through placing an advert in her local newspaper.

Persuaded by the benefits of our service YourAdPlus, she decided to place some of her trust in the on-line universe. But, still to be completely won over, she also placed an advert in her local newspaper. Old habits can die hard.

What was the result in this friendly battle of print versus pixels?

YourAdPlus yielded four exceptional candidates. After interviewing all four and being delighted at the calibre of each person, our client made an offer that was immediately accepted by her favoured candidate. Although we don't know whether they lived happily ever after, we do know that their working relationship, although in its infancy, is a positive and harmonious one and our client is delighted that she took the leap of faith to advertise on-line with YourAdPlus.

And what of the newspaper advert? It turned out to be a waste of money on this occasion because the few candidates that did respond were completely unsuitable.

And the moral of this true story? If you're looking to recruit some exceptional people, but like many small businesses your budget has been trimmed to the irreducible minimum, take a closer look at how we can help you with our unique on-line recruitment solution from just £185 plus VAT.

Letter 3

Dear Mrs Collins,

Do you want more from your printing company?

In the current challenging climate, businesses of all sizes are looking for even more value from their professional partners and they need their marketing communications to really pack a punch. If your marketing literature is printed externally, then **now is the time to compare the service you currently receive with the service we can offer you.**

As you know, Quentin Press provide a wide range of print services to hundreds of local businesses in the local area. Over the last 10 years, we've built a fantastic reputation for being reliable, cost-effective and, most importantly, for producing superb quality print to tight deadlines.

Here's just a small selection of current projects we're working on for local businesses like yours

- **Project managing** and printing several hundred bespoke folders and their accompanying dividers, pages, labels and envelopes
- **Printing full-colour pamphlets**, newsletters, novelty shaped promotional flyers, sales leaflets mini brochures and sales flyers
- **Printing postcards**, brochures and presentation folders

We offer a huge range of printed finishes from high-gloss and bio-degradable lamination to the standard stuff. We're also accredited by the Forest Stewardship Council (FSC) - your assurance that you are working with an environmentally responsible printer.

Quality and great prices aside, what sets us apart from many other print companies is that we really do look after you with one-to-one dedicated account management. Often, you want your marketing literature right now! Come Hell or high water we will meet your deadlines. We're confident that you will be thrilled with the finished result. ***When it comes to creating an impact with both clients and cold prospects, nothing grabs their attention like a professionally printed document.***

The next step
Please contact us to arrange an informal meeting. We'll bring along two of these fabulous pantone mugs for you, filled to the brim with organic chocolates. We look forward to hearing from you and to working with you again.

Yours sincerely,
xxxxxxxxxxxxxxxxxx

AB Managing Director

Letter 4

Dear Mrs Simmons,

Have you missed the delicious nutty taste of our linseed pods that are bursting with Omega 3?

It has been a little while since we have heard from you so we hope that you are well. But, are you still getting your Omega 3? If you are not, then please enjoy the complimentary seven day supply of High Barn Oils linseed pods that I have enclosed with this letter.

As you know, there are many health giving benefits to linseed and when you buy your linseed from our farm, you know that you are enjoying a product that has been **grown on our farm and naturally pressed in our barn using traditional methods**. It all adds up to the most delicious taste and of course many health benefits ranging from strong nails to clear skin and more supple joints.

Why get your Omega 3 from fish oil or even from linseed grown overseas when you can get it from linseed that's been grown and freshly pressed in Sussex?

Take a peek at our brand-new website

We have received some lovely feedback on our new website from both existing customers and from new people finding us for the first time. You can download recipes, read our latest news and even order on-line. And of course, you can still place your order by telephone.

I hope that you enjoy the enclosed linseed pods and I look forward to hearing from you again,

Kind regards,

Durwin Banks
Farmer

Letter 5

Women Leading The Way Conference - how to be outstanding and get outstanding results! Will you be attending?

Dear Mrs Jennings,

I would like to invite you to the Women Leading The Way Conference, a one day event on XX date. Held at the stunning headquarters of the Business Design Centre in Islington, London, this conference is aimed at women that are involved in working in children and young people's services. It promises to be a thoroughly enjoyable day in which you can network with other like-minded women, join in with the animated audience discussions, listen to three inspirational keynote speakers and enjoy learning in a stimulating workshop environment. And delicious refreshments are included in the modest delegate fee, courtesy of the Good Eating Company.

Why Is the Conference Being Staged?

The Women Leading The Way Conference will present a blend of new and innovative approaches to management and leadership in an engaging format. Its remit is to empower women that are aspiring managers and leaders in the provision of services for young people and young adults. It will also give you the opportunity to network, learn and to share ideas in a vibrant and relaxed environment.

What Is Happening on the Day?

After registration, refreshments and informal networking you can listen to three inspirational speakers, followed by question and answer sessions.

We are delighted to have secured…

- **Dr Terry Ryall, the founding Chief Executive of V,** the National Young Volunteers Service. This service was launched in May 2006 with a mission to mobilise a new generation of volunteers aged 16-25 and to revolutionise the youth volunteering landscape..... And with a staggering target of raising £50 million from the private sector! Terry is a compelling and engaging speaker.
- **Julie Bentley MBA, the Chief Executive of FPA,** formerly Family Planning Association, a national charity with a wide service portfolio including a national helpline, training, and a range of nationwide community projects. Julie believes that great leaders gain respect through fairness, transparency, clear boundaries and consistency.
- **Dinah Cox OBE, Executive Director of ROSA,** an organisation that forges vital links between the women's sector and other sectors from which funding may be sourced. Dinah became a feminist at the age of 12, after realising that many women were being held back from fulfilling their potential.

On the day, you can also choose from five workshops. Each one is facilitated by an experienced trainer.

- **Coaching for Change** - strengthen your career aspirations with key self coaching techniques
- **The Power of Influence** - learn how emotional intelligence can help you to influence others
- **Recruitment and Selection** - discover how to make the shortlist and manage the interview process
- **Image Consultancy** - how to develop a powerful and personal brand
- **Inspire Your Audience** - learn powerful presentation skills that will engage your audience

The conference has been jointly organised by Charlotte Blant, the Managing Director of Youthforce, and Roland Azor, the Director and founder of Innovations at Work. Youthforce is one of the UK's leading providers of accredited and non-accredited training courses, designed to inspire and motivate professionals of all levels, from volunteers to managers. Roland is a highly skilled and experienced practitioner specialising in integrating and mainstreaming equality into organisational change and staff development programmes.

How to Book Your Place on This Pivotal Conference

The conference is now two thirds full so early booking is essential to secure your attendance. The cost of attending, including refreshments, lunch, workshops and handout material, is just £XX plus VAT, a total of £XX. If you book two places, a third delegate comes free! Book three places and a fourth delegate comes free. You can book on-line at xxxxxxxxxxx or call xxxxxxxxxxxxxxxx.

We look forward to hearing from you and to meeting you on the day. Please do not hesitate to contact us if you have any questions about the event. You can speak to any member of the Youthforce team, on 01273 776 779 or e-mail xxxxxxxxxxxxxx

Yours sincerely,

Charlotte Blant
Managing Director

PS: It has probably not escaped your attention that we have included a Cocoa Loco chocolate gift tag with this letter. Cocoa Loco is an award winning small family business that makes the most scrumptious organic vegetarian chocolate. Visit the Youthforce stand at the Women Leading The Way Conference with your gift tag and we will give you a complimentary jumbo bar of Cocoa Loco's divine chocolate.

Letter 6

We Know That We Are Not Your First Choice...Could we be your Second Choice when You Need an Urgent Back Up?

Dear Mr Davies,

Whilst we would like to be your preferred vehicle adaptation specialist, we appreciate that you are loyal to your current vehicle adaptation specialist.

However, there may be occasions when your adaptation specialist is unable to adapt a customer's vehicle. For example when they are on holiday or when an adaptation is complex. We say this because in recent months we have spoken to over 50 new Motability dealers. Each one has told us that whilst they are satisfied with the specialist they are currently using, they would also like to use Techmobility because *we can handle any adaptation*. From Multiplex wiring, indicator switches and infrareds to swivel seats and bespoke adaptations.

We would be pleased to provide our services to you on an occasional basis, augmenting the service you are already receiving. **You may like to know why 500 Motability specialists trust us as their preferred adaptation specialist.**

- We have 20 years' experience in adapting vehicles for disabled motorists.
- We have a disability accessible workshop in Sussex. We can adapt several vehicles at any one time.
- We have *two fully equipped mobile workshops*, operated by qualified engineers. **We can adapt your customer's vehicle at your dealership.** The mobile workshops are equipped with welders, grinders and cutting equipment. Any adaptation can be undertaken on site including discreet hand controls, left foot accelerator pedals, infrareds, hoists, swivel seats and multiplex wiring.

So, the next time you need to call on a powerful reserve please contact us. We would be delighted to offer our services to you.

Yours sincerely,

Ryan Walker
Managing Director

Letter 7

It's crammed with high-value ideas to promote your business. Welcome to the 2011 Creative Vision Promotions' catalogue. Check out our very special offer for the first 50 customers to place an order in 2011!

Dear Mike,

2011. It's going to be a good year, a year in which successful businesses like yours continue to gain market share through being positively different. And promotional gifts have a huge part to play in achieving this.

When blended with your existing marketing communications, promotional gifts can

- Create a real and positive impact
- Build loyalty with cold prospects and VIP customers alike
- Dramatically increase responses to both on-line and off-line communications

It's time to recycle your 2010 catalogue

Why? Because our 2011 catalogue is packed with thousands of brand-new promotional gifts to suit every budget, including an incredible variety of striking pens, a range of eco-friendly key rings and an assortment of gorgeous mouse mats - still the ideal blank canvas for promoting your brand and revealing your sales message.

And have we got a fantastic offer for you!

If you are one of the first 50 customers to place an order from our new catalogue **you will receive free one colour personalisation on up to 3 different products-saving you £90**. ***Additionally, the first two customers to place an order will also receive a signed first edition copy of the Amazon bestselling business book; Powerful Marketing on a Shoestring Budget for Small Businesses, by Dee Blick.*** It's time to order! We look forward to hearing from you and to working with you in 2011.

Kind regards,

Paul Sheldrake
Managing Director

'I'm always impressed with Creative Vision Promotions' ability to recommend the right promotional gifts for our business, at the right price and to deliver them in a short time frame.' JS, Catering Business

Letter 8

'It's advisable for any workshop to stock Kalimex K-Seal HD.' Commercial Vehicle Workshop Magazine

Dear Mr Stephens,

Kalimex is a family-owned business, founded 16 years ago. We supply our award-winning products to over 1,500 motor factors, including hundreds of commercial vehicle motor factors - But not yours as yet. **So I'd like to introduce you to one product that commercial vehicle motor factors can't get enough of - K-Seal HD permanent coolant leak repair**.

- It mixes with all types of antifreeze and is ideal for HGV, heavy plant, agricultural and **all** large water cooled engines ***up to 56 L capacity***.
- It ***permanently seals*** the vast majority of leaks in engine blocks, cylinder heads, head gaskets, radiators, freeze plugs and heater cores.
- ***No other product can beat*** K-Seal HD. It's consistently recommended in trade magazines as a high quality, innovative product that works time and time again.

We'd like to send you a free full-size sample of this high margin bestseller. You buy K-Seal HD at £8.33 plus VAT and sell at RRP £15 plus VAT. To receive your free sample, simply contact us on 0800 783 3717 mentioning this offer, e-mail info@kalimex.co.uk or complete the form overleaf and fax it to 01273 890704. **This is a genuine limited offer that closes on XX date.**

Yours sincerely

Mike Schlup
Managing Director

Stop Press... Stop Press... Stop Press... Stop Press... Stop Press…

In an independent market research survey conducted in January 2011 with over 200 stockists, 98% said that Kalimex was an excellent or a good company to do business with.

Now, please turn over for the 3 questions that new CV stockists always ask Kalimex.

Letter 9

Your free sample of K-Seal HD is enclosed with a special offer when you become a stockist of Kalimex products

Dear Mr Stephens,

I'm pleased to enclose your **free, full-size bottle** of K-Seal HD permanent coolant leak repair and your new customer credit application form. Simply complete this form and return it with your first order to us at the freepost address below. ***As a thank you we will send you a Kalimex goody bag including a thermal drinks mug filled with jellybeans.***

Why do thousands of motor factors stock our award winning products?

- Our products come highly recommended by the trade, and independent testing in trade magazines consistently rate them as being the best products your customers can buy. Did you know that the leading roadside recovery service uses K-Seal for roadside head gasket repairs?

- You make decent money when you sell Kalimex products. They will fly off your shelves through word-of-mouth recommendation and ongoing PR and advertising. They also have **generous margins**. For example, you buy K-Seal HD at £8.33 plus VAT and sell at £15 plus VAT.

I look forward to welcoming you as a new stockist and helping you to increase your sales. Please don't hesitate to contact us if you require any further information.

Yours sincerely,

Mike Schlup
Managing Director

PS: There is free delivery on all Kalimex orders over £95

Letter 10

Dear Joan,

I'm sure that you share many similarities with the talented individuals that attend our Essentials of Project Management workshop. You have many valuable skills and attributes including being conscientious and organised, with an eye for detail. You're open to new ideas, to exploring how you can improve the way in which you manage your tasks. Never one to hide away, you will step up to the plate if asked to manage and coordinate a diverse group of people or to consider doing so.

You thrive on doing your job well. Job satisfaction means a great deal to you.

I would also hazard a guess that you are pretty self-aware and recognise when you need external help if you are to successfully manage your projects and bring them in on time and to budget. You know that projects require a high level of organisational skill and discipline to manage.

Now, if project management training is something you are currently thinking about, you may be unsure where to start. There are many training organisations offering Project Management workshops and training programmes that, on the face of it, look similar.

That's why writing this letter to you was something of a challenge for me.

You see, Youthforce offer Project Management training that really is genuinely different. For starters, it is so straightforward, so easy to understand and apply that you will absorb the information, the tips and the advice with ease. You will have that great feeling when something is presented to you and it seems so straightforward that you wonder how it could have bypassed your learning radar before. You will find the practical templates and the professionally written workbook to be of real value in your everyday working life. In fact, not only will you enjoy attending The Essentials of Project Management workshop, you will walk away feeling empowered to tackle both current and future projects.

This is because you will have learned how to successfully manage projects of all sizes, taking into consideration the four basic elements of resources, time, money and scope.

At this stage, if you are interested in finding out more about The Essentials of Project Management workshop, there are two things to help you further:

1. Take a look at the attached workshop outline. It goes into more detail about what you will be learning and how your learning process is structured.

2. Pick up the phone and have a chat to any member of our team. Tell them what you are looking for from your training, the types of projects that you either manage now or you are being asked to manage, and what is really important to you. Ask them how you will benefit from The Essentials of Project Management workshop.

We look forward to hearing from you.

Yours sincerely,

Charlotte Blant
Managing Director

'Furious activity does not necessarily equate to progress and is no substitute for understanding.' Anon

Letter 11

'*All I want for Christmas is...* the debts I'm owed by customers recovered and paid to me in full'

Dear Mr Stretford,

It's that time of year when most businesses have to dig that little bit deeper into their pockets. Entertaining clients, staff parties, thank you gifts for key customers - it can all add up.

That's why, at this time of year especially, it pays to be really on top of your aged debtor list. **If you currently have unpaid invoices that are stretching beyond their payment terms, pass them over to us.** And, don't consider writing any of those debts off just because you've reached the end of your tether. **At Direct Route we achieve miracles each day for clients that had all but given up on ever having the money they were rightfully owed.**

You don't have to accept bad debt as an inevitable part of business. Instruct Direct Route again today to pursue your outstanding debts – either on a zero cost debt collection basis or the more traditional no win no fee commission basis – Why?

1. **Our recovery rate is outstanding -** it takes our skilled account managers an average of just 33 days to recover outstanding debts.

2. **7 out of 10 debts are collected by us** without the need for further legal action.

3. **The unique Register of Outstanding Invoices (ROSI)** is excellent in accelerating the collection of your unpaid debts and prioritising your business at the head of your debtor's queue. An example of the written warning that your debtor will receive as part of our demand process is enclosed with this letter. This alone significantly increases the likelihood of your debt being paid.

4. **We were the pioneers in zero cost debt collection services,** providing an alternative to the more traditional commission based debt collection services. It is now possible to have your outstanding debts recovered, without paying a penny.

5. **Our team have over 80 years' experience** in debt collection. Where others may falter through a lack of knowledge, experience and qualification, we succeed. We have built our good name on service and results.

6. **We are renowned throughout the debt collection sector for being ethical,** professional and tenacious, and for delivering exceptional service levels to our clients. You will be allocated your own experienced and dedicated account manager, responsible for pursuing your outstanding debts.

The next step

If you would like us to act on your behalf right now, please complete and return the attached registration form with your details, together with the overdue invoice/s and the contact numbers for your debtor/s. You can fax this to 01274 223191, e-mail to newdebts@directroute.co.uk, or post to the address above. Alternatively you can register and submit on-line at www.directory.co.UK/free_membership.

On the day that we receive your instructions, a demand letter will be sent to your debtor.

If however you would rather talk to a member of our team beforehand to discuss our services further, please do not hesitate to contact us on 01274 223190.

Yours sincerely

Richard Price
Director

'In the 3 years that we have used Direct Route's services, an incredible *90% of the debt value* that we have passed to them has been collected. **Out of £52,191.61 worth of debt, £46,948.55 has been recovered** ***at a cost of just £855.61*** plus VAT to us.' LB, Financial Director, Transport Company

Letter 12

Dear Mrs Sanderson,

As someone who appreciates traditional handmade fruitcakes, I'd like to share our summer fruitcake collection with you.

The last few months in our family bakery have been very busy indeed as the word about our exquisite fruitcakes continues to spread. We are now baking to order the Old English Mead Cake, the Sussex Countryman's Cake and the Kentish Harvest Cake - three of the most delicious and moist fruitcakes you will ever taste. Each one is beautifully presented in packaging that can be recycled or composted when the last slice has been devoured. *The unique signature cake band represents a typical Sussex scene and adds the finishing touch to a fruitcake that has a taste like no other.*

A special offer to tempt you – half price postage and packing

If you order between now and August 31 you will pay just £2.95 for delivery to a UK address. You can place your order on-line at www.countryfarmcakes.co.uk quoting the special code HPO, or by telephone on 01403 741466.

You can order by post too. Please make your cheque payable to Country Farm Cakes and include the name and address of the recipient. You can order one cake or 20 cakes and still pay just £2.95 if your order is being delivered to one UK address! If you would like your cake to be sent overseas, please contact us for more details.

Why not make your summer coffee mornings and afternoon tea something extra special with a Country Farm Cakes handmade Sussex fruitcake?

Yours sincerely,

Sean Tulett
Managing Director

'I have eaten many cakes in my 18 year career as a chef. I can honestly say that Country Farm cakes are the best I have ever tasted.' Dan Clarke, Master Chef of Great Britain

Letter 13

Dear Mr Davies,

I am sure that you, like me, are often approached by businesses offering unique services (that turn out to be anything but), which is why writing this letter to you was something of a challenge for me.

You see, there is a unique service that I would like you to consider, one that I believe in my role as your professional bookkeeper will make a measurable difference in ensuring that your bad debts are kept to a minimum and that your invoices are paid more promptly. *And because this service requires no upfront financial commitment, there is absolutely no risk involved.*

AccountAssyst, the name of the service I'd like you to consider, is an incredibly powerful, simple to use, on-line credit management solution for businesses that offer products or services to other businesses.

Because you supply on credit, you will benefit from the highest levels of protection at all stages of the credit management process. This will ensure that your chances of being paid are maximised and that any write-offs are reduced.

What ***really impressed*** me when I was invited to test this service on behalf of my clients is that it does more than simply provide you with accurate information on the credit worthiness of potential and existing clients – so much so that I have now purchased a branded version of AccountAssyst for my clients.

For example it includes:

- new customer account opening
- existing customer account reviews
- the unique ROSI monitor early warning system
- an on-line automated overdue monies chase process
- the most up to date credit reports for limited companies and sole traders

However, at this stage, I don't want you to make any commitment to using AccountAssyst.

I would like you to do what I did, which is to take advantage of a two-week trial so that you can put the system through its paces and see for yourself just how unique it really is, and how your business will benefit.

I have also arranged for you to receive ***eight free business credit reports*** *when you register at www.accountassyst.com/xxxx* . You may want to look at the current credit status of some of your existing customers or perhaps some potential customers. Maybe even check out your competitors. **However you choose to use them, eight free business credit reports is a good enough reason to look more closely at this incredible system.**

I appreciate that you may be quite comfortable evaluating AccountAssyst without any help. On the other hand, you may prefer to have the system demonstrated to you. Either way, please contact me and let me know how you would like to move forwards. I can arrange a demonstration for you. Of course, when you have trialled AccountAssyst, I would like to know your initial thoughts.

If you have any other questions, please do not hesitate to contact me personally.

Yours sincerely

Xxxxxxxxxxxx

Managing Director

Chapter Summary

1. Your sales letter is an intimate, targeted communication. Make it charming and relevant.

2. You must inspire the recipient to respond.

3. Time spent researching and planning your content is time never wasted.

4. If appropriate, group your intended recipients then identify their needs.

5. Stand in the shoes of each one. Why should they respond to your letter?

6. Make sure you know what's happening in the marketplace of your target audiences.

7. Spend time researching competitors to understand how you compare.

8. Avoid making extravagant statements. Being positively good can be good enough.

9. What are the main benefits you are offering? Do they differ depending on who you're targeting?

10. Consider making an offer; time bound, for a limited number of responders.

11. When writing a letter get the basics right; make the layout interesting and easy to read. Avoid gimmicks. Professional, crisp and clean.

12. Always write in a friendly and engaging manner. Jargon free.

13. Consider using the space on the back of your letter to include another message.

14. Can you increase responses using lumpy mail?

15. Make your envelope the same quality as your letterhead paper.

16. Plan your sales letter campaigns using the 'Power of Three'.

17. Increase the impact of your campaigns with your website news and blog.

18. Study the successful letters in this chapter. What can you learn? Which approaches are relevant to your business and your target audiences?

19. Allocate time to write your sales letters.

20. Don't be afraid to edit your work and, if necessary, pay an editor.

CHAPTER 4

BEYOND THE BROCHURE

For many businesses, knowing how to promote themselves beyond sending out e-mails and handing out flyers is a mystery. For others, a glossy brochure is their default option. This can be expensive, often costing as much to send as it does to write, design and print. Also, because so much was spent creating it in the first place, the business owner often sticks with the brochure well beyond its sell by date, unwilling to jettison something so costly to start the whole process again.

This is at odds with the entrepreneurial culture prevalent in small businesses. Small business owners seek gaps in the market and then change and improve their existing offering accordingly. Because they don't require the consent of others to implement their ideas, they can forge ahead quickly. Suddenly that glossy brochure is woefully outdated. But being too expensive to discard, it continues to be used and handed out with a number of flyers promoting the latest offerings. It doesn't create the right impression.

At the other end of the spectrum, a business owner may believe that a flyer is all that is needed to convey adequately what they have to offer, especially if they are voracious on the networking scene. But a flyer has its limitations too. It has often been designed by the printer as opposed to a professional designer and because of its size, its impact is limited. The message it carries tends to be very general and lacking in sparkle and charm. It often amounts to little more than a shopping list of the services or products offered by the business, plus some contact details.

There is another way!

In this chapter, we are going to look at 12 of the most powerful, low-cost communications that I have used in the last 26 years. With one or two exceptions, they can be produced in a printed format or issued on-line.

As you read through this chapter, don't be tempted to dismiss a communication if at first it seems unusual or not relevant for your particular business.

Ask yourself instead:

- Could I use this communication to market my business effectively with some or all of my target audiences?
- How will this communication fit into an integrated communication campaign? If this is to be one element in the 'Power of Three', what other two communications should I use?
- If I can see a merit in this communication, will it have greater impact if I use it on-line or if I have it printed? Should I consider a mixture of on-line and off-line communications?
- Could I use lumpy mail to increase the impact?
- What professional help will I need to implement this communication? Do I need to consider using a copywriter, an editor, a designer, a printer?

Using These Communications Effectively

- They can reinforce the message being carried by your sales team when at seminars, trade shows, in meetings with potential clients, cold canvassing etc.

- They can open up a dormant or cold sales channel, generating awareness and interest in what you have to offer.

- They can be used to maintain sales momentum during the time that often exists between meeting with a potential client and the subsequent sign up.

- They are ideal as a follow-up to your telemarketing. These communications will often have a far greater impact than the standard e-mail sent out to confirm the conversation that has taken place.

- They provide you with something interesting to hand out at networking events, something to support your 60-second presentation.

- At exhibitions, they can be used to inspire conversations with the people visiting your stand and can be included in your goody bags.

- They are ideal for your targeted direct mail campaigns. They can be used with your sales letter or as stand-alone communications.

- Some may be perfect for adding to your website, helping to keep it interesting and worthy of repeat visits.

Integrating Off-line and On-line Sales Communications

As mentioned earlier, there are no hard and fast rules as to whether your sales communications should be printed or used on-line. Sometimes it will pay to do both. If you produce a Questions and Answers sheet, it is always a good idea for the printed version to be complemented by a similar document or page on your website.

It can be tempting to focus your efforts solely on creating on-line communications simply because it's cheaper and easier. This is not always the right decision. You don't want your communications to just be efficient, they need to be effective too. I have worked with organisations that have received no response from their e-marketing campaigns, yet have generated thousands of pounds worth of new business when they switched to printed communications, despite containing the same information and targeting the same audience. With print costs plummeting and e-mail fatigue growing, it would be a mistake to shy away from printed communications, especially if your on-line communications are not delivering. It's impossible to replicate on-line the experience of someone opening up your envelope to find a high quality, relevant sales communication and gift or special offer.

Consider a blend of on-line and off-line communications and ideally have them working together to create an integrated campaign. For example:

- A printed voucher can be used to drive people to buy from your website or to find out more about you on-line.
- Your sales letter can encourage the recipient to go on-line and complete your survey.
- Your biography could be an individual document or could be included within any number of the communications included in this chapter. On your website, your biography could be accessed through your 'About Us' page.
- Your press clippings sheet can promote the 'News' page on your website, or your blog.

If you decide that concentrating purely on either on-line or off-line communications is a good idea, you must be absolutely certain that you're not limiting your chances of success in doing so. Are you reaching the right people in the right quantities at the right time in order to build a profitable business? Continually ask yourself this question. We did cover this in more detail in Chapter 1 so re-visit it if you're unsure.

12 Powerful Communications

1. A Customer Survey

I've started with this communication because it's always wise to find out what your existing customers think about you before embarking upon your marketing communications programme. Another benefit of a customer survey is that if you have been doing your job well and delivering exceptional service to your customers, your survey will produce some excellent feedback that you can include in other communications.

Don't confuse a customer survey with a market research survey which is usually a more formal exercise undertaken by a suitably qualified professional. A customer survey is a simple exercise that can be undertaken each time a customer buys from you. Asking how they rate their experience is a survey, albeit an informal one.

I would suggest that once a year you undertake a more structured survey in which you ask a number of specific questions. This is the type of survey I have focused upon here. I have categorised a customer survey as a sales communication because if you create it properly, it will enhance your reputation with your existing customers and could well act as a trigger for customers to use you more often. This applies equally whether you supply products or services.

'I haven't got all day.'

Customers often don't have the time to answer all the questions you would love to ask them. Even if they did, they're unlikely to study every question with intense scrutiny. Ask too many questions and you'll experience a diminishing return in the quality of the answers. Your survey must be succinct, relevant and genuine.

Whilst you seek the reassurance that you're on the right tracks and exceeding your customer's expectations, it may also be useful to know of their relationships with other providers of similar products or services. Similarly, if you're planning something important such as rebranding your business or launching new products, your survey is the perfect opportunity to solicit your customers' opinions.

Aim for 8 to 12 questions in your survey. Make it easy for your customers to give their opinion by using a rating system, something simple like scoring 1 to 10. Make sure that you explain how the rating system works.

Always provide space under each question to encourage the person to explain the reasons for their score and to write any additional feedback. Although the rating system will enable customers to complete the survey quickly and it is therefore likely that you will receive a high number of returns, it is the customer comments that provide the greatest insight.

Which Questions Would You Like Answered?

Your questions will usually fall into 5 categories. For each category you must encourage customers to be specific in their responses. For example, telling you that they are not happy with your service is too vague to be of much use. Letting you know that they find it frustrating that they can't get hold of you when they call at 9.00am, however, is very helpful. You can only make improvements to your business if you receive feedback that enables you to identify the problem.

Category 1 - These questions relate to your performance and your service levels. They may encompass asking customers how easy it is to contact you, how responsive you are to their questions or problems, and, if you have a customer service team, whether they deliver the same high consistent levels of support each time.

Category 2 - These questions relate to the quality of what you actually deliver. You want to know whether your products or services always meet expectations. Do they exceed them? What improvements can be made?

Category 3 - These questions are about your competitors. Do your customers use other providers that offer the same or similar products or services, and if they do, how do you compare?

Category 4 - I call this the 'did you know?' category. These questions provide an opportunity to introduce your customers to other products and services you offer that they may not be aware of. It's sufficient just to ask a customer if they know that you offer these other products and services, and if they don't, would they like to find out more. You can also ask for their feedback on your proposed plans to improve your business. Only do so if the customer can see that you are genuinely interested in their opinion and will take their feedback on board.

Category 5 - These questions provide the customer with the opportunity to share something with you that has not been covered by the previous questions. Don't exclude this section. The most valuable information can often be found here. Usually the feedback is both positive and helpful. A customer may share something that causes you to make some changes sooner rather than later. Finding out what's in your customers' minds can stop minor irritants becoming major problems further down the line. Asking something simple, such as *'Is there anything else that you would like to tell us?'* or *'Have we missed something that is important to you?'* should ensure that nothing is left out.

How to Deliver your Survey

There are four ways in which you can deliver your survey:

- You can print and post it.
- You can create it and send it on-line, using a software survey provider such as Survey Monkey (*www.surveymonkey.com*)
- You can opt for both on-line and printed which should enable you to reach your entire customer base.
- You can opt instead to contact each customer by telephone.

Whichever method of delivery you choose, your aim should be for the survey to reach as many of your customers as possible.

To receive the maximum possible response (which is likely to be in the region of 25%) as opposed to the usual rate of 2% to 3%, you will probably need to telephone those customers that have not responded and ask whether they have time to answer the questions on the phone. This can be challenging for you to carry out personally. You are very close to your business and it can be difficult to be on the receiving end of constructive feedback without becoming defensive or veering off course. It can be equally difficult for your customers to share feedback with you - good, bad or indifferent. So instead, consider asking a person that you trust to make the calls. Perhaps recruit a marketing student from a local university who would appreciate the work experience. If you do this, make sure they are given some training about your business, your values, your customer base and the importance of conducting your survey in a friendly and professional manner.

When calling those customers that have not yet responded to your survey, the person representing your business should explain the following to them:

- That their answers will not be shared with another third party.
- That they are calling only to understand your customer's thoughts on your services and not to trying to sell something.
- That you will issue a report on the survey responses and detail any changes being planned as a result of the feedback.
- That completing the survey will take only a few minutes of their time.

You may need to arrange another more convenient time with the customer to gather their feedback. Don't assume that they have time to down tools at the precise moment you call. I've found that the word 'feedback' rather than 'survey' elicits a more positive response. When you have concluded the survey, if the customer has been really positive it's worth asking if they are happy for some of their comments to be used in your marketing material. Are they happy for their name to be used in full or would they prefer to be anonymous when the feedback is reproduced? If they don't want their testimonial to be used in this way accept their decision with good grace.

Our Survey Said – The Follow-Up

The main reason for carrying out a survey is to ascertain your customers' thoughts about what you deliver and your overall service. When you are in possession of their responses, be sure to scrutinise each answer carefully. Identify where improvement is needed and where praise can be bestowed upon your team. Set a time limit for implementing the improvements and don't forget to keep your customers informed, so demonstrating how their answers contributed towards your decision to make these improvements. In short, let your customers know that your survey was not a hollow PR exercise.

Using the Results in your Sales Communications

You don't need the permission of your customers to summarise the positive results from your survey as these businesses did:

> '95% of the Motability dealerships we surveyed said we are the only adaptation specialist they use.'

> '9/10 of our customers rated our customer service team as very good or outstanding.'

> '9/10 motor stockists recommend Kalimex K-Seal as their preferred coolant leak repair.'

Your simple rating system will enable you to calculate statistics like these. You don't need a minimum sample to use these statements with confidence in your marketing communications. The next time you are watching the television, keep an eye out for the small print at the end of the adverts promoting hair and beauty products and you'll see how this works. Even the big brands trumpet their positive results based on a customer sample as small as 30.

2. Questions and Answers (Q & A)

A questions and answers document can be used to encourage a prospect to contact you by addressing many of the perceived barriers to a sale. It also works well as a refresher communication for a customer that may not have been in touch with you for some time.

There is one proviso.

The questions must be genuine. They should be real questions that people have previously asked you before they have done business with you. A very good Q&A sheet will succeed in removing those barriers to a sale that exist simply because a person doesn't know enough about you. It's unlikely that anyone will buy from you if they either don't know enough about you or are unsure about your ability to meet their needs. So, if your questions lack credibility because they are not the questions that prospects usually ask but instead are a regurgitation of your benefit statements, you're not going to enlighten anyone.

To re-iterate what has been written in Chapters 2 and 3, when creating your Q&A sheet you must stand in the shoes of the people that you'd like to convert to customers. Look at your business through their eyes. What do they need to know?

If you're stuck for inspiration, take a pad and pen with you to your next networking event and jot down the questions that you're asked by people that don't know what you do and are curious to find out more.

How many questions should you include in your Q&A? Try not to go beyond 12 questions. Your answers to each question should vary in length. If you can answer a question in one sentence, do so. Don't be tempted to expand the answer unnecessarily. A short answer will break up those questions that require more explanation.

A Practical Example

I offer a one-day intensive Marketing on a Shoestring Bootcamp to small business owners and I use the Q&A format to explain to potential clients what they can expect from the day. By doing so I aim to answer those questions that business owners may ponder over before committing to the day, whilst also managing their expectations of the day itself. I also send out the Q&A communication as a follow-up to any telephone call I receive from an interested prospect and print it on the back of a sales guide promoting the workshop.

To help you compile your own Q&As, I list below the 10 questions that I ask and answer in my bootcamp Q&A.

1. Do I need to do any preparation before the session?

2. Do I need marketing experience to benefit from the session?

3. Can any members of my team attend as well as me?

4. Where is the session held?

5. What time does the session start at and when does it finish?

6. Do I need to take notes during the session or will you follow-up with a report?

7. Will any handout material be available on the day for me to work from?

8. Is this session tailored to my business and my specific marketing needs?

9. Do you provide any follow-up after the session?

10. What are your payment terms?

Bear in mind that the purpose of this document is for it to be useful, informative and helpful. If you can stick to these basic rules you will create a customer-focused sales document that will reinforce your selling efforts.

3. Your Biography

It may seem unusual to include your biography as part of your sales communications tool kit, however there are circumstances when it is a wise move. If you are personally linked to the services or products that you are promoting, perhaps you actually deliver them or are involved in their creation, your biography is an opportunity to share relevant information about yourself to prospects and customers. This will help to build a positive opinion of your business. Also, if you promote your business in local or national media, you will usually need your biography on standby. Some journalists and editors will expect this from you before deciding whether to cover your news.

How and When to Use your Biography

- You can add it to your website, maybe include it as a separate page accessible from your 'About Us' page.

- You can include it in your sales literature or provide it as a stand-alone document with a nice image of you accompanying the text. This is especially important when you are launching new products or services and want to demonstrate your credibility. The audience will be more open to your overtures if they can appraise your skills and experience at the same time as reading about what you're offering.

- When you are pitching for a project - your biography could be the deciding factor in you being awarded the business.

- When asked to speak at a seminar or an event. It is a good idea to provide the organisers with a copy of your biography to include within the pre-event communications.

What to Say...

Examples of detailed yet concise biographies can be readily accessed on the back of most business books. The author will have composed the biography with the aim of impressing the reader sufficiently for a purchase to be made. The reader may not know of the author, so within a few lines the biography needs to communicate that this is a book written by somebody worth reading. Have a browse through a few author biographies for some inspiration.

To help you further, here are two example biographies. Mike Collins is the MD of AccountAssyst and Nicola Sales is the MD of YourRecruit. Although they differ in content, both biographies build a credible picture of the experience, values and business acumen of each person.

Biography of Mike Collins

Mike has spent his entire 20 year career in the field of business to business credit management and debt collection. He held senior positions at Midland Bank, GUS Group and Dun & Bradstreet before embarking into private practice and taking up Managing Directorship roles at the Guardian Group and The Direct Route Collections Group.

In 2008, Mike began the pursuit of his long-held ambition to radically change the 'shambolic' system of credit management that exists in the business to business community, and became the driving force behind AccountAssyst. He approached the internationally renowned insolvency practitioner, Gerald Krasner, with the AccountAssyst concept. Gerald is now a partner in the business.

Mike is a recently appointed credit management Education Tsar under the government backed Enterprise4All scheme. His role encompasses mentoring small businesses and helping each one to establish good credit practices.

Mike is widely regarded by his peers as being one of the leaders in the credit management industry and is seen as the ideal person to drive forward the AccountAssyst concept.

Biography of Nicola Sales

Nicola Sales is a Fellow of the Recruitment and Employment Confederation, the world's largest recruitment body. Fellowship is the highest status that can be awarded to any recruitment professional. Less than 6% of recruitment professionals attain this level.

Nicola has 22 years experience gained working within recruitment and at a senior level in HR where she worked for Canon UK and Makro. At Makro, Nicola was responsible for the national recruitment programme and for developing induction and training programmes for new recruits. This wider people experience has proved to be a real asset for YourRecruit clients.

After being headhunted by a national recruitment brand, it took her just six months to realise that she had the skills, experience and integrity to establish her own recruitment business; something that Nicola accomplished 16 years ago.

Today Nicola is the Managing Director of YourRecruit, one of the South East's most successful independent recruitment consultancies. She heads a professional and friendly team of permanent and temporary consultants. In the last year, Nicola and her team have developed a range of online recruitment solutions that in her own words 'Knock the spots off the job boards by helping businesses to recruit online on a shoestring budget.'

What is Nicola's recipe for success? 'It's to treat our clients and candidates at all times with integrity and respect....to continually look for ways in which we can improve and deliver our services and in doing so out-innovate our competitors,' she says.

Keep your Biography Up-to-Date

Your biography should not be a document that is written once and never re-visited. Keep it updated with new achievements including any new qualifications, new positions of responsibility with relevant trade associations and committees, enhanced accreditations for both you and your business and any completed projects of particular distinction and merit.

4. A Post-It Note

You may think it's strange that a post-it note has made it onto my short list of powerful sales communications but I can assure you that it does work wonders in certain selling situations.

- It can add an extra special personal touch when affixed to your letter with a neatly written message along the lines of: 'Dear (name), It was lovely to talk to you today and I will contact you as agreed in a few days' time.'

- It can highlight something within your mailshot that you want the recipient to pay particular attention to. 'Please make sure that you read the Q&A section as discussed, especially question 3.'

What's the effect of this? In most cases the person that you are writing to will pay particular attention to your message and provided that you are not asking them to do anything out of the ordinary, they will do as you ask.

The secrets to using a post-it note successfully as a sales communication are:

- Use it judiciously. Not every communication warrants this extra touch.
- Write your message with care making sure that your handwriting is neat and legible.
- Ensure that your message is sincere. Don't be over-gushing.
- Make the message personal. Think about the business that you are writing to. Don't write the same message every time, with only the recipient's name being changed. Write something that you think will grab their attention by being relevant to them and their business. Be charming.

Mantra Magazines, a publisher of several high-quality monthly magazines, uses post-it note messages really well. When a member of their sales team is sending a copy of the rate card for one of their magazines to a potential advertiser, they affix a post-it note to a copy of the relevant magazine alerting the recipient to the pages that feature their competitors' adverts and to the editorial pages that demonstrate how their own business would be presented. This really does arouse the recipient's curiosity. It triggers them to explore what's on offer in the magazine and to evaluate how they could benefit from advertising.

I recommend that you use the larger-sized post-it notes rather than the small square ones. Don't skimp on the quality of either the post-it note or the pen used to write the message. And never try to save time by printing your message rather than writing it. This will reduce its impact immediately. Always write the message by hand and avoid WRITING THE MESSAGE IN CAPITALS.

Follow these simple tips and you'll be surprised at the positive results!

5. A Voucher

The humble voucher is probably one of the earliest sales communications that I can remember. My Mum used to cut the vouchers from various magazines each week and redeem them at our local supermarket. Whilst adverts, direct mailshots and sales communications have increased in sophistication over the years, the sales voucher is still a popular tool, used by the biggest and most successful brands. And vouchers don't need to be used solely to provide money off incentives. There are many ways in which you can use a voucher without reducing the price of what you are selling.

A voucher can be sent out as a separate sales communication, as an accompaniment to your sales letter or as an item on your website for people to download and print. The purpose of the voucher is to highlight the offer that you are making. What types of offers? Here are some examples to inspire you:

> *'To benefit from half price postage on your next order of one of our beautiful handmade Sussex fruitcakes, simply visit our website and quote the reference code xxx.'*

'To take advantage of your complimentary 60-minute coaching session, you must contact us today on xxxxxx.'

'To benefit from your five free business credit reports, you must register on our system by xxx date.'

'You can claim your free goody bag when you visit our exhibition stand on xxx date. But you must bring this voucher with you!'

'For your 3 free invaluable marketing reports containing over 70 proven marketing on a shoestring tips, go on-line now or contact us on xxxxxx.'

'Download the voucher from our website to benefit from a free starter or a free pudding with every main course ordered in September.'

A voucher can accompany another sales document, the most obvious ones being your sales letter and newsletter. Simply earmark approximately 25% of the space for your voucher wording and separate it from your letter with a line of printed perforations. This way the reader will know where the letter ends and the voucher takes over.

A voucher can be used as a stand-alone sales document for your sales team to hand to customers and prospects. Or why not consider mailing your voucher together with a free gift as the very first stage in generating a prospect or customer's interest sufficiently for them to visit your website or pick up the phone to contact you?

Vouchers that work also include the following:

- Clear and explicit details of the offer you are making.
- Clear, easy to follow instructions on what the recipient must do to benefit from the offer.
- A close date to encourage early responses and discourage procrastination.
- A limit on the number of people that can benefit from the offer.
- A code that the person must use if they are to benefit from the offer. This enables you to track the effectiveness of the voucher.

If you are considering using vouchers as a sales tool, please enlist the help of a designer. Unless you are an absolute dab hand on the computer, a homemade voucher will generally convey a poor impression of your business and the integrity of your offer will be called into question. Don't sabotage a great idea with a clumsy or amateurish execution.

6. A Quiz

If you'd like to vary the content of your sales communications and at the same time encourage your prospects and customers to interact with your business, then a quiz is a great idea. Like your Q&A sheet, your quiz can be short and sweet, containing just a few multiple-choice questions, or can extend to 15 questions or more. Try to make it relatively simple to complete as the aim is to receive as many responses as possible. By setting questions that are too difficult, you will be limiting the success of the exercise. However, the same issue can arise by setting questions that are too simple. This will take away any sense of challenge and therefore remove the fun in completing the quiz. Aim for the middle ground.

The type of quiz you run depends on the experience that you want to create for the prospect or customer, and the message that you want to communicate. A quiz works well when combined with other sales communications. For example, the call to action in your sales letter could be to entice the recipient to complete and return the enclosed quiz for the chance to win a prize. Your quiz can be printed on the back of a sales sheet promoting a particular product or service, or located on your website.

A quiz can be serious or slightly frivolous. Let me illustrate this with two contrasting examples of businesses that have used quizzes in a smart way to promote their services.

AccountAssyst

AccountAssyst used the quiz format to encourage small business owners to self-diagnose their need for the AccountAssyst on-line credit management system. Called a 'Credit where Credit's due Compatibility Test', it comprised of 10 questions about the business owner's current credit management processes. A business owner was asked to answer 'Yes' or 'No' to each question. On completion of the quiz, they were shown how to add up their scores. An explanation of how to translate the score into a verdict on how watertight or otherwise their credit management processes are, was delivered on the back of the quiz. Three or more 'No' responses indicated that their credit management system was in need of improvement.

The quiz also included a strong call to action. The business owner was provided with an incentive of eight free credit reports to trial the

AccountAssyst system. Many small business owners signed up for a trial of the AccountAssyst system after completing the quiz. The self diagnosis and evaluation quiz and the free credit reports combined well to make this marketing exercise a real success.

Techmobility

Techmobility wanted to promote their vehicle adaptation service to motor dealerships at one of the busiest times of the year for dealerships, that of the new vehicle registration. A sales flyer was created to highlight the many benefits that motor dealerships and their customers would enjoy by referring their customers to Techmobility. On the reverse of the flyer was a 15 question multiple-choice quiz. Each one of the 15 questions was an advertising slogan for a brand of motor car. The dealer had to match the correct motor brand to the right slogan. The first six dealers with the correct answers won a gift voucher and a goody bag. The quiz also had a time limit for responses.

A whopping 25% of the dealerships responded.

Many of the dealers also took the time and trouble to compliment Techmobility on this initiative.

Why did Techmobility use a quiz? They knew that sending out the same message each month to the same audience using the same format would not inspire dealers to read this particularly important sales message. The quiz was instrumental in bringing the attention of the dealer to the Techmobility brand. As a result of this simple low-cost communication, Techmobility experienced their busiest ever period.

How to Make your Next Quiz a Success

- Make sure that the questions you are asking are connected with what you do.

- The questions should be neither simple nor complex. Aim for the middle ground.

- The quiz must be of interest to the people you are targeting and it must be relevant to their needs.

- Multiple-choice questions or those requiring a simple yes or no answer are always successful.

- If returning the answers is part of the process, make it easy for the person to do so. If possible offer e-mail, fax, and postal options. This will increase the likelihood of a high return.

- Offer a gift or incentive either to everyone who returns the quiz or to a limited number of people on a first come, first served basis.

- If appropriate, publish the correct answers and the details of the winners on your website and in your next newsletter.

7. The 10 Reasons Why

This communication can be as small as a bookmark, or as large as an A4 flyer, with a myriad of sizes in between. 'The 10 Reasons Why' is a punchy sales communication that shares the 10 key reasons why customers choose your business. If you want to be short, snappy and to the point, then your 10 key reasons could run along similar lines to the following example of those for an on-line retail business. With a few tweaks, it will work equally as well for your business.

10 Reasons Why You'll Love Being our Customer

1. A no quibble guarantee.
2. Free delivery on all orders, large and small.
3. Our secure and encrypted website.
4. Our helpful and professional team.
5. Regular and genuine special offers, giving you more for less.
6. Lowest price pledge - you won't find cheaper anywhere else.
7. You'll receive our free information packed magazine including many offers.
8. Thank you discounts and rewards when you recommend us.
9. Same day dispatch of your order.
10. No minimum order.

Contact us today. Go on-line at xxxxxxxxxx or freephone xxxxxxxxx between 8 am and 8 pm, seven days a week, and speak to a member of our team - no call centres! Why not check out our very special brand-new customer offer overleaf.

This communication works well on its own. It's ideal to hand out when you are networking because it contains more information than your business card. It can be combined with a special offer, enclosed with your sales letter and added as a page on your website.

8. Your 'Raving Fans' Charter

There's nothing quite like having your existing customers enthusing about your products or services to persuade a new customer that you can be trusted with their money. You see it working every day on websites such as *amazon.co.uk*, where purchasers are encouraged to leave their feedback on items that they have bought. However, it is never a good idea to fabricate customer feedback, even with your customer's consent!

If you want your customer feedback to deliver an impact and to warrant being used as a stand-alone communication, it *must* be genuine, unedited, up to date and specific.

With positive customer feedback from, say, just five of your customers, you have the makings of a powerful sales communication. This could be used on its own as a separate document or combined with any other communication mentioned in this chapter.

How to Request Feedback from Your Customers:

- Ask someone that you trust to speak to your customers on your behalf to gather feedback. It can sometimes be awkward for you to ask your customers for their opinion of your services and similarly difficult for a customer to tell you honestly what they think. When a local design agency asked me if I would contact a handful of their clients for this purpose, I discovered that one of their clients had won an award thanks to the work of the design agency. They had forgotten to pass this news on. Customers will often feel more comfortable sharing the good things they think about you and your business if they are able to do so through a third party.

- Before asking somebody to start gathering feedback, call your customers or send them a nice e-mail to let them know that they may be contacted by someone acting on your behalf, and the reasons for the call.

- Always try to use the telephone for this exercise. You will receive far more information on the telephone than you would if relying upon e-mail. With the best will in the world, your customer may just never get round to answering an e-mail.

- To avoid woolly and generic customer testimonial, it will help if you ask your customers specific questions such as these:

    1. *What made you choose our business?*
    2. *How would you rate your experience of working with us?*
    3. *What have the results been so far?*
    4. *Is there anything else that you would like to add?*

- The quality and depth of the feedback gathered should warrant a separate sales communication. However, you can also sprinkle the feedback throughout other on-line and off-line communications, including your website. Rather than the usual 'we are delighted with their services' testimonial, yours will be tangible and specific. Readers will recognise that it is genuine because each snippet is written in a different way, with a style unique to the person that shared it.

- When sharing your positive customer feedback in your on-line and off-line communications you will make it an even more engaging read if you frame it within a few lines of explanatory text. Here's how Ashley Law Crawley Independent Financial Advisers did just that:

When we recently asked our business and personal clients why they continue to use our services, we received many positive comments, including:

'We use your services because the level of service is second to none and the quality of advice is always excellent.'

'I like working with you because you have a good understanding of our business and our needs. This enables you always to provide the right advice at the right price.'

'My company expects and strives to be the best in all we do. We expect no less from firms that provide services for us and I'm pleased to say that your company comes in as one of the best.'

'You provide a sincere friendly service without undue jargon and a deep understanding of pension issues and legislation.'

'The knowledge and information you provide is easy for us to understand and it enables us to make decisions.'

Ashley Law Crawley include this testimonial on the inside cover of their sales folder. They also used the feedback from other clients to create a separate sales document. This now accompanies their targeted sales letters and is included in the goody bags handed out to people attending their regular seminars.

There is, of course, another subtle benefit in asking your customers for their feedback on your business. It encourages them to take the time to recognise the good service that you provide, and enhances the relationship as a result. When you have created your sales communication encompassing their feedback, make sure that you send a copy with a personal note of thanks to every customer that took some time to help you.

9. Press Clippings Document

What do you do with any media coverage that your business receives? If you just share the good news with your networking colleagues and family, you're not making the most of the opportunity that such coverage provides.

Whether your business is mentioned in local, national or trade media, you need to publicise it. Start by promoting any media coverage on your website. Add a line to your e-mail details with a link through to your website, or to the website on which your coverage can be found. This will help to build a positive impression of your business.

Why not go one step further and create a Press Clippings Bulletin? An A4 sized document showing interesting snippets from your media coverage is a powerful, low-cost document and one which can be used in a number of ways.

- Hand it out at exhibitions – it will act well as a conversation starter with visitors to your stand.

- Use it as an accompaniment to your sales letter. It can be enclosed separately or reproduced on the back of your letter.

- Enclose it with any orders that you dispatch to your customers.

- Use it as part of your formal sales presentations.

- Use it to inspire journalists and editors to cover your next story.

Simple to Create

Firstly, come up with a title for your press clippings document, such as:

'Where have we been making the headlines recently?'

'Recent media coverage of our new services.'

'Some recent media coverage for XYZ Company.'

If you are lucky enough to have received some national media coverage, just one or two examples will be sufficient to have an impact. If your coverage has been in the local press, a few more examples are probably required to give this page some credibility. It is not necessary to reproduce each item of news in full. Instead, select the most interesting elements of each news piece and signpost the reader to where they can read the piece in full - your website or blog for instance. This is another example of how on-line and off-line communications can work together.

The layout of this document is important too. Again, it must not resemble a home-made production. Ask a designer to provide you with a fixed price for what should be a very straightforward job. They will be able to come up with an eye-catching design such as making the bulletin look like a page from a newspaper or designing each snippet of news to look as though it has been torn from a newspaper. Do keep your press clippings document up to date, though. Readers will not be inspired by media coverage of your business if it is several years old.

10. Did You Know? - The Top Tips Guide

In recent years, the growth in the number of businesses using the Internet as a source of free information has been phenomenal. Consequently, in order to meet this demand, an almost unlimited supply of free articles, top tips, health checks, wealth checks etc. have been published on-line. If you are looking for some of this free business advice, pop a few relevant key-words into a search engine and you will be deluged with matching results. The quality of this free advice does vary, however. Some articles will be top-notch, packed with great information, easy to absorb and read. The quality of others can be more dubious with so-called top tips turning out to be simply a clumsy sales pitch with no real value to the reader.

If you plan to write articles for publication either on-line or off-line, resolve from the outset that each article will be of top quality. Giving away some of your knowledge and expertise by supplying a steady and targeted stream of top tips will help to promote your business and build your reputation as an expert in your field. And this will in turn lead to new clients.

Top tips can be posted on-line or provided in print. They can be used as the basis for a blog post, included in a newsletter or accompany your sales letter.

Here's how to create a top tips article that will be welcomed by your audience.

- Before you start writing, revisit your marketing plan. Who are you writing these top tips for? Your tone and content should always be influenced by your audience.

- Draw up a shortlist of topics and tips that you are confident will be of interest and use to your audience. Be different if needs be. You don't have to follow what others are doing.

- Aim to share sufficient knowledge and expertise with the reader for the information to be valuable and credible. You want them to become loyal readers of all of your top tips articles and not just the first one.

- If you have plenty to say on a subject, rather than trying to cram it all into one set of top tips, consider breaking it into several. Drip feed the information over a few months.

- Top tips work particularly well when promoted on your website. Alternatively, they can be sent out to your contacts via e-mail if they are happy to receive them this way.

- Aim to write 350 to 600 words worth of top tips. How many tips? It is up to you but the popular figures are usually 3, 5, 7 and 10.

- This particular sales communication complements your biography. Include a shortened version of your biography at the foot of the top tips article or print it on the back. Add a couple of positive client testimonials and you've combined three powerful communications in one document!

A Practical Example of a Top Tips Article

Each month I write a top tips article for the 60,000 readers of seven local magazines, many of whom are ideal prospects for signing up to my blog and for buying my books. The article that follows, '10 Top Tips for Writing the Perfect Press Release' can be used as a guide should you be planning on writing top tips articles for the first time, or looking to make your current top tips articles more effective. You will see that the article concludes with a concise biography, a promotion of my first book and a recommendation that readers subscribe to my blog. Don't be afraid to add a similar footer to your own top tips. Look upon this as your rightful reward for sharing your expertise with readers. Bear in mind also that many readers will want to find out more about you.

> ***10 Top Tips for Writing the Perfect Press Release****, by award winning Chartered Marketer and business author, Dee Blick*
>
> *Contrary to what you may have been told, many newspapers and magazines are open to featuring your press release. But there is a proviso. The subject matter must be relevant, topical, newsworthy and of real interest to their readership. The way to a journalist's or editor's heart lies in presenting a professional and attractive press release that really packs a punch.*

1. ***Find a Hook***. *A good press release requires an interesting angle. Whether your message is topical, you've gained an accreditation, won an award, secured an incredible deal in a challenging climate or even downsized your successful business by moving into a home-based office. If you don't have an interesting story to interest the readers, you don't have a genuine press release.*

2. ***Use a strong headline.*** *If you're stuck for inspiration, study the business headlines in newspapers and magazines. They tend to be succinct and they summarise the story that follows. Keep your headline to one line of text.* ***'Local business woman interviewed by The Financial Times.' 'Local bookkeeper secures multimillion pound client.'*** *Make the headline grab attention.*

3. ***Include a strong opening paragraph.*** *Define the compelling messages that your press release hinges upon in the first paragraph. Make sure that your website is mentioned as there is every chance that whilst the journalist is scanning your press release, they will be looking at your website too. If you can reinforce your opening paragraph with relevant statistics from a reliable source, do so.*

4. ***Use quotations wherever possible.*** *You can add real human interest to your press release with a genuine quote. 'We were delighted to secure this project after a challenging but exciting tendering process.' Sometimes a journalist will highlight your quotation in the published piece if sufficiently impressed.*

5. ***Keep your press release to around 450 words.*** *You're not writing a book. Focus on communicating the key points. Three or four paragraphs should do the trick.*

6. ***Ensure your press release looks professional****. Use bold and italics sparingly but resist the temptation to use different typefaces and type sizes.*

7. ***Make sure that your press release is checked before sending it****. Don't ask for praise. You want to be alerted to spelling mistakes, clumsy grammar and typographical errors before sending it.*

8. ***Include a brief company description at the end of your press release under the heading 'Editor Information'****. Include your name and full contact details. Don't attach any high resolution images but mention that these are available.*

9. ***The e-mail that accompanies your press release should summarise its contents.*** *If a journalist or editor receives your release after their publication date, you want it kept back for future coverage. A persuasive e-mail will help.*

10. ***Pick up the telephone*** *and chat to the journalist about your release. Focus on communicating the one or two strong messages that you know will interest readers. Journalists and editors are continually looking for good press releases.*

About Dee Blick

Dee is a Fellow of the Chartered Institute of Marketing, the world's largest marketing body. She has 26 years of marketing experience. Dee specialises in working with small businesses. If you want to read more of Dee's marketing wisdom, buy a copy of her bestselling book: Powerful Marketing on a Shoestring Budget for Small Businesses. There are over thirty 5-star reader reviews on Amazon. Subscribe to Dee's blog at www.theblickblog.co.uk and you will receive free fortnightly marketing tips.

11. Your Newsletter

I realised the immense potential of printed newsletters six years ago after being approached by a recruitment business concerned that their newsletters were no longer generating any responses whatsoever. This business specialised in recruiting care staff from the European Union for care homes in the United Kingdom. They had purchased a mailing list of care homes and were mailing all the homes listed with their monthly newsletter. Although they had managed to gain some new clients from their efforts, their mailing costs always absorbed any profit. It was not hard to see why this was the case. Their newsletter comprised of three or four paragraphs of rambling text about their services, accompanied by a few visuals. It was most definitely a home-made creation and as far removed from a polished, professional and engaging newsletter that you could get. I was quietly confident that there was sufficient mileage and potential from their mailing list to warrant a further attempt. We developed a brand-new, professionally designed newsletter, and mailed it to their complete mailing list. Over £40,000 worth of sales followed, from both their existing client base and from brand-new customers. The total cost of this newsletter - copywriting, design, print and distribution -

amounted to £800. After that experience, I have been a firm advocate of newsletters and have continued to witness incredible results from such a simple tool.

So, why did that newsletter work so well when the previous one had not?

The new newsletter:

- Looked the part. It was attractive, well laid out and the copy flowed nicely.
- Had interesting content that was relevant, useful and informative for the targeted recipient - the manager of each care home.
- Was accompanied by a brief letter that summarised the contents and highlighted the special offer.
- Had clear calls to action - the reader knew what they had to do if they wanted to use the business for their recruitment.
- Clearly explained the benefits of doing business with the agency.

A newsletter is a flexible communication and can be used in many ways:

- You can keep in touch with existing clients, informing them of what is happening in your business, keeping your name firmly in their mind.

- You can keep in touch with warm prospects you have previously pitched to, but are yet to buy from you. Pestering continually by e-mail or telephone runs the risk of sounding needy.

- It's a fantastic tool for reviving your lapsed clients, gently reminding them that you are still around and ready to do business with them again.

- Direct mail, exhibitions, seminars, networking events - your newsletter can only add value to your existing marketing activities and complement your existing communications.

One question I am often asked by a business owner contemplating their first newsletter is how regularly they should be sending one out. There is no hard and fast rule as to the frequency of your newsletters. For example, I work with one business that sells promotional gifts and corporate clothing. In this case we create a newsletter on a quarterly basis. Because there are always new products and clothing ranges to promote, each newsletter generates new orders that way outstrip the cost of production. The regularity of the communication keeps the business name alive in their clients' minds, while at the same time prompting the reader to consider making an additional promotional gift or clothing order.

Is a newsletter appropriate for your own business? Ask yourself the following three questions.

1. Are your competitors producing regular newsletters?
2. Do you work in a sector in which communicating regularly with your customers is important in maintaining their loyalty and gaining repeat sales?
3. Are your products or services frequently changing?

If you answer 'yes' to any one of these questions, then a newsletter is appropriate for your business.

If you are new to writing newsletters or the ones that you have created previously have not been particularly successful, set yourself a goal of producing one high quality newsletter this year. A newsletter that is targeted, professionally designed and well written. After sending it out to your current clients, follow-up by asking for feedback. This should help you to decide whether your newsletter had the desired impact, and if so, when your next newsletter should be issued. It is better to produce just one or two excellent newsletters each year, crammed with articulate and relevant content, than it is to push out a lacklustre monthly newsletter that is struggling to communicate anything of value.

Top Tips for Producing a Profitable Newsletter

- **Your newsletter must have a clear direction and tone.** As with all your marketing communications, you should start by defining the audience that is going to be receiving your newsletter.

- **With your audience firmly in mind,** it's time to decide upon the content that you think will be of genuine interest to them. It's natural to want to cram your newsletter with as much information as possible about your products or services, along with several sales messages and calls to action. However, you want your newsletter to be read and acted upon. An overdose of sales talk will turn off any audience. Although the newsletter should of course include articles designed to sell your products and services, try to restrict these to approximately half of the newsletter overall. The other half should be devoted to interesting, information-rich content relevant to the sector in which your business is based. The clue lies in the name of this communication. It's a newsletter, not a sales flyer. For example, one of the much improved newsletters for the care home recruitment agency included:

- A three question quiz with Marks & Spencer's vouchers as the prize.
- A feature on the benefits of meditation for residents.
- An article from a guest writer on storytelling in care homes.
- An explanation of colours and the impact of colour in a care home setting.

along with the sales content, which included:

- An article on the company's unique 12-month replacement guarantee.
- A client case study.
- A summary of their services.
- An article on the benefits of doing business with them.

- **Do not overburden your newsletter** with too many words or too many visuals. By the same token, a newsletter that has an abundance of white space may suggest that the business has struggled to provide sufficient material. As a general guide I usually allocate 500 – 600 words for each page, based on an A4 size sheet. This allows ample space for imagery, design and branding. You may want to run with a two-page newsletter or produce a larger four-page issue. Your decision will probably be based on the amount of content that you want to share and how frequently you plan on producing your newsletter. Once you have finalised the content, it's a good idea to spend a little time thinking about where you want your articles to be positioned rather than simply abdicating the task to your designer. There may be a synergy between certain articles and features and these should appear on the same page. The best place for your competition is the back page, and your most important features, those that you are very keen for readers to notice, should sit on the right-hand side of any page.

If you want your newsletter to be well received, it must be useful, informative, relevant and a good read. I would also suggest enlisting the services of a professional designer and, unless you are confident in your own writing abilities, the services of a local copywriter capable of turning your ideas into sparkling prose.

The care home recruitment newsletter benefited from a professional designer and copywriter whose fees were more than covered by resultant sales. Determining the actual content of the newsletter, however, is something that you cannot really delegate. Here are some ideas that usually work well in any newsletter:

- **Include a top tips feature**. As outlined earlier in the chapter, top tips are always popular if they impart genuinely useful information rather than sales waffle. You may want to consider writing three top tips in your newsletter and signposting readers to your website or blog for the remainder. Think about what you can share that would lend itself well to the top tips format and that your readers will find interesting.

- **Publish an article written by a guest writer**. This always works well if your guest writer complements what you do and is asked to share useful information too. For example, Independent Financial Advisers could use an accountant as their guest writer, sharing tax tips. A business selling promotional gifts could have a marketer sharing top tips on how to use promotional gifts wisely. An interior designer could have a guest writer discussing soft furnishings. A printer could include a column from a designer; a weight loss specialist could have a personal stylist as a guest writer. The possibilities are endless. You may want to consider lining up a number of guest writers to keep your newsletter fresh or alternatively you may be happy sticking with the same person, especially if they prove popular with your readers. You will also enjoy the benefit of reaching your guest writer's audience too, as you can be sure that any guest writer will be happy to see themselves in print and will therefore promote your newsletter to their own circle of influence.

- **Consider including updates or media coverage** about what's been happening in your sector that would be interesting and helpful to your readers. Changes in legislation, the way in which your products or services are sold, any independent favourable media coverage including reviews of what you offer. Again, you don't have to provide all the details in your newsletter. You can signpost to your blog, your website or any fact sheets that you have prepared that cover the topics in more depth.

- **A focus on you, a member of your team, or your entire team**. Corny but true, people definitely do buy people. So using your newsletter to introduce your team will always go down well, especially if most of your communication with clients takes place remotely. You could answer questions in the style of a mini interview as an alternative way of introducing yourself. Stuck for questions? How about... *'What inspired you to start your business?', 'What are the highlights of running your business?', 'What are your plans for the business moving forwards?', 'What would you say is the secret to keeping your clients happy?', 'Tell us about your new service/product.'* An interview of a few hundred words can have a really positive impact, especially when it's accompanied by a nice photograph. Similarly, a photograph of your team taken in an unusual setting is always attention grabbing. The Personal Injury team at Bennett Griffin Solicitors are based in Worthing, just a few hundred yards from the sea. Their first newsletter included a really striking image of the team on the beach, accompanied by a brief description of what each team member specialised in.

- **Include a Questions and Answers section**. Even if your newsletter is aimed squarely at existing clients, don't assume that they know everything about your business. Use your newsletter to include your top three Q&As and signpost readers to your website for any others.

- **How about a feature on a client and your achievements with them**? This has two benefits. Firstly, you could feature your VIP clients and in doing so, strengthen your relationship with them. Secondly, a great client case study can work wonders in galvanising prospects to do business with you. It also keeps existing clients loyal. You can't give them too many reasons for continuing to use you. Ideally your feature should focus on what your client wanted, what you actually delivered and what made your delivery so special. Include a couple of lines of genuine testimonial from this client to give added authenticity.

- **A competition is always popular**. These always go down well in newsletters provided that the questions being asked are neither patronising nor onerous, and the prize being awarded will be genuinely appreciated by the readers. You may want to ask two or three multiple-choice questions, the answers to which can be found within the newsletter. This is a good way of ensuring that the newsletter is read. You may also want to consider having one main prize and two or three runner-up prizes.

- **Consider writing an article that focuses in detail** upon one specific aspect of your products or services. This can take the format of a 'did you know?' article and it works particularly well if you have recently made improvements or additions to your products or services.

- **Provide a summary of your products or services** and the key benefits of them. This has a place in any newsletter. It is always worth reminding and informing readers what you offer. Cold prospects will be introduced to your products and services for the first time and existing clients will be reminded. This is beneficial in both cases. Aim to provide the information in a few concise paragraphs or bullet points.

- **You can provide a summary of your blog**, your website and what readers will find when they go on-line. Your newsletter is a good way to introduce readers to your on-line presence. A few lines summarising the topics covered in your blog and testimonial from people that subscribe would be a good way to do this. Have you improved or upgraded your website recently? What are the goodies on your website that readers need to be informed of or reminded about?

- **How about providing a voucher**? We covered the benefits of a voucher earlier in the chapter. Your newsletter can be used to promote an on-line voucher or can include the voucher itself. Be aware that by choosing to include a close date on your voucher you will be rendering your newsletter redundant after the voucher expiry date.

- **Motivational and inspiring quotes** can work well, especially if you provide services such as business coaching, mentoring, training etc. Quotations are short, easy to read, and work well at breaking up blocks of text.

- **Don't forget your clear calls to action**. You should conclude each sales-oriented article in your newsletter with one. 'Contact us ... for an informal chat; a quotation; to request a free health check'. 'Go on-line to ... complete our survey; find out more about our latest product; download your voucher' and so on.

- **Testimonial from happy clients is always worth including.** This works well if you place the testimonial in different areas around your newsletter as opposed to listing it in one column. I'd like to emphasise again that it's important that the testimonial is genuine, unedited and, whenever possible, that the name of the person providing the testimonial is included.

- **Sometimes an introduction from you is appropriate**. You don't have to accompany every newsletter that you send out with a personal letter from yourself in order for it to have an impact. Instead, you can include a short introduction from yourself on the front of the newsletter in which you provide a brief summary of the contents and your reason for sending. Perhaps accompany this introduction with a nice photo of you, plus your signature.

The Name of your Newsletter

Your newsletter needs a memorable title, something other than just your business name. It can, of course, be accompanied by a strap line to anchor its title to you and your business. (Strap lines are covered in detail in Chapter 5.)

Here are a few examples of newsletters and accompanying strap lines, with the type of business detailed within brackets.

InForm - Personal injury advice and guidance from the personal injury team at Bennett Griffin *(specialist personal injury solicitors).*
Techmobility Talk - The Motability Dealer Newsletter (*vehicle adaptations specialist).*
Hot off the Press - The printed word from Quentin Press *(printing company).*
Let's get creative! The brand-new, new-look newsletter from Creative Vision Promotions *(promotional gifts).*
FM Focus. The newsletter from Dyno-Pest for facilities managers in the Greater London area (*pest prevention and management).*
Loving Linseed. The brand-new health and vitality newsletter from High Barn Oils - the home of naturally grown and cold pressed linseed oil rich in omega three *(Linseed Oil farmer).*

What's Stopping You?

If you can put these tips into practice and distribute to the people that you want to target, give a newsletter a go. You should see an increase in your sales for a relatively modest outlay.

12. Your Business Card

During your professional lifetime, thousands of business cards will be pressed into your hand. When attending a networking event, a business card is usually the first sales communication you encounter. Yet how many business cards actually have an impact and inspire you to find out more about the person that presented it? Very few is the most likely answer.

Whenever we receive a business card, either by hand or attached to a letter, we tend to judge the person it belongs to based on the impression we are given by that card. If the card is thin and flimsy and appears to be cheaply produced, we are unlikely to be impressed. If the card does not clearly advertise what the person does, we are unlikely to spend time trying to find out. Yet a business card can be a powerful door opener and an excellent conversation starter. A well designed and attractive business card that includes the right information about a person will immediately grab attention. If we don't have an imminent need for that person's services at the time we receive the card, we are more likely to put it to one side for a later date if the card itself is appealing.

Here are some tips for creating a striking, relevant and attractive business card.

- **Get the basics right.** Make sure that your business card is professionally designed, carrying through your logo, business name, associated imagery and strap line if you have one.

- **Don't opt for cheap and cheerful.** The weight of your card and its texture is the first thing that will be noticed by the person receiving it. The difference in cost between a good quality business card and a poor quality one can be just a few pounds. Opt for a good quality board. If you're not sure on the finish of your business card, fish out those business cards that you've kept. Use the most appealing one as your guide, and ask your designer and printer to quote costs based on that template.

- **Use both sides of your business card.** The front of your card should include your business name, your job title, contact details, website and blog if you have one. Increasingly, people are also adding the details of the social networks that they belong to. If you want to be found on-line, include your social networks. The back of your business card is a mini blank canvas and should not be ignored as a further opportunity to sell yourself and your business. For example, you can use it to:

    - Highlight two or three benefits of your product or service.
    - Promote your latest book, seminar programme, workshops, Masterclasses etc.
    - Let people know how much stock you carry in your on-line shop and any permanent price pledge - *'over 500 of the latest hiking products at up to 30% off the retail price.'*
    - Highlight a powerful customer testimonial or a couple of lines of positive media coverage.
    - Promote your website - two or three lines that will motivate the reader to go on-line 'Visit our website to view our stunning handmade jewellery collection.'
    - Promote any useful free resources that you offer - white papers... top tips... how to guides. 'Download

your free guides to building a successful small business from our website.'

- List the services or products that you provide. Be aware that if you go beyond a few lines of text, it's going to be very difficult for the person to read what you're offering and this in itself will create a negative impression of your business.

If you need some further inspiration to make your business card really stand out, how about...?

- Including your company's mission statement.

- Including a photograph of you - this can work really well if you deliver workshops or you're a public speaker.

- Printing the same information on the back of your business card as on the front... but in a different language if you regularly work abroad.

- Including a quotation or saying that reflects your business philosophy.

- Asking a question... 'What business challenge keeps you awake at night?', 'What would you like to gain from your free 60-minute session with me?'

Let your imagination wander. How do you currently grab the attention of people when you're marketing your business? What are the things that you say that stops them in their tracks? Distilling this into one line and adding it to your business card could really give it that extra 'oomph', making it stand out amongst a sea of corporate blandness!

Double-up Your Sales Communications to Increase Impact

When printing sales communications, consider combining two of those described in this chapter into one document. For example:

- As outlined in Chapter 3, the back of the sales letter is a blank canvas. Don't let it go to waste. Consider including your list of Questions and Answers, a quiz, some testimonial, or a selection of press clippings etc.

- A voucher advertising your special offer can be built into your sales letter or newsletter.

- A survey can be on the reverse of your press clippings.

If you do decide to combine your sales communications, let the reader know this.

'Make sure that you enter our competition overleaf.'

'Please turn over to read some genuine customer feedback.'

Chapter Summary

1. Be open to promoting your business with communications that you may not have previously considered.

2. Don't favour on-line communications or off-line communications. Be open to using both.

3. Consider the variety of ways in which your sales communications can be used - on-line and off-line.

4. Consider combining two sales communications together to increase impact.

5. Make your customer survey simple, thank your customers, and act on feedback.

6. Use the positive comments from your survey as testimonials.

7. Keep your questions and answers genuine and helpful.

8. Your biography can influence a journalist to cover your story so make it a good one.

9. A neatly written post-it note can highlight a key message within your mailshot.

10. A voucher can encourage the undecided to respond.

11. Use a quiz to diagnose your customers' needs for what you offer.

12. Use the '10 reasons why...' sales communication to advertise why your customers choose your business.

13. Your 'Raving Fans Charter' is simply genuine, unedited and positive customer feedback.

14. Your press clippings document should be up to date and professionally designed.

15. A top tips article enables you to share your expertise and build your reputation.

16. Your newsletter can be a huge income-generating tool if you spend time planning and promoting it.

17. Your business card can do more than simply yield your contact details. Turn it into a mini selling tool.

CHAPTER 5

HOW TO BUILD YOUR SUCCESSFUL BUSINESS INTO A SUCCESSFUL BRAND

'Brand building starts with understanding the key attributes of your products and services as well as understanding and anticipating the needs of your customers.' Philip Kotler

Branding is a subject that regularly confuses small business owners. They are either unsure about the meaning of a 'brand', or don't believe that branding is relevant to small businesses.

If there's one myth that I would like to bust in this chapter, it's that branding is only for blue-chip businesses. I hope to persuade you that branding is relevant to your business too and will show you the simple steps that can be taken towards building your small business into a brand. I will also underpin these steps with case study examples of small businesses that are successfully developing brand awareness of their company.

Firstly, it is important that you are customer-focused and open to change. You need to recognise the importance of customer care and understand that there will be times when you need the support of other professionals, including designers, web developers and perhaps copywriters.

What Does the Word 'Brand' Actually Mean?

Occasionally I will hear a business owner saying 'I've got my brand sorted out.' What they are usually referring to is the design of their logo and business name. These details are only two of the many aspects that contribute towards defining a brand. Branding was encountered as far back as Anglo Saxon times, originating from the word 'brandr' meaning 'to burn'. The Anglo Saxon farmer used branding as a means of stamping his ownership on his livestock. Those farmers that enjoyed an excellent reputation would find that their brand was in demand, whereas the farmers with poorer quality livestock would struggle to sell their cattle to trade buyers.

And it's not that different today.

Businesses that enjoy an excellent reputation are the ones we gravitate towards when we have available funds. By contrast, the businesses that make the headlines for their poor customer service or inferior products are invariably ignored. Many go out of business or spend a considerable period of time and money on re-building a positive reputation.

Philip Kotler is one of the world's most highly regarded marketing practitioners, and he offers the following definition of a brand:

> ***'A brand is a promise to your customers, the totality of perceptions about a product, service or business, the relationship customers have with it based on past experiences, present associations and future expectations...brand reality is always defined by the customer's view.'***

Kotler's description suggests that at the heart of a successful brand is the delivery of a fantastic customer experience every time. This is because the power of your brand ultimately comes down to what your customers think about it.

Perhaps one of the best examples to illustrate the impact your brand can have upon your business is that of the Ratners Group. Ratner jewellery had always been extremely popular with the public until Chief Executive Gerald Ratner made his infamous speech about the jewellery on offer in his chain of shops being cheap and of poor quality. The perception of the Ratner brand plummeted overnight and this nearly resulted in the firm's collapse. And yet nothing had materially changed to the jewellery on sale in the High Street in those few hours. What had changed, however, was the perception of the Ratner brand on the High Street. It was now regarded as a firm selling cheap and nasty jewellery and making fools of their customers. Consequently, customers no longer wanted to be associated with it.

This example shows the power that customers wield in building or breaking a brand and how important it is for an ambassador of the business to recognise this fact.

The Benefits of a Brand Over a Business

The vast majority of small businesses have competitors. In a growing crowd of businesses offering similar products or services to yourself, a good reputation is something that puts your business in the spotlight and helps it to stand out from the rest. Customers take notice and are drawn to you. Satisfying customer needs and delivering great products or services help generate that good reputation and so provide the foundation of a strong brand. And with a strong brand your business will benefit in the following ways:

- Your customers will thank you with continuing loyalty even when tested by a competitor. Loyal customers are also likely to recommend you to others, something worth its weight in gold.

- Your customers will be more willing to pay a price premium for your products or services because they can see the added value in what you deliver. Value they believe they would be hard pushed to find elsewhere.

- Your customers will be less sensitive to your price increases. Whilst price does matter, it's usually not the major issue.

- You will close sales more quickly. Prospects will need less time to make the decision to do business with you as they trust your name and your reputation.

- Customers will be willing to award a larger share of their available spend to you.

- In tough economic times, customers will be reluctant to stop using your services and will prefer instead to part company with suppliers with whom they have not forged such a strong relationship.

How to Start Building Your Business into a Brand

There are four key areas to consider, namely:

Visibility - how your customers view your business. This encompasses your business name, your logo and any associated imagery. The quality and relevance of your on-line and off-line marketing communications are also crucial factors.

Consistency - consistently delivering an outstanding level of service to your customers. It does not matter where, when or how a prospect or a customer comes into contact with your business, they need to be assured in the knowledge that each time they do so, they will benefit from the same high levels of care, delivery and attentiveness.

Clarity - understanding exactly what your business stands for, why customers buy from you and why customers continue to buy. Don't overcomplicate your messages and always view your business through the eyes of the customer when developing key benefit statements.

Corporate Social Responsibility - it is no longer enough to deliver value to customers and make a profit. Reach out into the local, national and even global community; reduce the impact of your business on the environment etc.

Let's look at each one in more detail.

Visibility

At some stage, most small businesses will review the image they present to prospects and customers. Over a period of time they become aware of any shortcomings in:

- Their logo.
- The typeface and style of their business name.
- Any supporting images.
- Their strap line.

Why is this? Usually, a business will have been set-up on the smallest of budgets, with any design work either handled in-house or passed to a printer with skills in printing rather than designing. And although this was perfectly reasonable at the start of the business, as the business becomes more established the home-spun nature of the imagery becomes increasingly apparent. Even if a professional designer had been used previously, the look may no longer accurately reflect what the business now stands for.

So with money allocated from the kitty and a designer from their networking group booked in for the task, the business owner embarks on a process of re-branding the business. This should be an enjoyable and rewarding experience, but often becomes an intensely frustrating one for all parties involved.

If you are about to embark upon the process of re-branding, it is important to make sure that you are personally involved in the design process, even if you don't have any specific ideas regarding the new look. Abdicating responsibility to your designer could result in many design hours being spent on developing a new image that you are not happy with and so reject. With no guidance or instruction, the designer may create an image that has no relevance to the ethos of your business. There is also the risk that you accept the image purely because you can't come up with a better one yourself.

To re-brand your business image successfully, it is important that you play your part in the design process, working closely in collaboration with your designer to create a design brief that you are happy with and have discussed in detail.

When creating a design brief, consider the following:

- **Are you looking for a whole new look or would you just like to improve what you already have?** It may not be appropriate to completely redesign your image, especially if there are elements that are still relevant and appealing. You may not be in a position financially to make all the necessary changes to your marketing collateral. For example, when Direct Route were going through this process, they realised that they did not want to lose their existing logo in favour of a brand-new one, but that they did want it to be redrawn by a professional designer so that it looked crisper and more professional in both printed and on-line communications. The original logo had been designed in conjunction with their printer and remained relevant to the business today. The revamped logo therefore retained the fundamentals of the original design but the image was sleeker and altogether more professional looking. It consequently had a greater impact on the eye.

- **Your budget may not stretch to a complete overhaul of your image** but this should not deter you from talking to a designer about improving it. A good designer can work wonders with your existing imagery and a few subtle tweaks can make a world of difference to the overall perception of your business. You may believe that a complete redesign of your logo and image is desirable but your heart cannot sanction such a dramatic step. If so, don't worry. I have seen the plainest, the most unprofessional and the most inappropriate images transformed into something quite stunning with just a few subtle design improvements.

- **What are the key words that define your business and your customer offering?** It may seem strange to include this in a design brief, but it helps to provide your designer with as much information as possible about your business. If you are able to think of a few keywords that encapsulate your offering, include these in your design brief. One word may be enough to inspire your designer to create something amazing and relevant. When ISM went through a re-branding process, the seven keywords delivered to the designer were: pioneering, innovative, powerful, flexible, reliable, quality and outstanding. These are the words that define their approach to business and the integrated security control room management systems they design and install. Interestingly, the designer placed each one of these words within the design of the company folder, providing real impact.

- **Are you looking for a fresh, modern, clean look?** How about a traditional look? Quirky, cheeky and irreverent? Try to guide your designer by providing a good description of the personality of your business. Describe your target audiences in detail and explain why existing customers use you. By providing this information, you are helping your designer to look at your business through the eyes of your customers. Don't be shy about sharing these elements of your marketing plan. Good design is not just appealing and attractive, it is relevant too. Many designers are given the slenderest of information to work from - in some cases they are provided with a list of competitors' websites and nothing more. The better the information that you can offer, the greater the likelihood that the new design will be just what you're looking for.

- **What are the colours that are *inappropriate* for your business?** Tempting though it is to choose the colours that you like on a personal level to represent the identity of your business, you should also be aware of those colours that are inappropriate for the nature of your business. For example, a dark colour to present a business that provides products for children could appear a little strange. Try to be open-minded about the colours you choose. It may be that a colour that you are not particularly fond of yourself is the most relevant one for your business. If a designer is able to present their ideas to you in a number of different colours, unrestricted by your personal likes and dislikes, the chances are that the best result will be found.

- **Make a list of everything that is going to be affected by your re-brand**. This will clarify your thinking as to whether you are going to completely change the look of your business, or improve what already exists. It's important that your designer has access to this list too. Their design has to work effectively across all of your marketing communications. You would usually expect to make changes to the following:

  - Your website.
  - Your e-mail template.
  - Your letterhead paper, business cards, compliment slips.
  - Your marketing communications - flyers, newsletters, brochures etc.

  You may also have signage, corporate workwear, exhibition banners and stands, and other business specific materials, all of which will need to change. An alternative option is to present contrasting images of your business and therefore not worry about re-branding everything. This is rarely a successful move, however. Calculate the total cost of making these changes. To do this you will probably need to have a conversation with your web developer, your printer and your designer, not to mention your accountant! If you're planning on making amendments rather than going for a complete overhaul, you may prefer to make the changes over a few months. Start with changes to the essentials such as your website, letterhead paper, business cards and marketing communications. The remaining changes can be implemented gradually over the coming months. However, if you are planning on a complete new look you should really bite the bullet and change everything at the same time. Calculate the costs of each approach before arriving at your decision. It may be that the figures staring back at you persuade you to wait for a month or two before starting the ball rolling. It's important not to discover midway through the process that you don't have enough money to effect all the necessary changes, leaving your image confused and inconsistent.

As Direct Route decided to make only subtle amendments to their existing logo and because the difference between the original logo and the improved one was not dramatic they were able to implement the changes over a period of six months. With many direct mail campaigns in the pipeline, the immediate requirement was to update their marketing literature. Spend some time deciding on how you want to approach your own re-branding exercise before briefing your designer.

- **Do you want to change your strapline or slogan?** Perhaps you want to add one. The main purpose of your strapline is to support your business name and your logo. It can play a vital part in communicating what you offer and a brilliant strapline will help you to stand apart from those competitors that simply rely on their business name. A business name that doesn't give any clues as to its purpose is at a disadvantage without the inclusion of a strap line.

  A good strapline can help make a business memorable. Think of Tesco. Their strapline, 'Every little helps' is extremely simple, but also annoyingly memorable. Your strapline should ideally translate what your business represents into a customer friendly language. As part of the Direct Route brand audit process, the decision was made to change the existing strapline from 'Direct Route Collections' to 'The Commercial Debt Recovery Specialists'. This decision was made after a dozen business people were asked to comment on what they thought Direct Route did, based purely on their logo and existing strapline. Most believed that they were a courier company! Change was long overdue and now the new, simple strapline, which sits directly underneath the Direct Route logo, clearly states what the business offers.

If your business name clearly represents what you offer, consider a strapline that includes three or four of the keywords that we discussed earlier to communicate your company ethos. Make it simple and clear. How long should your strapline will be? Try not to go beyond eight words.

To provide further illustration, here are some examples of simple and effective business strap lines.

'Anything fresher is still swimming' - from a fishmonger. There's no mistaking the brand promise in this strapline is there? This is one of my favourite straplines.

'World leader in paper-based packaging' - from a packaging company, as I'm sure you guessed. It's clear from their strapline what they do and their brand promise is included, i.e. that you won't find anything better because they are the world leader.

'Commercial vehicle services & parts' - this is a simple but essential strapline as it was impossible to know the nature of the business from the business name. The strapline therefore removed any confusion. This business has a fleet of vans so the vehicle signage acts as an advert, attracting the attention of potential new customers whilst the drivers are servicing their existing customers.

'Private and Commercial Property Management' - this is another strapline which describes in five words what the business does. Again, this was necessary because their business name was that of the Managing Director.

'World pioneers in integrated security management' - this is a punchy strapline from ISM, a business that operates in a fiercely competitive global marketplace. In just six words the strapline tells their target audience what they do and the leading position that they occupy. No room for shrinking violets!

'Making your business leaner, fitter and more powerful' - this is the strapline from my own business, The Marketing Gym Ltd. I will let you be the judge on this particular one.

It's important to decide whether to use a strap line before you brief your designer because they will need to integrate it into the overall design. A good designer will usually present your strapline in a number of different positions so that you can see what options are available.

If you do decide to use a strapline, don't settle on one that has been hastily conceived and could easily be applied to any business. And don't be tempted by one that is cute but says little or nothing about your particular product or service. Here are some examples of straplines that I feel fall into this camp.

'Because we care'

'You've tried the rest, now try the best!'

'Unique IT solutions for your business'

'Pride in delivering'

'Simply the best'

'Putting our customers first every time'

Although catchy, they are all rather too generic. Instead, invest some serious thinking time on creating a strapline that supports your business name, your logo and your company ethos. You want to arrive at something that is individual and describes succinctly what you provide to your customers. If you need further inspiration, take a closer look at business cards, vehicle signage, adverts in newspapers and magazines, websites and of course, the television. And remember, above all you want your own strapline to be a positive and relevant reflection of your business.

- **A good design brief should include a concise but informative paragraph on each of the following**:
    - The products and services you offer.
    - Your target audiences.
    - How, and from where, you gain most of your business.

- Formal and informal feedback from customers on your service and on your current image.
- The specific reasons why you are considering making changes to your image.

Armed with this information, your designer will be able to deliver their very best work for you.

Tips for Choosing a Designer

- **Don't appoint the first designer that you meet** unless there are compelling reasons to do so; for example they come with many trusted endorsements and their portfolio includes outstanding examples of what they have achieved for businesses similar to your own. Ask a handful of business people that you trust if they can recommend a designer. Then look at their websites and draw up a shortlist of three.

- **How do they react to your brief?** If they are enthusiastic, taking notes, asking questions and actively listening to your ideas and freely sharing their own initial ideas, you are off to a promising start. A good designer will not coerce you into agreeing with their own views, nor will they agree with you on every point. Spend time looking through their portfolio, asking about the inspiration for their designs.

- **Ask for a fixed fee in writing.** This will usually be presented in three parts. The first element of their fee will be to redesign your logo or improve it. You need to clarify the number of changes that you can request before incurring additional charges. Grey areas can lead to unexpected bills. It is likely that several changes will be made to the original design before both of you are completely happy with the final look. Will you be presented with one logo or several? I usually ask my designers to put forward three initial designs from which a favourite can be chosen, and tweaked if necessary. These should also be presented in a range of different colours. The second element of the fee will be to reproduce the final agreed design across all your marketing communications, and to create the artwork for use by your printer and for your website. If you would prefer your designer to manage your printing, this will constitute the third element of your quote. You can't expect your designer to liaise with the chosen printer at their own expense so they will usually add their management fee to the print cost. It is also wise to clarify beforehand that the fee you pay your designer will entitle you to the artwork they are going to create and any photos and images that they buy on your behalf and bill you for. Some designers can be sensitive about this, especially if they suspect that you are making the request because you are going to use another designer in the future, or manage the print yourself.

- **Treat your designer with respect.** They are a trusted and valued business partner, not a commodity supplier. If you can work harmoniously with your designer and commit to what should be an exciting and rewarding process, you will build a mutually beneficial relationship that should last many years. Great design can be instrumental in boosting your bottom line and enhancing what people think about your business. Look upon good design as an essential business investment, not an expense.

The second element of building a successful brand is:

Consistency

Most of us are creatures of habit. There are reasons why we buy our clothes from the same outlets and why we prefer to meet friends at our favourite coffee bar. We feel comforted and secure in the knowledge that by repeating our actions, we're going to enjoy the same experience every time. We like our loyalty to be rewarded with good feelings and great experiences. Businesses that become successful brands understand the importance of delivering a consistent and positive customer experience. These businesses make it their mission to ensure that each customer has an enjoyable experience regardless of when, how or where they come into contact with the company brand. So your favourite coffee shop is likely to offer more than simply selling good coffee. The atmosphere is likely to be warm and convivial, and the staff welcoming and friendly. Perhaps they will have made the effort to learn your name and know your preferred coffee choice. And should you ever spill your coffee, they replace it without question or charge. They will have recognised that the taste of their coffee alone is not enough to turn you into a regular customer.

There are, of course, always exceptions to this example of a customer-driven business. Those brands that concentrate on delivering their services or products at the lowest possible price often forego the niceties that result in an improved experience. In those cases, customers are largely willing to lower their expectations in exchange for a very low price. But most of the time, customers want it all – value, first-class service and a consistently great experience.

Building Consistency into your Business.

Identify the interactions that a customer has with your business at each stage of their relationship with you. These are known as your customer touch points. Review how your business performs at each of these touch points. Many businesses tend to focus on delivering positive experiences in two key areas - recruiting new customers, and delivery. Other areas, such as after-care and building the relationship after the sale can be neglected to some extent. Consequently, inconsistencies can creep in and sabotage what has been a positive experience to that point. You may find that this exercise reveals that your business is one of those that is over-delivering in some areas, and under-delivering in others. Could this be a good time to revisit Chapter 4 and whip your survey into shape?

Once you have identified the touch points, group them into the following categories:

- The prospecting stage.
- The sign up stage.
- The delivery stage.
- The immediate post-delivery stage.
- Ongoing relationship building.

Having done this, identify within each category how many times a customer interacts with your business. Can you see any inconsistencies in the quality of the service they are receiving? Does the speed and courtesy of your response to e-mails and phone calls vary depending on how busy you are? Customers will ultimately become disenchanted with your business if they can't be sure what to expect from you each time. This will also make them reluctant to recommend you. Similarly, your business will experience fluctuating degrees of success with new prospects if you are quick to respond on some occasions but are impossible to get hold of at other times. If you employ people, check that there are no inconsistencies of service delivery within your team. Put your customer touch points under the microscope and evaluate whether each one delivers a consistently good experience.

Once you have gathered the evidence, and it may be a matter of a few hours or longer depending on the size of your business, aim to implement any improvements swiftly. One business that I worked with, a commercial photographic laboratory, had an exemplary and consistent record for responding to customer e-mails and phone calls. When a new customer came on board, they processed their order within 12 hours compared to the industry average of three days. However, at the immediate post-delivery stage they did not follow-up the orders with a phone call to check whether the customer was happy and if they had a need for any additional services. When they started doing this, sales increased significantly. New customers had often not realised at the time of placing their first order the breadth of services that the business was capable of providing. Having a friendly and knowledgeable employee at the end of the line proved to be a hit, especially as the remit of the employee was to ensure that the customer was happy with their order rather than obtaining further sales.

Another business, Kalimex, scored very highly on their customer service at the point of delivery. However, after surveying their customers they realised that at the new customer sign-up stage they were not providing enough information about their payment terms, discounts and the delivery schedules for their products. A simple question and answer sheet, combined with a friendly welcome letter and a follow-up telephone call addressed this and it led to a steady increase in sales.

This is not an academic exercise. It's an opportunity for you to stand back from your business and look at where and how you can raise your service levels to the same high standards across the board. Try to set aside some time in your diary to perform this review, otherwise there is a risk that your good intentions will never materialise. By striving for high levels of consistency in your customer experience, you will be moving your business several steps nearer to becoming a brand.

After identifying the various interactions that customers have with your business and satisfying yourself that you are handling these to a consistently high standard, it's a good idea to document this information. It will be invaluable when you are training staff. It's important that they understand what is expected of them and it will reinforce your commitment to placing the customer at the centre of your business.

Let's now look at the second way in which you can build consistency into your business.

Whether you employ staff, use associates to deliver your products or services or are a sole-trader, it is essential that everyone in your business radiates a positive and enthusiastic attitude. Attitudes, both positive and negative, have an influence on your customers and as a consequence, your reputation. The manner with which the phone is answered, how your business is presented at a networking event, how your sales people introduce your business to cold prospects, how your telemarketing agency builds relationships in your name – nothing should be dismissed as unimportant. Successful businesses become successful brands from the inside. And it starts with you as the figurehead of your business.

Every single person that joins your business should understand from the very outset what your business stands for, your customer service philosophy and how you are building your brand. Today, it may simply be a matter of having a coffee with your telemarketer and impressing upon them the need to build relationships rather than trying to hard sell. In a few years time, it could be a more formal meeting with your newly appointed sales team. Make sure that you start off on the right tracks because further down the line your good habits will have become firmly entrenched. Keep that document up to date too – it will reinforce those conversations.

How can you ensure that your values and customer-centric principle is understood and implemented by everyone? Dyno-Pest manages to achieve this by including the following in the training programme for all new members of their sales team:

- **Branding awareness**. An explanation of what the Dyno-Pest brand stands for, how Dyno-Pest differs from other pest control companies and how they will be expected to present Dyno-Pest to potential clients.

- **Telephone training**. A guide to handling calls with potential customers and dealing with incoming enquiries. This is particularly important if they have previously worked in an environment in which they have been expected to take a hard selling approach as Dyno-Pest has a different philosophy, based on building trust and relationships over a period of time.

- **A think tank discussion forum.** If a new salesperson has a background in pest control, the think tank provides an opportunity to discuss the differences between Dyno-Pest and their previous employer, and for them to outline the training they received in their previous role. It is then made clear that anything inconsistent with the Dyno-Pest ethos must be left behind. This ensures that any bad habits are eliminated early and the importance that Dyno-Pest places on its good name is clearly established.

- **A brand guidelines portfolio.** Included in this portfolio are templates for standard letters and e-mails. Each template has been professionally written, and so using these template communications ensures that the Dyno-Pest brand is represented consistently. The communications are accurate and without spelling or grammatical mistakes.

Another successful small business, Mantra Magazines, ensures that all new recruits complete an induction training programme. Part of this programme is a special project designed to prompt the new recruit to study what the Mantra brand stands for, how customers perceive it and what makes it positively different from other publishing brands. Like the Dyno-Pest salesmen, the Mantra sales team are given a set of template documents - adverts, letters and e-mail wordings and articles to send to existing and potential advertisers. This saves time and it ensures that the Mantra brand is always delivered to the same consistent high standard. When one of my clients commissioned a telemarketing company to generate leads for their sales team, they spent some time writing a brief for the telemarketers. The brief included their values, the benefits of the services they wanted the telemarketers to promote, an explanation of the potential barriers to a sale and their customer service philosophy. In my client's eyes, the telemarketers were an extension of their brand and so were assuming the important role of brand ambassador.

Returning to your own business and thinking again about those customer touch points, are there any areas in which you and the people associated with your business could benefit from training? Here's some food for thought:

- **Is there a need for customer care training - either new training or refresher sessions?** Pleasing customers is vital to the success of every business, and is at the heart of building your business into a brand. Customers remember their personal interactions with you and your team, especially those in which they were less than satisfied with the service they received. You and your employees are likely to remember only a fraction of these interactions and will probably be unaware of occasions when you unwittingly under-deliver. Customer service training teaches your team how to interact effectively and appropriately with customers and makes a clear statement that you take customer satisfaction seriously. In a competitive marketplace, good customer service can set you apart from other businesses, and those businesses that do not take customer satisfaction seriously enough to invest in delivering it, invariably suffer in comparison with those businesses that do.

- **What customer care training should you consider?** Naturally this will depend upon your business, how you deliver your products or services to customers, how many customers you have and the service standards that you have established. But most small businesses have a need for customer service training that encompasses one or more of the following:

    - Telephone skills.
    - Rapport building.
    - Handling awkward and challenging customer situations.
    - Understanding customer needs.
    - How to delight customers.
    - Written communication skills.
    - Listening skills.
    - Positive tone of voice and body language.

Start with the most pressing training need in your business currently. Identify the individuals in need of this training and if not sure how to deliver the training, use the Internet to search for local training providers. Ask your networking group for recommendations, or contact your local Chamber of Commerce. It may be that government grants are available.

- **Is there a need to train some or all of your employees in the intricacies of your products and services?** There may be a need simply to brush up on existing knowledge levels or to start from scratch if you have a relatively new team. Don't assume that everyone in your business is equipped with your knowledge. Find out by asking or testing them. And nothing beats asking your customers for their feedback. The results of your customer survey should pinpoint those areas in which improvement is needed and this, combined with your employees' feedback, should help you decide upon the most effective training.

- **Do you need to develop an induction training programme for new recruits?** This should be part of your knowledge management process designed to help your new starter become a useful and integrated member of your team. Don't throw people in at the deep end and expect them to learn on the job if they will be interacting with customers in your business. Your induction programme should cover how an employee should do their job, how their role fits in with the rest of your business and the part they play in building harmonious customer relationships. It should also establish immediate training needs. Letting a brand-new employee loose onto the telephone to deal with existing customers or handle enquiries from potential customers without any training can result in immeasurable damage to your brand.

- **Consider scheduling regular team meetings.** Whether you decide to hold a monthly meeting or one on a less regular basis, make sure that you stick to the schedule. This sends a message to your staff that you recognise the role they play in the development and growth of your business. Team meetings can aid the ongoing process of building your business into a brand by providing a forum in which the values and vision of your business can be re-stated. The best team meetings are vibrant, interactive and informative, blending updates and progress with bursts of training and lively discussion. Use your team meetings to discuss real-life customer case studies, both good and bad. Share and introduce best practice and encourage feedback from employees. Your team meetings can become a mechanism for developing and improving your Customer Care Charter.

Let’s now look at the third element of building a successful brand:

Clarity

Coupled with consistency of message is clarity of message. Successful small business brands deliver clear and simple messages - on-line, at networking events, through the printed word - at every customer touch point. They do not risk causing confusion over their core benefits by overcomplicating their key messages. In Chapter 1, we looked at why you must define who you want to reach before creating simple, clear and compelling communications centred on addressing the needs of those potential customers. To help understand the importance of clarity within a business context, grab a piece of paper and jot down your answers to the following questions in no more than a few lines:

1. What do we do as a business?
2. What are our values?
3. What is our story; how have we evolved to where we are today?
4. What is our Vision Statement?

Okay, you may have found it pretty straightforward to answer the first two questions, but let's look at that third question, your story. This is something that we have covered in previous chapters, but it's well worth re-iterating now. Your story, what led you to launch and grow your business and how it has evolved from those early days, has to be told. It is your business DNA. Your story makes you unique. Telling your story establishes your business as something personal and real. The biographies of Michael Collins and Nicola Sales detailed in Chapter 4 included their individual business stories.

Whilst I was having my hair cut recently, I asked my hairdresser, Vince, if he would tell me his story as part of my research for this chapter. I had often wondered what inspired Vince to open his own hairdressing salon in a town already well served with hairdressers. Vince explained that his father had been a successful barber and that he was always eager to follow in his father's footsteps. Unlike his father who was risk averse, however, Vince is quite the opposite. So despite the existing competition in town, he made the decision to open his own salon and a few years later to use the premises below his salon to open a cafe. In both the salon and the cafe, Vince is very keen to ensure that each customer feels as though they are the most important person there. To help achieve this, Vince earmarks a separate budget for customer service training which is delivered on an ongoing basis to all his team. He believes that his Italian upbringing is the reason behind his conviviality and his desire to make his customers smile. Having been told Vince's story, I find that I now have an attachment to his salon, something that I do not share with other salons in the town. My knowledge of Vince and his history means that his salon becomes my hairdresser of choice for reasons other than quality of work and customer service. I now feel a personal involvement.

This is the effect that telling your business story can have upon your customers. They will feel more personally involved with you and will therefore be more likely to remain loyal to your business.

Storytelling is embraced by many successful blue-chip brands. The next time you visit the website of a well-known national company, look out for their story. It won't take long to find it. Many high profile speakers will start their talk by giving you a glimpse into their early years. They will explain how they started with nothing except a burning desire to accomplish something big and, if told with humility, their story will captivate and inspire you. It will make you want to find out more about them, to get closer to them.

You may want to include part of your story on your website. You don't have to go overboard on the detail. Give the visitor a glimpse into your experiences and how your business has evolved from that initial idea. Your story will be one of passion, inspiration and frustration. Everyone loves a drama – your story deserves to be told.

Now to consider the fourth question, your Vision Statement. According to a Japanese proverb,

> **'Vision without action is a daydream. Action without vision is a nightmare.'**

A Vision Statement is a sentence or short paragraph that articulates your hopes and dreams for your business. It has its roots in your story. Your Vision Statement should enrich your business, your customers, your suppliers and even the wider world in general. It gives you differentiation by adding depth, meaning and credibility to what you do. Better still, it can make you as an individual even more likeable and credible.

Here is my own Vision Statement as an example.

> *'To carry the message to all small businesses that marketing is the life blood of their business and that it's possible to achieve incredible results on a shoestring budget.'*

And here are the Vision Statements from some well-known global brands to inspire you:

> ***Google:*** *'To organize the world's information and make it universally accessible and useful'*

> ***Toys 'R' Us****: 'To put joy in kids' hearts and a smile on parents' faces'*

> ***Microsoft:*** *'To enable people and businesses throughout the world to realize their full potential'*

Once you have created your Vision Statement make sure that everyone connected with you - associates, team members, suppliers, customers - is aware of it and can see the purpose in it. Look upon it as your company's inspiration. It is there to steer your business in the right direction, to influence your actions, to continually aspire to. It must be genuine and something that you passionately believe in. It should stimulate the people that come into contact with you. Inspired and driven teams are at the heart of building a business into a brand.

Let's now turn to the final element of our brand building process:

Corporate Social Responsibility

The 21st century has witnessed the emergence of ethical and socially responsible marketing. You may be familiar with the term 'corporate social responsibility' (CSR) that has been coined to define this. It was initially the focus of large corporate organisations looking for ways in which they could improve their image with many different groups connected to them: their own employees, their customers, prospective customers, the media, and other influential groups.

The actions of organisations under the banner of CSR are various, ranging from sponsoring charities and organising charitable events to lobbying government. Under the umbrella of CSR, these organisations also look at how they can actively involve their employees in the running of the business and in the making of key decisions in order to give each individual a sense of purpose and connection. Many organisations are also now starting to look at how they can reduce their negative impact on the environment.

You may wonder how corporate social responsibility can be relevant in your efforts to build your business into a brand. If your team is small or non-existent and you have very little money to spare, it may seem impossible to take part and therefore largely irrelevant.

However, in the last few years I have worked with a number of small businesses that have successfully built a credible corporate social responsibility policy. This has ranged from supporting local or national charities to considering whether they can make and deliver their products or services in a more environmentally responsible manner. These actions help to make a tangible and positive contribution to the brand building process. Customers are looking for more than just the reassurance that their needs can be met. They want to see that a business has a heartbeat, a conscience, is committed to the community, to its employees and to the environment.

If you can go that extra mile with your own business and focus on taking some small but positive steps, you will certainly help your brand building efforts.

If you are interested in helping a local or national charitable cause, you don't have to earmark thousands of pounds to do something that will be appreciated. Recently I have witnessed local small businesses helping local charities in all manner of creative ways that don't involve shelling out huge sums of money. For example:

- A financial advisor donated £15 for every delegate attending their evening seminars and £15 for each new client that mentioned the charity they were supporting.

- A baker made a donation of £1 for every cake that was sold to a person mentioning the charity when they placed an order.

- A fashion retailer made a donation of 10% of her profits on clothes sales from specially arranged fashion events to the charity she was supporting.

You may want to commit your CSR policy in writing and to use it as part of your marketing communications tool kit, including adding it to your website. This will again help you to stand out amongst your competitors. With a growing expectation on small businesses to define themselves through their good works, it's worth giving this some serious consideration. It can only enhance your brand building efforts.

As an example, overleaf is Dyno-Pest's documented CSR policy. It encompasses how they treat their employees, customers and suppliers, and their commitment to the environment.

Social Responsibility Policy

Dyno-Pest is committed to operating in a socially, environmentally and customer-focused way. We believe that ethical behaviour should be at the heart of our business and that by respecting our customers and the wider community we will achieve sustainable growth and maintain our reputation as a quality business.

In practice, this means that we will:

- manage our business with pride and integrity.
- ensure full legal compliance in all that we do.
- aim to provide a safe, fulfilling and rewarding career for all our employees, treating everyone with dignity and respect and ensuring that our equal opportunities policy is constantly upheld.
- actively assess and manage the environmental impacts of all our operations and policies and objectives to help us achieve this.
- balance the needs of long-term sustainability with short-term profitability.
- value our customers and take their needs and concerns into account when making business decisions.
- value our suppliers and build long-term professional relationships based on mutual respect and trust.
- support sustainability through our purchasing decisions, choosing Fairtrade, local, or recycled products wherever feasible and choosing suppliers who operate with the same ethos and values as ourselves.
- develop our standing as a responsible business in the community.
- measure and monitor our performance to evaluate what we do in order to improve our CSR performance each year.

All staff are aware of our social responsibility policy and are encouraged to suggest new ideas to help us to develop closer relationships in the community. We measure and report on our performance annually.

Signed: Ralph Izod

Managing Director

To conclude, building your small business into a brand is attainable. There is no need to spend huge sums of money, but you must be committed to the branding cause and you should not focus on one area to the detriment of another. In Chapters 6 and 7 we look at how to grow, nurture and protect your brand on-line.

Chapter Summary

1. Myth: branding is only relevant for big businesses. It's not. It's relevant to small businesses too. Even the biggest brands had humble beginnings.

2. Branding goes much deeper than logos and image.

3. Your customers have the power to make or break your brand.

4. Building your business into a brand will increase customer loyalty, require less time to close the sale and provide many other benefits.

5. The four key areas of branding are: visibility, consistency, clarity, corporate social responsibility.

6. Visibility means getting your look right. Logo, imagery, on-line and off-line communications.

7. Make sure that your designer has a thorough written brief and that you work closely in collaboration with them.

8. Being consistent means rewarding your customers with a great experience every time they come into contact with your business.

9. Evaluate the quality of your service at each customer touch point and be swift to make improvements.

10. Successful branding starts on the inside. All employee training should reflect your values and your customer ethos.

11. Clarity is about knowing what you stand for, why your customers buy from you and why they reward you with their loyalty.

12. What is your genuine story? Are you telling it?

13. Your Vision Statement must capture your deep-seated passion and purpose, beyond making a profit.

14. Corporate social responsibility has a part to play in your business. Explore the good works that you can do without denting your profits.

15. Look at simple ways in which you can reduce your impact on the environment and how you can foster closer relationships with your employees and your suppliers.

16. Consider creating a corporate social responsibility policy. It will help you to stand out amongst competitors for all the right reasons.

CHAPTER 6

HOW TO BLOG FOR BUSINESS SUCCESS

You may be considering blogging to promote your business but are unsure how to start. Alternatively, you may have started blogging with the best of intentions but have since abandoned doing so in the light of a distinct lack of reader interest. It is easy to fall into one of these two categories. Blogging is one of those subjects that seems to be talked about an awful lot, but also seems to be surrounded by much confusion.

So, let's shed some light on the whole subject of blogging so that you can decide whether it is going to be of value to you and your business. If you decide that it is, we look at how to approach it in the right way later in the chapter.

What is a Blog?

There are many definitions of the word 'blog'. A couple that I like are:

*'Short for 'We**b log**', a blog is a Web page that serves as a publicly accessible personal journal for an individual. Typically updated daily, blogs often reflect the personality of the author. A Blogger is a person who blogs.'*

'A blog is a direct communication from a single person, like a letter or a note. It has more freedom of expression (ideally) than a corporate summary or sales pitch.'

So in effect, a blog is an on-line communication that enables the blogger (the title for the person writing the blog) to share their knowledge, opinions and information on topics that they enjoy writing about, and that they know people enjoy reading about. Today, many business people have cottoned on to the power of blogging within a business context. It has now expanded beyond the hobbyist and computer geek sharing their enthusiasm with likeminded fellows, into the business world.

A business blog should never be a 'flog' – in other words an on-line regurgitation of your latest sales flyer, your 60-second elevator statement, or a précis of your brand new products or services. Nor is it a reproduction of your newsletter or your latest press release. Don't confuse your traditional sales communications with a blog. Sales communications are designed to sell and the recipients of your sales material understand that. Business blogs are designed to share information or opinion and invite feedback, without the expectation of any imminent return in the shape of an upswing in sales. You can blog about whatever takes your fancy, but for your business blog to be successful, to build a loyal following and be recommended by others, it must be an enriching, relevant and well-written communication. Business blogs eschew the traditional calls to action such as 'Buy Now!' or 'The First 20 people to respond will receive this special gift' and so on. Astute business bloggers know that if they are to attract a loyal audience, their blogs should continually give without the expectation of a return. This begs the question, 'Why should I divulge my precious knowledge and expertise in a blog if I shouldn't expect anything in return?'

The Benefits of Blogging

- **Low or no cost.** Small businesses rarely enjoy the luxury of huge marketing budgets. They can't afford to invest time and energy on expensive marketing tactics without being reasonably certain they will recoup their costs, at the very minimum. Each marketing activity has to pay for itself and deliver a return. Blogging is truly a 'marketing on a shoestring' activity. This is because your blog site and page can be set-up free of charge, yet within a matter of hours your thoughts can be made available to a worldwide audience. With the only expense being your time, this makes blogging a low risk marketing activity.

- **Simplicity.** Blogging is a simple process that requires no technical skills for its successful accomplishment. You don't necessarily need to involve your web developer and once your blog is up and running it takes minutes to keep it updated. You are in complete control of the blogging process. The power to blog is literally at your fingertips.

- **Reputation building**. Blogging helps a person or business to build a positive and powerful reputation. By offering great tips and useful advice to your audience, you start to be seen as an authority in your field. This status can lead to sales further down the line, as customers are more likely to buy goods or services from a person they consider to be an expert. Your blog is an important part of your positive on-line reputation. The first place that many potential customers will go to find out more about you nowadays is on-line. A well-stocked blog, with well-written and interesting content and enthusiastic reader responses, communicates a positive message about you and your business.

- **A leader not a laggard**. A blog enables you to demonstrate that you are current. You can respond to news literally as it is breaking. You can write a blog on something highly topical and within minutes of receiving the news yourself, your interpretation of it is available for people to read.

- **Relationship building.** Over a period of time a feeling of trust will be built with your readers. As a result, should they be looking to buy what you sell, they are more likely to feel confident in approaching you. Your readers have got to know you, to trust, admire and respect you. They have built a very positive impression of you through your blogs. They have got to know your philosophy on life and business, and feel that they know you as a person before they have even met you. In effect you have created the ideal conditions for a sale without doing any overt selling. This is why blogging complements your more traditional sales communications. It adds value.

- **New audiences.** Blogging can introduce you to people that are interested in your expertise, but that you have previously been unable to reach. This is because their preferred channel for seeking information is on-line. By offering your blog you are enabling them to communicate with you and find out more about you in a way that suits them.

- **Strengthen existing relationships.** Your blog makes you more accessible to your existing clients and prospects. It's an opportunity to impart your wisdom in between existing communications, to keep in touch and to add value to what you already provide.

- **More visitors to your website.** If your blog is part of your website or provides a link to it, you will see a rise in the number of visitors to your site. This is provided, of course, that you are posting regular and relevant material. And in the list of regular readers of your blogs you will have built an audience that has *chosen* to receive information from you. These people have consequently already progressed some way along The Continuum of Behaviour. They are aware of you, interested in you and have made a positive evaluation of you.

How to Set Up a Blog

You can set up a basic blog for free on a publishing platform such as *www.wordpress.com* or *www.blogger.com* Sites such as these enable you to dip your toes into blogging without spending any money.

It is a simple process but if you are not comfortable with setting up a blog yourself, talk to a couple of local web designers that have experience in creating blogs for small businesses. Take a look at the blogs that they have created before deciding with which designer to work. Should you wish to have your blog added to your website, your web designer should be able to help with this too. In either case, however, the designer is likely to require some payment.

Once your blog is up and running, you won't need to be technically minded to manage it. Adding new blog content and moderating the responses that you receive from readers is a very straightforward process. If you are comfortable using Microsoft Word, you will have no problems managing your blog.

What Type of Businesses Benefit from Blogging?

The simple answer is that any, and indeed every business can benefit in some way from blogging - some more so than others, though. A business that provides a very niche product or service can benefit from blogging in the same way that a provider of more mainstream products or services can. But whilst a great number of businesses seem to have been bitten by the blogging bug, it doesn't necessarily mean that they are suited to blogging.

Before you decide to blog, there are some key questions that you need to consider.

1. **Do you enjoy writing?** This is the most important question because blogging is primarily a writing medium. You don't want to view writing your blog content as something of a chore; something that you keep putting off or that takes a huge amount of time as you struggle over each sentence. If you don't enjoy writing but still want to blog, consider using a copywriter that specialises in writing blog content. You will still need to provide them with the topic for each blog, however, if you want your blog to reflect you and your business. Don't underestimate the power of writing. Great writing has real impact on-line as well as off-line. Articulate and well-written material will encourage people to subscribe to your blog, to share it with others, and to get in touch with you. Great writing gives the impression that you are a credible player in the blogsphere.

2. **Can you commit to your blog?** Blogging takes energy and time. You will need to allocate the time necessary to write and edit new content and to manage your reader responses. Managing your blog includes responding to comments that people make to your blog content and, of course, promoting it. You need to make a commitment to blogging otherwise your blog will fade and die. You cannot afford to treat blogging as a hobby or chore. Instead you must view it as a powerful marketing tool. It will help if you subscribe to some blogs yourself and keep in touch

with the latest blogging etiquette. This way you will be learning whilst you are blogging. You don't want to become complacent with your blogging and in doing so become outdated.

3. **Do you want to place yourself in the public spotlight**? Your blog is there for the world to see. On the plus side this means that the potential for your blog to have a positive impact is limitless. But you must also be aware that the impact can be just as damaging if you write something that you later regret. Any suggestion of questionable integrity or poor judgement can be detrimental to a brand and lead customers to take their business elsewhere. Blogging is a very public act.

4. **Can you be consistent**? Consistency is about blogging regularly and to a schedule. Your readers need to know when they can expect your blog. They will soon lose interest in you if they detect that you are losing interest in them. It's also about establishing an individual style and approach, and sticking to it. It may be serious, quirky or humorous, but it needs to be authentic and cover topics that are related to the nature of your business.

5. **Do you enjoy communicating**? It helps if you derive real satisfaction from offering your thoughts to an audience. As mentioned earlier, blogging is all about giving without the prospect of any immediate return. You are aiming to build long term relationships with the people that subscribe to and read your blog. And that means enjoying communicating and imparting nuggets of wisdom and value for the sake of it! It's no good becoming frustrated

that you are sharing so much for so little return. Successful bloggers are in it for the long haul and love the broad and unrestricted platform that blogging provides.

6. **What do you really want to gain from blogging**? Establishing a few objectives that you want to gain from blogging will provide you with clarity and purpose. If you simply want to reach a greater proportion of your target audience on-line and to build up your status as an expert, these are strong enough reasons to start blogging. However, blogging may not be suitable for your business if your target audience is not interested in social media. If they are unlikely to spend time on-line, then you are unlikely to reach a sufficient number of them to make blogging worthwhile. If you're not sure whether your target audience is 'blog friendly' why not ask them? And don't assume that what they tell you now will hold true in six months time. Keep on asking.

7. **Can I write creatively about my core topic on a regular basis?** This is the niggling doubt that besets many new bloggers. It can usually be resolved by spending a little time on planning the topics that you would like to cover. For inspiration, take a look back over your working week. What have you discovered or learned that you can share? Is there something in the news that you can write about to engage your reader? At the start of your blogging journey it may help to come up with the topics that will cover your first six blogs. After that you are likely to find the challenge of coming up with blog topics on an ongoing basis much less daunting.

8. **Who am I blogging for and what can I blog about?** You don't want to start a blog that's not aimed at anyone in particular, and is not about anything in particular. A blog that's designed to enhance your business reputation should naturally be aimed at the type of people that do business with you or that recommend you. These are the groups that you outlined in your marketing plan. They will comprise of your existing clients, warm and cold prospects, influencers and referrers. You are simply using blogging as an on-line communication channel to reach more of them. Rather than communicating sales messages you are imparting some of your expertise, wisdom and knowledge. Start by thinking what you stand for, not just in your business but in your field of expertise. What really enthuses you? What keeps you awake at night with excitement and makes your heart beat just that little bit faster? Standing back and looking at the knowledge, skills and experience that you have built up over the years, what do you think would be of real interest to the people you are hoping to reach through your blog?

The Importance of Enthusiasm and Finding your Niche

The people that read your blogs need to be able to connect with your enthusiasm, knowledge and passion through the words that you write. If they do so, they will come back for more and recommend your blog to others. Writing about subjects that sit comfortably within your field of business expertise but do not inspire you will lead you to lose interest in what you are writing, and your blog posts will communicate this lack of genuine enthusiasm. It can take several months for your blog to build up a base of regular subscribers, so you can't afford to lose interest in your subject matter after writing just a few blogs.

Once you have determined what inspires you and what will interest your audience, it's time to produce content that falls into one or more of the following categories. Your blog content should be capable of:

- Educating your readers.
- Entertaining your readers.
- Informing your readers.
- Inspiring debate amongst your readers.
- Reflecting and sharing the latest relevant news or thinking.

What do you think that your readers are most likely to want from your blog? It may be that they are looking to be educated. Perhaps they like debating. Do they want to be led by you? Do they want to find out your opinions on the latest thinking in their sector and the latest news? Perhaps your audience likes a bit of everything - education, entertainment news and so on. Use your knowledge of your sector and your target audience to shape the content for your blog. You want to produce material that you're fairly confident your readers will enjoy reading.

Can you tap into the latest trends as they are emerging? Unsure what these are? Don't guess. If you can subscribe to the publications read by your target audience, not only will you find out which trends are emerging, you'll also uncover plenty of material upon which to comment. Why not ask your customers what they would like to read about in your blog? Search on-line to see if any of your competitors are blogging. Don't be put off if a competitor is blogging about topics similar to those that you are planning to write about. Your unique style will ensure that your posts remain individual. The on-line universe is limitless. If you can write articulate, topical and informative blogs, you should soon build a loyal following. By the same token, don't be afraid to blog about topics that are not currently being covered by competitors if they appeal to your target audience. You can carve out a niche.

Suggestions for Blogging Content

- **What is currently happening in your sector** that would be of real interest to your readers? Form an opinion, share it and invite feedback.

- **Think of your knowledge as a diamond,** with many facets. Share one facet at a time. You don't need to cover several topics in your blog. In fact, the more simple and focused you make each blog, the better.

- **Two or three tips - concise bites of your knowledge.** For example, a personal stylist could share tips about colour, the latest fashion trends, style, grooming and self-confidence. A chef could share tips on seasonal produce, cooking on a budget, buying and cooking local produce. An accountant or an independent financial advisor could share taxation and wealth planning tips. A life coach could share tips on self-esteem and personal improvement. The tips format in a blog works very well for any type of business.

- **Can you put some meaningful research under the spotlight,** research that would be of interest to your audience? Summarise this research to make it accessible to your readers, and ask for their opinions.

- **Can you provide clarity on forthcoming changes in legislation** that will impact your target audience?

- **Can you express an opinion that won't alienate your audience** but will encourage lively discussion? Your blog is not a place to sit on the fence.

- **Have you read an inspirational business or self-improvement book** in the last few months? Why not review it with the purpose of helping your readers to decide if they should buy it too?

- **Don't be afraid occasionally** to write a blog in which you share your journey or your story with your readers. For example you may have overcome a setback in business that has taught you a valuable lesson. You may have learned some new self-improvement skills that have changed the course of your business. What did you learn from your setbacks, opportunities and challenges? Sharing on a more personal level can move people and encourage them to share some of their experiences too.

- **You may choose to use your blog to introduce occasional guest writers.** Not only does this give you a break from writing, it gives your readers the opportunity to learn something from a guest writer who shares your values and complements your expertise.

- **Outline a client case study.** Do so in a factual way, avoiding lavishing praise upon yourself. Write objectively, making sure that the case studies you share are relevant to your readers. What will they gain from the case study? Will they be inspired, educated, entertained... a blend of all three.

- **Answer a frequently asked question.** What are the questions that people ask you at a networking group or when they contact you through your website? You can even establish a regular blog post of Q&As.

- **Review a website, a forum, a publication, a newsletter** – anything that your target audience would be interested in and that you have sufficient confidence and expertise to comment upon.

Grab Attention with your Titles

You will need to give some thought to the title of each blog that you write. The title you arrive at may not be that dissimilar from the headline of your advert or press release. You have to make the reader curious enough to click through and read more. Therefore, your blog title must have impact.

To get you thinking, here are a few of the titles of my blogs.

The 7 secrets of successful sales letters

What are journalists and editors looking for?

How Christmas came early for this client

By Royal Appointment or not?

Why successful sales people are in the minority

PR or RP?

When substance triumphs over sizzle

The art of public squeaking

Mary Portas and the Pilot

How Long Should Your Blogs Be?

There are no hard and fast rules. Your blog can be a few lines or a few thousand lines. Bear in mind however that a lengthy blog demands more time from your reader and needs to be compelling from beginning to end to maintain their interest throughout. If you have a lot to say, consider breaking your blog up with bullet points, numbers and paragraphs. Aim for variety too. You may put readers off if each post runs into several pages. My blogs range in length from 100 words to 600 words. If you can communicate in a concise manner, you will keep your readers engaged. When you have written your blog, leave it for a little while then review and edit it. If you overload your reader with too many themes in one long blog, you will unwittingly train them not to pay attention. One topic or one theme per blog is perfect. Don't get carried away with the sound of your own voice.

How Frequently Should You Blog?

Again, this is something that's down to you. Some bloggers post only once or twice a month whereas others write something every day. There are, however, two reasons why I would discourage you from writing a daily blog unless you are confident that you can maintain the commitment, the enthusiasm and the quality of these daily blogs.

- **Readers can become desensitised to your blog if it appears too frequently**. Their enthusiasm wanes and eventually they stop reading your blogs even though the content may still be relevant and sparkling. One well-written, thoughtful and considered blog published every couple of weeks will have more impact on your readers than a hastily assembled daily blog.

- **Your time is precious too**. Without even being aware of it, you may get carried away with blogging, spending hours writing and promoting your blog only to have very little to show for your efforts. For most small businesses, blogging is not the road to riches. You need to focus your attention on the marketing activities that are going to yield the highest returns.

How to Encourage People to Find and Read Your Blog

It usually takes time to build a loyal following for your blog. It may be several months before people start signing up to it. Don't be disheartened by this. There will be many more that stop by and read your blogs regularly without subscribing. As mentioned earlier, blogging is not about selling yourself and closing deals! It's about building your reputation, credibility and integrity, and establishing you as an expert in your field - a trusted person that people can look to for useful advice, a well reasoned thought and an insight into a topic of interest to them. It also forms part of your on-line CV, adding value to the material that people can already access about you on-line.

Some Simple Ways to Drive People to your Blog

- **Include a link to your blog as part of your e-mail signature.** This way you will be promoting your blog with each e-mail you send.

- **Add your blog address to your business cards,** letterhead paper, and compliment slips etc.

- **Promote your blog in all your sales communications** – your newsletters, vouchers, surveys, Q&As, prospect letters, prospectuses, flyers and so on.

- **Consider writing a feature on your blog** in your newsletters to build reader awareness. Let readers know the topics that you cover, perhaps featuring shortened versions of some recent popular posts to whet their appetites.

- **In one or two lines encapsulate what your blog delivers** and communicate these both on-line and off-line. I promote my blog on Twitter as: 'No hype, exaggerated promises or sales spiel. Just a fortnightly dose of practical and proven marketing tips that deliver.' You can add your blog strapline to your newsletters, sales letters and flyers and include it as part of your 60-second introduction when speaking at a networking event.

- **Ask for feedback from the people that subscribe to your blog** and add this to your sales literature.

- **At public speaking engagements,** let the audience know that they can have even more of your wisdom and experience for free via your blog!

- **Add the details of your blog to any press releases.** A journalist is more likely to read your blog than your sales communications.

- **Make sure that you include the details** of your blog in your adverts and any accompanying editorial.

- **Publicise your blog via** the on-line social networking sites that you use. Twitter, LinkedIn and Facebook are ideal for promoting your blog. You can promote the same blog post several times over a few days in order to drive a steady stream of traffic to it. Always include a link to your blog in these messages. Add your blog address to your Twitter background.

- **Ask your readers to respond to your blogs.** A blog with reader comments arouses the curiosity of other readers and shows that you are inspiring debate, a sure sign that your message is hitting the spot. To encourage responses, ask the reader a question or two within each of your blogs. Encourage them to share their thoughts. Do they agree or disagree with you? Can they share a similar experience or a contrasting one? Once people start commenting on your blogs, they are more likely to become regular visitors to your blog and to recommend it. When you do receive comments from readers, respond and thank them. This will also encourage them to become regular responders. You may even want to feature your top reader responders in a column on your blog site.

- **Promote on social networking sites** the fact that some interesting comments have been added to your latest blog. This can arouse interest and help direct traffic to your blog. I do this regularly on Twitter. 'So why is John Smith enthusing about this particular blog post?', 'I've caused some real controversy on my latest blog post....'

- **Ask your suppliers,** and even your clients, if they would consider promoting your blog on their website and provide a link to it.

- **When commenting on other blog sites** include the web address of your own blog.

- **Ask your readers to** recommend your blog.

- **If your blog is separate from your website,** provide a link between the two. And ensure that visitors cannot possibly overlook this link by using an image as well as words to promote it.

Practical Advice on Blogging - From Two Expert Bloggers, Sue Atkins and Dawn Brewer

I am lucky to know many people with vast experience in the blogging world, and I have asked two blogging experts to share their tips on blogging.

Sue Atkins

Sue Atkins is a renowned parenting expert and the author of Raising Happy Children for Dummies. Sue regularly appears on *BBC Breakfast* and the Jeremy Vine Show on BBC Radio 2, and her parenting articles are published all over the world. Sue is an experienced blogger (you can access her blog at *www.theSueAtkins.com*) and her daily parenting blog is read by parents, trainers and educational professionals. Sue's blogging tips are:

- **Readers are drawn in by a strong, engaging voice** that sounds confident, knowledgeable and approachable. Make sure that you write well, that you are constantly checking your spelling and grammar for inconsistencies and mistakes. Use bullet points and short paragraphs to maintain reader interest.

- **A conversational tone will have the most appeal** with your readers regardless of your subject matter. When you write, imagine that your readers are in front of you. What would you say to them? Can you communicate this in your blog?

- **You might not consider yourself a writer,** but it's your writing skills that will ultimately make or break your blogging career. Don't overanalyse everything that you write or you'll never get started, but do reflect on what you have written. Is there a flow and a rhythm to your writing that makes it easy to read? If you're not sure, ask for feedback.

- **Find your own voice.** You may want to write the same post in several different styles and experiment until you find your authentic voice. However I find that through writing regularly, my style and my confidence improves. So relax, have fun and experiment with your writing style until you find your own voice. Leave the jargon behind and don't adopt an academic tone unless your audience expects this. Focus on the problems that you are solving for your audience.

- **Blog regularly.** Talk to any writer and they'll tell you that to find your true style, you need to write regularly but not necessarily every day for the reasons that Dee outlined earlier. Consider writing once a week, a fortnight or even once a month. You will almost certainly fare better writing slightly less often and putting more time and effort into your post. Wouldn't you rather your readers were eagerly looking forward to your next in-depth blog instead of skipping past yet another mediocre piece that you've churned out?

- **To get into a regular blogging habit,** think about setting up a blogging calendar. I encourage the people that I mentor to brainstorm 12 topics for the year. They can also use their blog as the basis for an article, a press release, a handout, even the topic of the month on their website.

- **As a writer, I do write a daily blog** and I have a regular system to my writing. I know that Monday is my weekly parent coaching question, Tuesday is my topic of the week, Wednesday is my parenting story to ponder, and Thursday is my podcast and so on. Some of my blog posts are quick and easy to write and to read whilst others take a little longer. What I find is that people like the variety. Once you've found a comfortable routine, it's easy to keep the momentum going.

- **You may want to set aside a regular time** each week to write your blog if this fits in with your lifestyle and grab a cup of coffee whilst you are doing so. Then just relax and enjoy taking some small action steps towards taking your writing forwards.

Dawn Brewer

Dawn Brewer specialises in on-line copywriting, writing web pages, blog posts, newsletters and articles for the on-line world. A Chartered IT Professional and Member of the Chartered Institute for IT, Dawn also has an MBA (Technology Management). Dawn set up her first WordPress blog in 2007 and currently blogs at *www.dawnb.co.uk/dawnb-blog*. Dawn's blogging tips are:

Add Some Power to your Blog Posts

Although words and writing are vital for a good blog, you can add extra power to your blog posts with these ideas:

- **Images.** Pictures add interest and help catch the attention of those readers skimming posts in search of the key points. Loading pictures into a blog is as straightforward as inserting an image in a document. Name your image something relevant - not DSCF0057.jpg for example but dawn_brewer.jpg – and fill in the information when you upload your picture. Typical information you can add includes: captions which usually appear below pictures and descriptions and keywords which are used by websites and other software in different ways. This information helps to enrich your reader's experience, meaning that more of them will enjoy reading your blog and will therefore come back for more.

- **Video and audio.** Consider an occasional video or audio post to add interest for your readers (or viewers!). Keep it short - a few minutes are usually enough. Keep your audience in mind (just like all marketing) and say what you're thinking. Spend a little time beforehand planning and then practicing because you don't want to be seen referring to notes and stumbling because you have lost your thread. The more natural your video presentation, the more impact it will have with your audience.

- **Links.** In your blog posts you can link to other material, such as pages on your website, other blogs you've written, recommended articles or news stories that you are commenting on.
  Don't use 'click here' instead make the action a link:
  'For comparison download the price chart to see

- **Search Engines.** Help your blog to be found by readers and search engines (Google, Bing, etc.) by using words and phrases that are relevant to your business. If you're enthusiastic about your subject this will happen anyway, but it's a good habit to incorporate into your writing.

Interact and Participate to Build a Blog

If you write blog posts and that's all you do, then you won't attract as many readers as you deserve for your efforts. One way to attract readers is to participate in relevant on-line communities.

- **Search out other bloggers** (including people in your field of expertise and, the people you are trying to attract to your blog) and engage with them on their blogs by leaving comments. Generally, leaving a comment links back to your blog too and that's how communities and relationships are built. Commenting is also a good way to enhance your reputation and may lead to opportunities for you to write guest posts on other people's blogs.

- **Use social media sharing devices** such as the 'like' button.

- **Add value by helping your readers** to find relevant information by building links from your blog to other blogs. Add links in your posts and also generally (e.g. on the sidebar of your blog). Ask other bloggers to do the same.

Be Aware Of and Manage Spam Comments

Once your blog has been found the likelihood is that on-line spam comments will arrive in with all of the genuine responses. The good news is that it's only the comments that you approve that will appear on your blog. But how do you know if a comment is genuine or spam?

All comments are listed for you to approve or delete. Generally, every comment has a link to show where it's from. Sometimes the comment itself or the words in the link make it clear it's spam.

If you're unsure, follow the link and see where it takes you. If you like the destination, approve the comment, otherwise delete it. Following the link may mean you visit a spam website, but that's better than automatically approving all comments.

If the comment is offensive in any way, delete it.

Comments that you don't agree with however can really add some interest to your blog and create some debate. Approve the comment and add one of your own welcoming the viewpoint, then explaining your view too. Don't get drawn into an ever-escalating unreasonable debate. Remember, this is your blog and you're in control. You can delete approved comments too.

Be Efficient and Schedule Blog Posts

It may suit you to write a series of blog posts at the same time. Most blogging software (like WordPress) allows you to 'schedule' blog posts to go live in the future. So, for example, if school holidays are important to your business, you can write a series of blog posts ready for each school holiday and then schedule them all to go live on future dates.

And Finally

Most bloggers are happy to help and share tips. If you get stuck, an on-line search for your problem will yield many solutions.

Thank you to Sue and Dawn for their strong and practical advice. Blogging is most definitely a marketing activity that is worthy of your exploration and subsequent evaluation at the very least.

Chapter Summary

1. A blog is not a 'flog'. Don't use it to sell.

2. A blog complements your traditional sales communications, adding additional value.

3. A blog can build and enhance your reputation as an expert in both the on-line and off-line worlds.

4. You can create and manage your blog using free software.

5. Successful bloggers enjoy writing and sharing their expertise freely. They are in it for the long haul.

6. Write about what inspires you and what your target audience wants to read about but make it relevant to your business.

7. Sparkling content should educate, entertain, inform and inspire debate.

8. Tap into the latest trends that are emerging in the marketplace of your target audiences.

9. Don't get complacent. Learn as you blog. Become a permanent student.

10. Top tips are always popular.

11. Consider using an occasional guest writer to add variety to your content and think about being a guest writer on other blogs, establishing reciprocal links.

12. Make sure that your posts have eye-catching titles to encourage click through.

13. Don't overload your readers with monologues of text.

14. Establish a writing routine and stick to it. But remember, less is more.

15. Promote your blog everywhere. In your sales communications, in your social networks and when networking.

16. Encourage interaction. Invite readers to respond to your posts.

17. Consider adding images and short videos to some of your blogs.

18. Boost your subscribers by adding your comments on other blog sites.

19. Encourage debate on your blog but remember you are in charge of what is ultimately published.

CHAPTER 7

PROMOTING YOUR BUSINESS ON-LINE

We are flooded with information about how to promote our business on-line at every turn, on the television, in the press, on the radio and of course, from the Internet itself. Making sense of this information can be a real challenge. On the one hand we are keen to learn, and intrigued to find out what our competitors are doing on-line. But on the other hand, when we search for advice we are bombarded with so much information from so many conflicting sources that it can be impossible to know what to do next.

This confusion can result in frustration and inactivity.

And what about social media? For many, social media intrigues and yet intimidates. Some small business owners are eager to learn more about social media marketing opportunities but struggle to find any practical guidance on the best route to take. Others dive in with gay abandon, and make a number of mistakes that could have been prevented with a little more guidance.

So if you want to promote your business on-line effectively and appropriately, where do you start? Well, first of all, do not abandon your traditional marketing tactics in favour of a wholesale shift to social media. This could have potentially disastrous consequences for your business. Approach social media in an exploratory way, looking at how it can be added to your existing marketing activities to enhance their impact and strengthen your name on-line. If after this investigation you are unconvinced that social media can benefit your business, carry on with what you are doing and simply keep an eye on developments in the social media world. Your customers and prospects may not be influenced by social media now, but as time moves on people can change their decision-making process, including their buying patterns. They can come to rely upon sources of information that they had previously shied away from. You don't want to be left behind.

The purpose of this chapter is to alert you to some of the more popular and inexpensive ways to promote your business on-line. In order to do this, I have enlisted the help of three experts in this field - trusted, professional people that specialise in helping small businesses to build their profile on-line.

Allow me to introduce my on-line experts:

Lesley Morrissey, On-line Copywriter (*www.lesleywriter.com*)

Lesley is a copywriter who focuses primarily on writing websites for small to medium sized businesses. She's had a fascination with words from a very early age, and this developed into a growing curiosity about what people read, and ***how*** they read. Learning from the world of advertising and from experts in web usability and observation, Lesley has developed a rare skill set, bridging that gap between website design and content. Two websites that demonstrate Lesley's skills are:

www.morestanservices.co.uk - this website is an example of working with a designer and developer who understand the concepts of readability.

www.rhodes2success.com/mentor/your-business-mentor - this is a longer sales letter style of web page that has been designed to generate leads.

Sam Garrity, Search Engine Optimisation Specialist (*www.elevatelocal.co.uk*)

Elevate Local are a family-owned business, founded by brothers Sam and Ben Garrity. They provide Internet solutions across four core areas - search engine optimisation, website design, pay per click marketing and social media optimisation. Prior to launching Elevate Local, Sam and Ben spent over 15 years working in traditional media within the advertising teams of The Daily Mail, Mail on Sunday and Express Newspaper Group. Sam and his team believe that Search Engine Optimisation (SEO) is a subject that unnecessarily confuses businesses due to the amount of conflicting information that shrouds it. It's their mission to remove the mystery and to give small businesses a powerful on-line presence.

Karen Skidmore, Social Media Specialist (*www.candocanbe.com*)

Karen Skidmore, founder of CanDoCanBe and creator of the Web Tech Marketing Club, is a marketing mentor and self-confessed web tech geek. A practical, down-to-earth business woman, Karen excels at making web tech marketing tools simple and accessible to small business owners, so that they can attract the right clients consistently. Karen was at the very forefront of the social media revolution. Since starting her first e-mail newsletter and launching her first blog in 2005, her on-line presence has grown significantly. It was only natural that she became an early adopter of social media tools such as Twitter, Facebook and LinkedIn. Karen is renowned for her excellent face-to-face and web based seminars on social media.

So, now that you know a little about these three experts, let's see what each one has to say.

The Key to Successful On-line Marketing – Making Sure that Your Website Delivers, by Lesley Morrissey

If you're planning to launch an on-line marketing campaign, your website is crucial to its success. Whether you're blogging, using social media, paying for Google AdWords or doing serious search engine optimisation, all that effort is wasted if, when people arrive at your website, they don't get your message. There's no point in driving people to your website if it looks dated, the copy is ancient, it's hard to get around and it is unattractive to the eye. You have wasted your time and energy.

Having a visually attractive website is part of the equation, but there are other equally critical elements. If you think of it as an equation there are four elements.

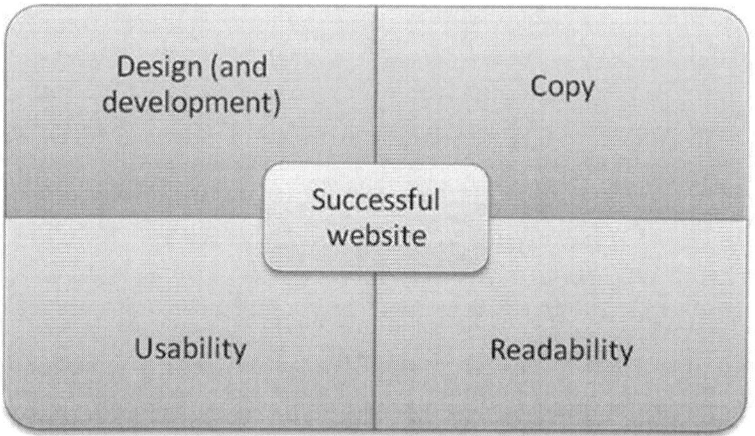

A website should be like a 'Derby', not a 'Grand National'. Both of these are horse races, but in the Derby the horses have a straight run from start to finish, with nothing in the way, until they cross the finishing line.

The Grand National is literally an obstacle race. There are huge fences where many people fall off, because they're just too big to get past.

Every time you place an obstacle in the path of your website visitor, it's a reason for them to 'fall off'. As web users are typically both impatient and lazy, it doesn't take much for people to leave your site. You might be surprised at how easy it is to dislodge them!

Having a successful website integrates all four elements to give your visitor what they want quickly and easily.

Let's look at how they interact with each other.

Design (and development)

There are two parts to the design of any website – the visual design aspects, in other words, what makes it look attractive, and the coding; that's the technical part that provides the 'instructions' for the Internet in how to present the design to the reader – known as 'development'.

The more complex a website is, the more work is required from the developer. When you get into websites with databases and e-commerce shopping carts, or integrated calculation devices, where the user can enter information and get a 'result' – then a good developer is required.

With a relatively simple brochure website, that is a website that's mostly about sharing information, the development is relatively straightforward and a good web designer can usually manage to load their design onto the web without a problem.

The design must:

- Be visually attractive to the reader, replicating the look and feel of your business right down to the typefaces, colours, straplines and images that you use in your existing on-line and off-line communications.

- Integrate the copy – which must present your message clearly.

- Provide a structure and navigation that makes it easy for the user to find what they want. Within one or two clicks the user must be able to get to where they want to go to on your website.

- Enhance the words rather than interfere with them.

Copy

This includes both the headlines and the words that help the reader to understand, not only what is on offer, but also how it might benefit them.

To create effective copy it's important that you understand what the reader is looking for and how you can address those wants and needs. If you are considering using a copywriter you must brief them thoroughly so that they can write copy that is targeted at meeting the needs of your visitors. Don't skimp on this!

There are a few rules to writing good copy:

- **The headlines need to engage the reader quickly.**
  Poor: We can reduce your bounce rate.

  Better: Get visitors to take action on your website!

- **The text needs to be focused on the reader – using 'you', not 'we', language.**
  Poor: We specialise in improving the readability of websites. This means that we understand the behaviour of readers and how they connect with both screen and paper. Even the best written copy (and we are professional copywriters too) doesn't work if the presentation gets in the way of the message.

  Better: If you really want people to get your message you need good copy presented to your reader so they can read it easily. If you've ever tried to read a web page or flyer and found it difficult to read, you'll have firsthand experience of poor readability. That's where you need help – and there's plenty of that here! (link)

- **The words should be simple, easily understood and jargon free.**
  Poor: If your website suffers from a high bounce rate, your SEO could be working, but the retention level is being affected by the website stickiness factor.

  Better: Do your website statistics tell you that people are leaving your website quickly? If you are getting many visits, but few enquiries, there could be a number of problems:

- The visitor doesn't understand your message quickly on arrival.
- The source from which they found your site led them to expect something different.
- The presentation of the information required them to work too hard to find out what they wanted to know.

The first step is to look at your website from the visitor's point of view and work out if the headline, content and visuals make them want to stay. This is known as 'stickiness'.

- **The sentences and paragraphs should be short and punchy – one thought per sentence and one idea per paragraph.**

  Poor: On arrival at your website, people expect to find the information they are looking for quickly and, if they can't see what they want immediately, many people are too impatient to spend much time looking any further and will leave your site in favour of an 'easier' site. This results in what is known as a 'high bounce rate' and means that any money invested in bringing traffic to your site with search engine optimisation or AdWords can be a complete waste of your budget.

  Better: Web surfers are lazy and impatient! If they don't see what they are looking for quickly, many of them will leave your site. They're looking for a site where it's easy to find what they want. If people 'bounce' off your site, any investment you make in bringing traffic to your site will be wasted.

- **There should always be a call to action – or people won't do anything.**

  Poor: We're very experienced consultants and have helped hundreds of clients to get their message to their target audience in written form.

  Better: If you'd like to join the hundreds of businesses who have got their message to their target audience successfully, give us a call on 01245 473296 or drop us an e-mail (link) with your challenge.

These examples demonstrate how easy it is to get it wrong – and how simple it can be to get it right.

The copy needs to fit into the design successfully so it all looks part of a single entity, not squashed into a space that is too small or floating about in a great big blank area.

Good copy should help the reader to find their way to what they are looking for. It needs to offer useful information about the things that people are looking for. It should also provide useful links to take people to where they want to go next with the minimum of effort.

The whole point of a web page is to get people to do something and many websites fail to include a call to action. If you don't ask, you don't get! In order to get this right it's essential that the website owner knows what they want people to do at each stage. That can be to navigate to a place where there is more information to engage them further or it can be to phone or e-mail them – or even just to sign up for a report or tips sheet. The copy can then be focused on persuading the reader to take that action.

Usability

Many people make the mistake of starting to create a website without a clear structure to work from. A website with no structure is a bit like trying to build a house with no architectural plans!

The structure identifies the pages and how they relate to each other. It also tells the designer what has to go on the main menu and, depending on the number of pages, may indicate whether you have a horizontal menu under the brand or a vertical menu on the left hand side.

The structure also takes into account where sub-menus are needed and how people find what they're looking for easily – without having to make too much effort.

Usability is assisted by:

- A creative design that integrates user-friendly simple navigation.

- A clear purpose for every page - with copy that ensures the message is easy for the user to understand and to take action on.

- A layout, use of colour and navigation that ensures that the message stands out and is easily found.

Readability

Very few people really understand what readability is – not web designers, not copywriters, not developers. Why not? It's supposed to be 'common sense', but it relates to **how** people read, rather than **what** they read, and it isn't taught in design, development or writing courses.

Readability links design and copy – unfortunately, it's frequently ignored, creating a big 'black hole' in the reader's ability to understand the message!

If you're still in the dark these are some of the examples where the lack of understanding of how people process information creates those obstacles that send people away from a website.

Getting attention

What we want when we arrive on a web page is to be sure it's going to deliver whatever we think we are looking for. This is the job of the headline; however, the page name doesn't qualify as a headline. 'Services' is not strong enough to engage the reader. What is needed is something that connects with them, so a strong headline is imperative; that's why a good copywriter can be invaluable.

So not **'Services'**, but **'Get your website to generate the leads you want.'**

Not **'Acme Widgets as Featured on the BBC'**, but **'You'll work with recognised experts.'**

Not **'We help clients achieve success'**, but **'You can achieve the success you want.'**

However, the designer needs to understand the importance of giving the headline space, size and position, to allow the reader to see it instantly.

In readability terms this means that the headline needs to be positioned roughly where the reader's eyes connect with the screen. Contrary to popular belief, that's not at the top of the page; most people's focus area is about one-third to two-fifths of the way down the screen and about 3 to 4 centimetres in from the left hand edge of the actual screen.

The headline needs to be big enough to focus people's attention – much bigger than 14 point bold! 18 to 24 point is much better, depending on the length of the headline.

It should never be squashed between the masthead and the first paragraph, but should be given plenty of space around it to really make it stand out. (The masthead is the area where the organisation's identity or brand sits – like a newspaper - 'Wall Street Journal'.)

Visual images

Pictures and graphics that enhance your message will give your page energy, but pictures used as space fillers and 'eye-candy' are more likely to hinder than they are to help your reader to understand your message.

These are common problems with images that reduce readability:

- Visuals that create a band across the page and that push the headline down, sometimes below the fold can result in some people not even seeing your message, let alone getting it! (Below the fold means below the area immediately visible when the page loads. Again, this is from the newspaper industry where the headline stories were always above the fold when the newspaper was folded in half for display on newsstands. The problem with websites is that, because of different screen sizes, it's difficult to know exactly where the fold is!)

- Moving images that distract the eye and take people away from your message. Excessive use of these on your website can irritate people to the point where they just want to get off your site, because it's getting on their nerves. Moving images includes:

    - Graphics that move around the screen.
    - Scrolling messages that run across the screen continually.
    - Bands of visuals – with or without words – that change every few seconds.
    - Photo galleries that replace the pictures either with fade in/fade out or just a straight picture replacement at regular intervals.
    - Talking heads – including a recent trend to have someone walk out from the side of the screen and start talking to you. This can work especially if you deliver the services being promoted on your website. The visitor can see you and form what is hopefully an immediate and positive first impression. However make sure that the visitor has the option of closing the presenter immediately or better still clicking to start the presenter. They may not want to hear what you have to say if they are visiting your site in a busy office.

- Images of people in suits smiling at the camera – or any other images that are obviously from a stock photo library –

don't actually say very much at all to the reader. They can also mislead people into thinking that the images are of you and your team!

- Pictures that are to the left of the copy: we read from left to right, but scan pictures on screen from top to bottom (usually). If your image is on the left, there is a danger people will scan down and continue reading underneath. This means that any copy to the right of the picture may not be read.

Pictures that help you to make your point including photos, graphs, charts, drawings or any other form of image - are great.

Two bits of advice:

1. Get original pictures – take them yourself or ideally get a photographer. Avoid the dreary corporate style pictures that look staged and cheesy.

2. If you have a gallery or a series of visuals you want to show people, put control of them in the hands of the user so they can view them when they want to.

Navigation

To anyone but the web designer that's the menu! Most people look for their navigation either horizontally, beneath the masthead or vertically on the left.

Menus that are placed on the right hand side of the screen are often not recognised as menus by the user, causing frustration as they search for a means to move to another page.

Menus that are above the masthead are not only virtually invisible, because people don't see the information that far up the page, they also disappear as soon as you scroll down the page.

Getting the navigation right relates to both readability and usability. Readability is to do with where we expect the menu to be, usability is to do with the ease of moving around the site. According to Jakob Nielsen, an expert in usability (*www.useit.com*) a good navigation system should tell the visitor:

- Where they are.
- Where they've been.
- Where they can go.

This means that the menu should show you the page you're on without the need for the page itself to state that. Any decent web designer can ensure that the button for the page currently being viewed stands out in some way.

Some web designers think that more menus provide alternative options for people – but, in my experience, more than one menu simply creates confusion! I have seen websites with six different menus all over the page, right at the top, horizontally under the masthead, on the left, in various places as hyperlinks in the text and also at the foot of the page. Some of these menus are the same as others; some have bits of one and bits of another. People don't know where to start and often give up and go looking for an 'easier' website.

With a horizontal menu, where there are sections with sub pages, it's fine to have that section's sub pages listed vertically on the left – but make sure the design is consistent and that every page looks the same. When you have a vertical menu, people seem to be less likely to look for the sections horizontally so a pop-out menu usually works better, as long as there aren't too many pages for people to look at (and be overwhelmed by).

Remember that the menu is there to help – not to confuse!

Layout

The way the words are presented can make reading easier – or they can make reading your website virtually impossible!

This is where the basic template for the website needs to take readability into account – and the most common area where web designers get it wrong, simply because they are completely unaware of the pitfalls.

These are the most common issues that cause problems and that you should avoid at all costs on your website.

Light writing on a darker background – whether this is white on black, gold on burgundy, yellow on dark green, pale blue on navy – they all create the same problem. Your eyes focus on the darker colour first, so the first problem occurs when you look *through* the words and have to try and refocus. This is compounded when your eyes have to handle a dazzle-effect when that dark background is cut up into little bits with the little lines criss-crossing it. Because your eyes are struggling to actually see the words clearly, your brain is getting a 'difficult information' message.

With a headline in a big bold font this is not a problem, because each letter has a defined shape and stands out from the background as a shape in its own right. With normal 10 to 12 size font, it's just too much effort for many people – they just leave the website to find something easier to read.

Justified text – this is where the paragraphs have all the lines the same length in pleasing-to-the-eye tidy blocks. Unfortunately, whilst it looks nice, it's also harder to read. The lack of 'shape' in the paragraph can trick your eyes into either skipping a line or reading the same line twice. When most people have done this twice in succession they give up – unless there's a compelling reason for them to make a big effort to keep reading. Most websites don't fall into that category!

The other problem that occurs from justified text is that it can force the words, or even the letters apart, resulting in oddly stretched words and big gaps between words making it look like a white 'river' running through the paragraph.

Centralised copy creates a different problem – that of your eyes having to search for the beginning of every line; that's just too much like hard work for most people! As we read on a subconscious level we don't reason our way through this process, we just get that 'difficult information' message, because the information isn't 'going in'.

Left aligned text is by far the easiest to read, providing both a shape as a bookmark for your eyes on the right and an anchor for the eyes to start from on the left.

The patchwork quilt effect – this is where there are many information points on the page, all fighting for attention. It's like offering someone a box of chocolates with many different centres – people can't make up their mind. With chocolates the lure of something delicious is usually enough to keep people focused until they've made their choice (and they can always come back for another one); with a website, people glance here and there, not really focusing on anything in particular as another coloured box or headline pulls their gaze away. You may be asking too much of them – to make a decision, without enough information – or sufficient temptation to give it another try.

Each page should have a dominant point – something that draws the reader's eye and engages their interest. At least you have their attention for long enough to tell them that you can deliver what they're looking for – ***then*** you can start introducing choices.

The Importance of Keeping your Website Up to Date

A website that hasn't been updated for years, even months, doesn't do the owner any favours. Worse still, many website owners haven't visited their own websites for so long that they can't remember what is on it!

It should be the responsibility of someone within your business to carry out regular reviews of your website. These are some of the things that need to be checked each time:

- **Currency of the content** – ensure everything is still accurate and relevant. What is missing? Have you added that new product or service or the latest review? Ideally you should freshen up your web pages from time to time too.

- **Links** – make sure that they work by testing them – both the menu buttons and the embedded hyperlinks on every page. A monthly task.

- **Customer testimonials** – add new ones and replace old ones with better ones (every 1 to 3 months). As Dee says, ensure they are genuine and unedited.

- **Personnel** – if you feature individual team members in your 'About' section (or anywhere else) ensure that someone who has left is not still featured and add any new team members promptly. Don't forget to update those team photos too.

- **Awards** – these should be up to date so if an award was presented two years ago it should not still be in a prime position.

- **Accreditations** you have gained and membership associations you belong to. Make sure you have the relevant logos and that you add new details without delay.

- **News** – ideally add news every week if you can but failing that a minimum of once a month. If you can't keep your news page updated, remove it. Nothing dates a website more than a news page in which the last piece of news was added several months ago. You can post news about your business - recent awards, accolades, client acquisitions and your industry in general. Keep your news short and sweet. One or two paragraphs and, include links if appropriate to other pages on your website.

- **Blogs** – these are a great way to update your site regularly. If you are new to blogging or, you're not getting responses to your current blog posts study the blogging tips in the previous chapter.

- **Case studies** – another excellent way of showcasing your capabilities, but just like your customer testimonial keep your case studies fresh, updating them as necessary and replacing them with new ones. Two or three paragraphs will be more attractive to your visitors than reams of text. Focus on what your client was looking for, what you delivered, any wow factors and conclude with a couple of lines of genuine testimonial from your client. Include images if appropriate.

Choosing a Designer and Developer

Firstly, let's establish the difference between a designer and a developer.

- A designer is an expert in graphics, creating the visual image and impact.

- A developer is an expert in the technology that operates your website.

Some designers do basic development for smaller sites perfectly adequately. Some developers have design skills. If you're planning a website that does more than move from page to page and maybe has the need for a database, e-commerce facilities, or programming to carry out any kind of calculation, it's worth working with a consultant who has both designers and developers in their team – or finding a project manager to bring together all the experts and manage the progress of your website.

As in most industries there are some very experienced designers and developers around – and some who are not so great. If you want cheap and cheerful, then don't expect a website that looks top end. You can pay anything from £100 to thousands for a website, so choose – and be prepared to pay for – a service that delivers the type of website you want.

Don't stick a pin in a directory; ask around. Look at websites you like and see if you can find out who created them. When people recommend their web designer or developer ask to see a list of the sites they've created – and get more than one quotation. Go one step further – pick up the phone and ask the owners of the websites that you are admiring a few questions. Would they recommend their designer or developer? Did they stick to the original budget? Was the whole process on time and fairly painless? What feedback have they had from visitors to their website? Make sure that when you are getting quotes that they are like for like too. Some companies will include things that others will leave out. Ideally, decide what you want and provide the same brief for the companies you choose to quote against. How many companies to quote? Three should be enough. You may also want to consider the services of a copywriter if you don't fancy writing your website yourself.

Make sure that your quote includes a content management system. This is generally referred to as CMS and it gives you access to your website, allowing you to update pages and add content including images. This means you don't have to pester nor pay your web designer to make changes.

If you want something simple and accessible the WordPress platform has far more flexibility than most people realise. The basic blog package is free, but with plug-ins (added features) that you pay for, you'd be surprised at what is possible (take a look at *www.Caipora.co.uk* which uses WordPress software).

The Secret of a Website that Works

It isn't rocket science – it's simply getting inside the head of the person visiting your website and contemplating the following.

- Why are they visiting this website?
- What are they looking for?
- What problems are they experiencing?
- What sort of mood might they be in?
- What are their expectations?

If you know the answers to these questions and if you can follow the design, copy, usability and readability guidelines in this chapter – you'll be able to create a website that really works.

Getting Loyal Followers

Whether you sell products, services or a mixture of both, if people visit your website and aren't ready to buy what you are offering right now, how do you persuade them to come back and perhaps buy in the future?

There are many ways of doing this, but one of the most effective is to stay in touch with them. In order to do that you need to know who they are and you need to remind them of your value at fairly regular intervals.

The easiest way to do this is to ask them for their contact information – but who will give you that without a very good reason? This is why you need a good 'carrot' to dangle in front of them; something that interests them enough to give you their name and e-mail details.

Asking people to sign up to a newsletter these days is not a very powerful incentive; most of us receive newsletters by the dozen every month. Most of them are deleted – and you'll find that the majority of people aren't prepared to sign up to something that has no perceived value. Today's Internet users want to know how to, what to, when to, or more in-depth information that will help them to make better decisions on everything from improving their life to buying a better bathroom cabinet!

The secret of staying connected to people who visit your website is to offer them relevant and useful information; something they see as having value. This might be a report, a white paper or a tips sheet – depending on what sort of product or service you're selling.

Using either a database built into your website or a separate external service you can collect their information, automatically download their report and then arrange for regular e-mails to be sent to them. These messages give them more useful information and they keep your name at the forefront of their memories when they do decide to buy the type of product or service you offer.

Yes, newsletters can of course also be sent to the same list of people; however, a word of warning about newsletters; each issue must provide real value or excellent entertainment for people to want to read the next one.

If you don't catch their interest with the first issue they read, they're unlikely to bother opening any subsequent issues. As you never know when people will sign up to your newsletter it means that every issue has to meet the high standard you initially set when you were full of enthusiasm.

The secret of getting automated messages and newsletters opened is – like any journalist knows – in the headline! Get good at writing really good headlines for your e-mail subject lines, brochure front pages, web pages and anything else you want people to read and you'll have taken a massive leap into successfully marketing your business. Make sure that before you plan your newsletter you study Dee's excellent newsletter tips in Chapter 4. They apply equally to your on-line newsletters as well as your printed ones.

I hope that you have found these tips useful and that they help you to create or change your website to generate the highest possible impact on your visitors.

The Key to Successful Social Media: Twitter, Facebook and LinkedIn, by Karen Skidmore

For many of you reading this book, this is the moment that you may start feeling slightly lost and a little bit overwhelmed. In fact, you probably shifted uncomfortably in your seat as you read the heading above, sucked in your breath and thought 'what the heck, I've got to do this?'

Social media is a lot like e-mail when it was first introduced into the world of business more than 25 years ago. It took many businesses months, if not years, to allow employees their own e-mail address and many more years after that to get their head around remote working. Now that we have social media sites such as Twitter, Facebook and LinkedIn, it's causing the same technical confusion and worries of privacy. Businesses no longer feel in control when faced with these new ways of communication.

What started off as a suggested fad, social media has now become integrated into our everyday lives. I'm not even going to mention any user statistics here because by the time this book is published, there will be another few zeros added as more people acquire smart phones and faster broadband speeds.

Like it or not, if you run a business you are going to have to learn the new rules of communication and embrace them!

What do you need to know before starting out?

1. **What your customers do.** Is social media an appropriate channel to communicate with them? How are they using Facebook? Are they signed up to Twitter? And are they using these platforms to connect with businesses like yours? It's essential you do the right market research before embarking on a social media project, so start with your current customers. It will save you money and months of time and energy.

   But remember; the research you do today may well be out of date within a matter of months. If your customers are telling you that they don't use any social media sites now, make sure you go back and ask them again in six months' time. It is incredible how fast society is changing and adapting to our new technologies.

2. **What your competitors are doing.** Check out your competition and see what they are doing. But just because your major competitors are embracing social media doesn't mean you have to. This 'copy them' mentality is the reason why certain advertising media, such as The Yellow Pages, have survived as long as they have. Do your market research with your customers first. Social media needs to be integrated into your overall marketing strategy, rather than it being about a race to have trendy Twitter logos stamped all over your leaflets.

3. **Your current marketing strategy.** The danger of jumping into social media unprepared is that it can be an all consuming activity. Many businesses will take resources out of one area of their marketing mix before starting something new. And if you take away resources from something that works already, only to get sucked in to the new technology hype – it could put you back even further. Add social media – don't replace it with something that works already just because it's perceived to be 'old hat'.

4. **What outcomes are you looking for?** Have clear goals and objectives to your social media plan. What results are you expecting? And how are you going to measure them? Just because something looks cool or pretty, doesn't necessarily mean that it's adding to your bottom line. Social media is not a place to do hard sales, but it's got to have a return on your investment, even if that investment is time rather than hard cash.

5. **A few tweets don't make success.** For those of you looking for a shortcut or for quick ways to make a fast buck, then

this is the wrong place to do it in. I hate to put you off before you begin, but successful social media marketing takes time and commitment. Setting up a Twitter profile, for example, and filling it with automated tweets, is just not going to cut it!

6. **You've got to be present.** Social media presents you with fantastic opportunities to automate and schedule your marketing. But over-automate and you'll lose friends before they even become close to being your customer. You've got to be present on which ever social media network you decide to focus on. So you will need to make sure you have the resources and time factored in to make this happen. You don't have to be on these sites all day and every day but as an experienced practitioner I would say that Twitter needs daily interactions; you need to be on Facebook three or four times a week and on LinkedIn at least once a week.

7. **You must get your house in order.** Before you dive in to the world of social media, you have to make sure that as Lesley has advised earlier in the Chapter, your website is a marketing machine. If you've still got a brochure style website that can't convert website visitors to paying customers, then get this changed first. You need to have a website that enables you to collect e-mail addresses and contact details. Because it's this mailing list that will enable you to turn your on-line friends in to paying customers further down the line.

Many on-line social network sites provide the same functionality as each other, but in different ways. There are many arguments for why one site may be better than another. The best tip is probably to try a number of them and decide what works best for you. You don't need to limit yourself to just one site, however. There are many on-line tools out there that enable your one message to be populated across several sites at the same time. Let's dive in and have a look at the three main social media networks: LinkedIn, Twitter and Facebook.

LinkedIn (*www.LinkedIn.com*)

Out of the three networks mentioned earlier, LinkedIn is the one that most business people feel comfortable with. It's professional and it's designed to be a business networking tool. LinkedIn is a free business-oriented networking site, designed primarily for professionals to exchange ideas, information and opportunities. Users develop a list of 'Connections' by inviting people to join their personal LinkedIn network. LinkedIn is primarily designed for professional networking and therefore registered users are looking specifically for business contacts. It includes a 'Recommendation' feature, a recommendation being a short, snappy rave review that one member can provide for another member, so beefing up their profile. It is easy to join LinkedIn groups, connecting with professionals from the same business background as yourself.

I liken LinkedIn to a business conference. It's the local networking event or annual trade show. People turn up suited and booted. And as everyone is there to do business, it feels okay to talk business.

What started out as a recruitment platform where people joined to be headhunted and look for new careers, LinkedIn has grown in to a global business community attracting small business owners right through to CEOs and Managing Directors.

LinkedIn is still very much a place where the headhunters hang out. And its paid-for subscription is designed to help people access the millions of people registered on the site. But for most businesses the free account is more than good enough.

Why is LinkedIn such a powerful network?

- **It is professional and business like**. Your profile is based around a CV format and the groups and discussions that happen on LinkedIn are around business topics, rather than what you had for lunch that day. For this reason, even the most senior business people feel it is appropriate to have a profile on LinkedIn.

- **It is based on the six degrees of separation**. If you haven't come across this theory (Google it to get the full story), the six degrees of separation likes to prove that we are all connected to each other by six people. By searching for key people you want to contact, you can easily see if they are already connected to someone in your network. If they are, it makes this an easier connection if that person can introduce you – rather than you attempting to approach the person stone cold. Interesting connections start to happen as your network grows.

- **Accessibility to inaccessible people**. You can bypass the gatekeeper and contact that 'hard to reach' person with a direct message that you can be sure they will receive. We are all more likely to read messages received through social media than we are emails from a cold prospect.

- **LinkedIn Groups**. Start diving under the hood of LinkedIn and you find thousands of active groups and communities. If you are looking to hang out with a particular target group of people, then LinkedIn probably has an active group of these people already. Search the groups by keywords or names to help you find what you are looking for. Find the groups that your hot prospects and customers are part of.

- **LinkedIn Answers**. Again, hidden under the hood there is a busy and engaging question and answer section of LinkedIn. Divided into specific categories, you can use these sections to ask questions yourself (particularly useful if you want technical questions answered) or, if you want to build your on-line profile, you can answer the questions yourself and start showcasing your expertise.

- **Google juice**. Because of its size, LinkedIn is indexed regularly (registered and checked by search engines so that relevant web links appear in search listings). If you want to be found quickly and easily on-line, a LinkedIn profile can be one of the quickest and most effective ways of achieving this. References to you on your website may not be indexed fully but a LinkedIn profile that's well connected will have you at the top of your name search in no time.

Top Tips for getting started on LinkedIn

1. **Professional headline**. At the top of your profile, you have what LinkedIn calls your Professional Headline. You have a limited number of characters to add here and this will appear next to your name in certain searches and newsfeed listings. Think of it as your answer to 'So, what

do you do?' Many people stick with 'Business Owner' or 'Managing Director' and frankly, this is dull! You've got the opportunity to stand out in searches and make yourself look more interesting for people to check you out. So make this your headline – not a full stop!

2. **Your photo**. Professional, headshot please! This is not the place to be adding your holiday snapshot with your partner's head quite obviously chopped out. People make snap judgements about what they see and your LinkedIn photo needs to sell you and your brand. Smile and look natural, not corporate and stuffy.

3. **Benefit driven profile – not a CV**. The challenge many business owners have with LinkedIn is its CV based profile. You are probably not using LinkedIn to find a job. But you do want people to stop and take notice of your profile when they view it. Avoid listing a whole load of things that you have done over the past few years. Focus on what's going to be of interest to your potential customers and influencers now. How can you help them to solve their problems?

4. **Website links**. You have the option of adding three website links to your profile. And, more importantly, the option of changing the text of the link to something more engaging than 'My Website'. What about adding a link to a specific page that outlines a number of successful client case studies? What about sending people to an example of your work or portfolio? What about a specific offer you can make to contacts from LinkedIn? Your website homepage is OK, but you have the opportunity to use this real estate far more effectively.

5. **Status updates**. Once a week, update your status and tell your contacts what you are up to. Mention a new project you've started. Tell people about your new product launch or workshop. Share a link to an article on your website or blog. This is your opportunity to sow the seeds and share what you do in a conversational way.

One of the easiest ways to start building your LinkedIn network is to start with your current face-to-face networks. When you meet someone, look them up on LinkedIn and invite them to connect. Start using it as a proactive networking tool and commit some regular time to using it and the connections will flow.

Twitter (*Twitter.com*)

Twitter is another free on-line service that enables you to broadcast short messages to your friends or 'followers.' It also lets you specify which Twitter users you want to follow so that you can read their messages in one place. You can easily follow thousands of users and by selecting those people that work in the same arena as you and your business, you can listen in and enter into conversations conducted between users with similar interests to yourself. On the other hand, of course, Twitter can also be actively used as a tool to push out useful messages about your business and your expertise to interested people. Part of the charm of Twitter is that all messages are limited to 140 characters and you can choose to allow your messages to be read by all, or limit them to be private and read only by a specific individual.

Twitter hits the headlines in the newspapers daily, with quotes from footballers' tweets in trouble (again!), politicians saying the wrong thing, or the latest trends, (last season's X-Factor was creating thousands of tweets every second).

I liken Twitter to a cocktail party. Tweets (the 140 character status update published on Twitter) are pinging around left, right and centre in their thousands. And like all good parties, if you try to participate in every conversation in the room, it's overwhelming and it gives you a headache!

Twitter is a 'dip in and dip out' site. You can't be expected to read every single tweet from every single person you follow. And nor should you want to. It's not e-mail.

You want to be logging in to your Twitter account a few times a day. Scanning through the latest tweets from the people you've followed, replying to your @ replies (public messages sent to you) and DMs (private messages sent to you) and adding your own tweets and @ replies to others.

(OK – I know that last paragraph may sound like a foreign language but I promise you, once you get past the perceived techno-babble, it all makes perfect sense. You've got to jump in and join the party to help you understand the rules and language.)

Why is Twitter such a powerful communication tool?

- **It is quick and easy**. With only 140 characters to each tweet, you have no choice but to be concise.

- **You have access to information.** Whatever your profession or industry, there will be buckets of resources for you to access. Blogs, publications, directories, news channels – presenting you with a free and easy way of keeping your finger on the pulse but... you don't have to read everything that comes your way. Much of it will skim over your head, but you will find some gems amongst the waffle!

- **You can find out what prospects and customers are saying** and thinking literally as it is happening rather than waiting for a few months or weeks to find out what matters to them.

- **Breaking news**. Stories can hit Twitter a good few hours before the national news channels have even checked their sources.

- **Global reach**. If you are looking to expand globally, Twitter can open the door to global connections for you. You can search for key influencers by location and even tweets by location. Because many smart phone users are now GPS tracked so are their tweets.

- **Local reach**. Twitter works locally too. I follow my local pet shop and my local cafe, both of which tweet their latest offers and events. I feel I know what's going on and I spend more of my money with them because of it.

- **Networking on steroids**. If you decide not to use Twitter as a direct customer marketing tool (and to be honest, it's not always the most effective way of using it), then do use Twitter as a networking tool. Twitter allows you to connect with other people. This can lead to mutually beneficial opportunities. I met Dee at a face-to-face networking event. But it was through Twitter that we got to know each other and the opportunity for me to contribute to this chapter was created.

Top Tips for Getting Started on Twitter

1. **Choose a Twitter name**. Choose your own name or your business name, but make sure it's short and snappy enough for including on your business card and sales communications. If your name has already been taken, opt for a shortened version rather than simply adding numbers to your name - for example karenskidmore78200. This just looks 'spammy'. The shorter your Twitter name, the easier it is for your tweets to be re-tweeted (this is when your tweet is forwarded on by one of your followers so it appears on their Twitter feed). With only 140 characters per tweet, you can't afford a long winded name!

2. **Photo of you**. Avoid using your company logo as your avatar (the image used with each one of your tweets) and get a professional headshot done instead, preferably of you smiling and looking at the camera. Unless you are tweeting from a group account, you are 'you' on Twitter, not a company brand, so be you in your avatar.

3. **Write your bio.** You have 160 characters to explain who you are. This appears on your Twitter homepage. Yes, do think about the key words that people use to find you on search engines. But write for human beings and not the likes of Google. Filling this space with a whole load of keyword phrases just looks ugly. It does nothing to engage other human beings and to encourage people to follow you. Keep your bio updated too.

4. **Create a landing page for your website link**. You have one website link to add to your profile on Twitter so use it wisely! Sending people to your website homepage is okay but you can be more personal. If you can, create a specific landing page on your website for your Twitter followers. Introduce yourself in more detail. Perhaps even tell them why you are on Twitter and what you tweet about. But always create an opportunity for someone to join your e-mail marketing mailing list. Offer a discount coupon, downloadable report, monthly articles – whatever is relevant and what might be an 'ethical bribe' and a thank you for them parting with their e-mail address and name.

5. **Decide on a tweet plan**. Plan out what sort of information you want to be tweeting about over the coming weeks. It could be a number of top tips. It could be articles listed on your website or blog that you signpost through your tweets. It could be links to recommended resources and websites that would be useful to your customers. It could be a combination of all these things, plus more. Brain storm and write down stuff that would be useful and of value to the people you want to reach. If you are not a rock star people are unlikely to be interested in a daily monologue of your eating habits and what you got up to at the weekend. Aim for 80% of your tweets to be about useful information and tips, 20% to be more social and relaxed in nature. If you are tweeting in a business context your tweets must be appropriate. They should not damage your business reputation in any way. Once clients know you are on Twitter, some of them will start following you. Bear this in mind.

6. **Follow some interesting people.** The easiest way to understand how Twitter works is to start following others and to see what they do. Read their tweets. Watch how they communicate with other Twitter users. See how they engage, re-tweet and reply to others. You will soon learn the do and don't etiquette of Twitter quickly.

7. **Become an established tweeter before you tell people.** A big mistake new tweeters make is to start telling their customers and their wider networks that they are on Twitter before they have created any tweets. Get 15 to 20 tweets published to give people an idea of why you are on Twitter, what you tweet about and why you would be interesting enough to follow before you broadcast your presence.

Once you've gone through these set up stages, have a play on Twitter for a few weeks. Get your head around the language that is used and the etiquette. And join in with the party. Remember no one is going to come up and talk to you if you've got your arms folded, with your back to the room. The easiest way to get involved with the Twitter conversation is to start it yourself. You will know within a matter of weeks if Twitter represents a worthwhile investment of your business time or whether it's just a bit of fun.....

Facebook (*www.facebook.com*)

At the time of writing, Facebook is supposed to be the third largest country in the world. What started out as a place for American college kids to connect with each other has now grown to be the largest and most dominant social network of our time. Facebook is now open to everyone and it's also becoming increasingly popular for business networking. The lines between business and personal have become blurred on Facebook. It now enables business people to meet their peers, find business contacts and raise visibility, thereby making it an easy and inexpensive way of reaching potential buyers.

I liken Facebook to a coffee morning or a gathering after work at the local pub. It's full of chit-chat, personal stories and observations on life. It's the place to share photos and videos, both personal and business and funnies from YouTube. The business world started adopting Facebook as a way of connecting and communicating with contacts from about 2007. And we haven't looked back since.

There are two main ways in which businesses can use Facebook: either through a personal profile or via a business page. There is no question that Facebook are encouraging businesses via their Facebook pages. You have Friends if you use a personal profile and 'Likers' for your business page (awful phrase but since pages lost their fan status and you are no longer a fan, 'Liker' seems to be the only way of describing people that follow your Facebook business page!).

Why is Facebook such a powerful communication tool?

- **Shareability**. Facebook is taking over the Internet via its Like button. As more and more people get a profile on Facebook, you are able to 'Like' stuff on websites and blogs and have this automatically fed into your Facebook updates. It may sound scary but personal recommendations and reviews are now driving our personal on-line shopping habits. It started with the likes of *TripAdvisor.com* and *Amazon.com* product reviews. Our word-of-mouth recommendations are now being translated into clicking the Facebook 'Like' buttons.

- **Photo and video sharing at its best**. There are lots of photo sharing sites, such as Flickr and Google's Picasa, but Facebook's photo and video sharing capabilities are so easy and simple. We are now part of a generation that shares images of our dogs, children, funny dances, freak weather... the list just goes on. The cuter, freakier, funnier a photo is, the more likely it is to be shared amongst our Facebook friends. And this is why we have seen some amazing viral marketing campaigns run through YouTube and fuelled by Facebook users.

- **Searchability.** If you want to find someone or something, Facebook usually comes up trumps. A teacher at my children's school researched the history of the school and its buildings for its 60th anniversary this year. Most of the interesting stories came via Facebook, including old photos and images for him to use in the commemorative book. As a business owner, Facebook creates a great opportunity to 'eavesdrop' on your customers' conversations and buying preferences.

- **Targeted advertising**. Much as Google AdWords work, Facebook has its own pay-per-click advertising option. You are able to hone in on factors such as geographical location, age groups, preferences based on 'Likes' – all in all, this presents you with a highly targeted advertising option that is worth exploring.

Top Tips for getting started on Facebook:

1. **Decide on whether to go profile or page**. You have to have a personal profile set up on Facebook to be an

administrator of a page, but there are no direct links or connections. This means you can be personally private on Facebook, whilst still building a business presence. For most businesses, I would recommend setting up a business page for your on-line brand and use a personal profile to connect with 'real' friends and family.

2. **Privacy Settings**. As much as you may hate Facebook's lack of opt-in openness (and believe me, I am not a big fan of this either!), once you get in to your personal privacy settings, you can be as private as you want. I strongly recommend you get your head around how your personal profile is set up, particularly if you are using it for your 'real' friends and family. Make sure you opt-out of GPS settings or allowing friends to tag you in photos, for example. If you are happy to be as public as possible, then that's fine. But don't assume anything you share on Facebook can only be seen by your on-line friends – because it will be available to all and sundry once shared and tagged, if you don't take control of your personal privacy settings.

3. **Share stuff to be shared**. As it has already been pointed out, photos and videos are what makes Facebook tick. So be aware of this when deciding on what content to share on your Facebook page. Automatically scheduling your tweets from your Twitter account to appear as a status update is inappropriate to the Facebook audience. So plan and think creatively on what your 'Likers' would like to 'Like'.

4. **Shared stuff is what makes Facebook work**. If your updates and content is not shared and liked, it is highly unlikely it will appear in your 'Likers' newsfeed. This is what makes Facebook algorithms work. Because the Facebook newsfeed for each person is defaulted to Top News, what most people get to see is the stuff that's shared and liked the most. If you post dull stuff and updates that people are not interested in then your communication with your Facebook audience will fall flat.

Like Twitter, play around with Facebook before deciding if it is a worthwhile investment of your time. You may opt for one of these social networks rather than both, or decide after a few months that your efforts are best spent elsewhere.

In Summary

LinkedIn, Twitter and Facebook are the most recognised of the social media networks, but are by no means the only ones. MySpace attracts music lovers, YouTube is the place for video sharing and location based sites such as FourSquare and Gowalla are just taking off at the time of writing. Who knows – by the time this book is published there may well be a whole load of new social media opportunities!

Social media can be seen as a minefield when you first start out. Technology can easily complicate matters and it's easy to feel overwhelmed by all the new language and terminology. But I hope this introduction to the world of social media and how to use the three most common social media tools will help encourage you to dip your toe in the water ... and get wet!

The Secrets of Simple Search Engine Optimisation (SEO), by Sam Garrity

An introduction to SEO

Search Engine Optimisation (SEO) is the process of improving the visibility of a website through an understanding of how search engines work and of the keywords that people use. The vast majority of people now search for products and services on the Internet using search engines such as Google and Bing. It is this behaviour that has made visibility on search engines a crucial element in many business marketing strategies. It is unusual for an Internet user to click through many pages of search results before selecting a site to visit. Therefore the higher a website appears in the search results, the greater the chance that it will be visited by a visitor looking for those products or services. SEO is therefore fundamental in directing traffic towards a site. Search engine optimisation encompasses two key areas - on-site SEO and off-site SEO. On-site SEO refers to work on your own website and it will include many of the tips that Lesley has shared, namely writing great content, having relevant links, a regularly updated blog and a fresh and relevant news page. Off-site SEO on the other hand refers to work on websites other than your own - such as generating links.

Ideally you should consider search engine optimisation (or SEO) before you build any on-line profile. A basic knowledge of SEO can ensure that:

- Your website is constructed in a suitable fashion.
- Your website is populated with great content.

- You can build a high profile SEO campaign.
- You can target the right audience.

Depending upon how competitive your market is, there are some SEO techniques that you can implement yourself that will produce good search engine rankings for your website. Here are 10 tips to get you started on the path to search engine success.

1. **Don't forget your website!**
   As Lesley advised at the beginning of this chapter, before working towards bringing thousands of visitors to your website you must ensure that your site will convert them into sales or enquiries. Start by carrying out a comprehensive study of your competitors' websites. An easy way to do this is to use a search engine such as Google to search for websites in your sector. For example if you are a driving instructor based in Southampton you should type into Google something like 'driving instructors in Southampton'. Once the search engine lists the results, you should visit most of the websites on the first few pages to assess them. When evaluating your competition you should remember your own ambitions. Are you a small local business or a national one? What message do you want to convey?
   If you know the core values of your business coupled with your ambitions you can evaluate your competitors and list what you liked and disliked about their websites. Ask yourself how well they convey their marketing message, how easy it was to navigate the site, and if you were a customer, whether the site would convince you to make an enquiry. Look at their websites in the light of Lesley's

tips. Ask your colleagues, business associates and friends if they will help you too. Once you have a good straw poll of opinion you will be well positioned to create a site that will turn visitors to sales.

2. Is SEO for you?

Before embarking on an SEO strategy it is crucial to ascertain whether this is in fact the right path for you. It's simple to find out. Start by drawing up a list of the phrases you think that people would type into a search engine to find companies in your sector (i.e. 'driving instructors in Southampton'). This list will be known as your 'keywords'. Involve your customers in this if you are not sure. What words would they type into Google when looking for what you provide?

Once you have a list of around five phrases, please visit the Google Keyword Tool using the address below:

https://adwords.google.co.uk/select/KeywordToolExternal

When on the site, enter your keywords list into the 'word or phrase' box with each phrase on a new line. You then type in the characters Google is prompting you to in the box below before clicking on the 'search' button.

Google will then list your keywords and any other keywords it feels is relevant along with some search data. The data you should look at is the 'Local Monthly Searches'. This refers to the amount of people that search for that keyword in an average month in the UK.

Once you have carried out this simple exercise you can ascertain if there are a robust amount of searches carried out for your product or service on-line. This will help you to determine whether SEO is right for your business.

3. Choose your keywords carefully

You should aim to have a defined list of targeted keywords that have been chosen with insight and care. You can achieve this with the help of the Google Keyword Tool that we identified in tip 2, by browsing Google itself looking at what Google prompts you to search for as you type and, by knowing your audience.

Very few websites have the diversity and power to get to the first page of the search engines for a large number of keywords. Hence your list should represent the size (amount of pages) of your website. If you have a small site (between 5-20 pages) and a defined target audience then five phrases will suffice.

Here is an example of a well targeted keyword list continuing with the driving instructor example:

- Driving instructors in Southampton.
- Driving lessons in Southampton.
- Cheap driving lessons in Southampton.
- Crash course driving lessons in Southampton.
- Advanced driving lessons in Southampton.

Once you have a list of highly searched for keywords to target you can start to incorporate them into your search engine optimisation work. It will help immensely if you can compose this list before reading any further because it will define everything that you do from this point onwards.

4. Website structure

Google and other search engines use an algorithm to judge websites. They use what we call ‘spiders’ or ‘bots’ and they visit websites sporadically to read and store the data they find. The best way to understand this is to imagine Google's millions of spiders crawling the World Wide Web. Every so often one of these spiders will visit your website and when it does you need to make sure that it's fed the right information.

To make sure the spiders are given the right information you need to practice good 'on-site' SEO. This simply means good SEO carried out on your website. We will tackle 'off-site' SEO (SEO work carried out on external sites) later. As discussed earlier, good on-site SEO includes the structure of your website and the content you publish. It also includes the title tags you use and how quickly your website downloads.

The way in which your website is built will influence a spider's ability to read the content. The content of some websites is invisible to spiders and has an adverse effect on SEO. Some common mistakes include:

- **The use of Flash**. Flash is used to create animation and is frequently used in introductions to sites and banners at the top of homepages. Search engines find it difficult to read text within Flash animations. If you have a core message that is important to your targeted keywords within a flash animation it might not be read.

- **Embedding content into pictures**. Search engines cannot read an image. So if you place text within an image, it will not be read by a spider. A simple way to see if text on your website can be read is to try and highlight it with your mouse cursor. If you cannot highlight the text character by character then your text is probably embedded within an image.

In some cases you can create animations/pictures with information that spiders can crawl. For a list of search engine friendly file types visit our blog at *http://www.elevatelocal.co.uk/blog/what-types-of-files-can-the-google-spider-index-1912474*

When assembling a list of pages for your website there will be the inevitable pages such as your homepage, about us, and contact us page but you should add pages that are relevant to the keywords you have decided to target. Using the same keywords from our earlier example - driving instructors in Southampton; driving lessons in Southampton; cheap driving lessons in Southampton; crash course driving lessons in Southampton; advanced driving lessons in Southampton – you could have the following pages on your website:

- Driving instructors.
- Driving lessons.
- Crash courses.
- Advanced driving lessons.

When creating these pages you should use unique content that reflects the keywords you are targeting. A suitable introductory sentence to the 'Advanced driving lessons' page could be:
'We offer a range of affordable advanced driving lesson courses throughout the Southampton area.'

This sentence balances the use of your keywords with essential information to the customer. Note – you should always consider your likely customers and never simply write content for spiders. If you overuse your keywords, you could be penalised by search engines for 'spamming' (overuse of keywords).

Once you have created your pages, you need to place 'title tags' on them. Title tags tell a search engine the title of each page. This is your chance to tell the spiders what you are targeting. To view your title tag you need to look at your website and read the text at the very top of the page (next to the logo of your Internet browser). If you are using Google's Chrome browser you need to hover your mouse cursor over the tab at the top of the browser.

If your title tags do not correctly target your keywords you will need to change them. If you have a CMS (content management system) there will be an area for you to do this. Other websites will require you to change the source code (note your web developer can help you do this if necessary – it is a simple job and should not incur any charge).

Within the source code your title tag is normally located as below:

```
<HTML>
<HEAD>
<TITLE>Your title tag is here</TITLE>
```

When creating your title tags you need to make sure you follow some simple rules. Make sure they reflect the page you are labelling and the keywords you are targeting. Each page's title tag should be different to avoid spamming. Your title tags should also be between 40 to

60 characters long as spiders will ignore text beyond this limit.

You can use a title tag to target a few keywords. A good example of a title tag is:

driving instructors Southampton - driving lessons Southampton

To increase the chances of a search engine spider finding their way around your website, you should include a sitemap. This is a page on your website that contains hyperlinks (hyperlinks, or links, are a reference to another page that a user can follow by clicking on the link). Once a sitemap has been created you should place a link to it in the bottom of all of the pages on your website.

Finally; search engines are interested in download speeds. You should aim to have a website that downloads quickly. To achieve this you must avoid placing large picture files or large videos files on your website. This doesn't mean you shouldn't have pictures and videos but that they should be compressed to make the files size as small as possible without compromising on quality.

5. **Links**

Search engine spiders place importance on the amount and type of websites that have a link pointing to your site. The perfect link is a one-way link pointing at your site from a site that is relevant to your business and that is deemed important by search engines. An example of a good link would be if you were a Garden Centre and you had a link pointing at your website from the BBC's gardening page.

You should avoid buying links as it contravenes Google's guidelines (for more on this visit *www.google.com/*

support/webmasters) but there are ways of cultivating great links.

Google and other search engines love content. If you write lots of unique interesting content that is rich in the keywords you have decided to target it will have numerous positive effects upon your website and business. These include the following benefits for SEO:

- Search engines will understand what you do, what keywords you are targeting, and think you are an authority on what you do.
- Visitors to the site will be captivated and then bookmark or link to your website.

Search engines give more precedence to sites that are continually growing and changing. For this reason we recommend having a blog on your website. If you provide a strong, topical, and unique blog it will help bring visitors to the site, generate natural backlinks and bookmarks. The search engines have a higher opinion of your site.

Please remember that you should not write copy purely for search engines. As Lesley has advised, you must construct your website copy with your target audience 'front of mind', continually asking yourself what they will think when they are reading it and their purpose for visiting your website. And remember - do not 'stuff' your content full of keywords as this will result in you being penalised by Google.

6. **Use social media to publicise your content**

The influence of social media on SEO is growing. Examples of how to use social media for your business include:

- Making professional or business to business connections through LinkedIn.
- Tapping into specific audiences through Facebook.
- Gaining followers from Twitter.

As Karen explained, LinkedIn, Facebook and Twitter are all very user-friendly sites that walk you through the set-up process in a logical way. Once you have these set up you can use them to connect with your audience and to publicise your website and blog content. If you are producing appealing and unique content you will find your message spreads organically and many natural links to your website will be generated.

Social media is incredibly dynamic so you should also research other social media websites and forums that will help you promote your business.

7. **Submitting to search engines and directories**

Listing your website on directories can help to drive relevant traffic to your website whilst being a great source of links. There are thousands of directories to choose from so be selective. Some good free directories include:

- The Open Directory Project (*www.dmoz.org*)
- Qype (*www.qype.co.uk*)
- Yelp (*www.yelp.co.uk*)
- Hot Frog (*www.hotfrog.co.uk*)

Visit their sites and follow their simple registration process.

You should also submit your details to the major search engines via their business listings. This will help you appear on the maps section of the search results. Here are the three we recommend using:

- *Google.co.uk/places*
- *http://listings.local.yahoo.com*
- *www.bingforbusiness.com*

8. **Remember other forms of Internet searches**

Search engines now allow you to search for videos, blogs, news, shopping items, and images amongst many others. You should identify which of these could be used by your business to target customers. An example of this would be a car repair garage filming a video on how to conduct vehicle winter safety and posting it on YouTube. People would find this useful and might bookmark it or link to it.

9. **Guard your on-line reputation**

With so many forums available and reviews of your product or service now being posted alongside the natural results it is crucial to protect your reputation. You can do this by following these easy steps:

- Visit Google's homepage and click on the 'News' link in the top left hand part of the page.
- Then type your business name into the search bar and click 'search news'.
- Finally scroll to the bottom of the page and click

on the link that says 'Create an e-mail alert for your business name' and follow the instructions.

This will allow you to monitor what is being said about you, enabling you to respond to any negative PR whilst capitalising on positive PR.

10. Google Analytics

Google Analytics is a programme that allows you to monitor the traffic to your website. By using this brilliant tool you will be able to see:

- How many visitors you have received on any timescale.
- How many pages each visitor looked at.
- How long they were on your website.
- Where they found your website (what search engine, directory etc). What they typed into the search field.
- The geographic locations of the visitors.
- What type of device they accessed your website from (standard computer, iPad, iPhone etc.).
- Whether they filled out a contact form or made a purchase.

Learning from Google Analytics will be instrumental in shaping your future decisions in Internet marketing. To install Google Analytics visit *www.google.com/analytics.* You may require the help of your developer to install this but it is an easy task, and they may have already done this when building your website.

11. **Help!**
    Don't let SEO distract you too much from your day job. It can become an obsession and if you are in a very competitive market you may need extra help. If you want a free audit of your website, or you'd just like to pick our brains please contact us via our website, *www.elevatelocal.co.uk*

Thanks to Lesley, Karen and Sam for their invaluable contributions. To conclude this chapter I would now like to share with you some advice on why and how you should protect your brand on-line.

Protecting and Nurturing Your Brand On-line

A statistic produced in a recent Microsoft report stated that 64% of HR managers are now browsing sites such as Facebook and Twitter to appraise the on-line profiles of candidates that they have interviewed or are due to interview for a position at their company. Furthermore, 41% of these HR managers are then rejecting candidates because of what these on-line profiles reveal.

And it's hardly surprising, is it? Within seconds, an HR manager can now obtain a different perspective of a candidate, one that is possibly more revealing and more accurate than anything established through psychometric testing or a stringent interview process.

So what does this have to do with the small business owner who's keen to forge a presence on the web?

Substitute the words HR manager for cold prospects and clients, and you have your answer. The people that you want to attract and your existing customers are now also likely to check you out on-line. Every communication that you send that includes your web address is a prompt for a person to find out more about you on-line. They may start by looking at your website, but with the Internet now offering a feast of information, they're likely to go beyond this and check you out more fully. Simply typing your name and your business name into a search engine can yield pages of results. It is important that the results portray you in a positive and professional light.

How to Protect and Nurture Your Brand On-line

1. **Start by seeing yourself as others see you**. Search for your name on the Internet and see what comes up. As Sam suggested, it's a good idea to sign up to Google Alerts so that you can find out what is being published on-line about you on a daily basis.

2. **If you are already using social networking sites** such as Facebook, Twitter and LinkedIn, it's a good idea to review your messages and social photographs, deleting any that you now view as being inappropriate or that portray you in a negative light. If your messages largely consist of bland updates on your daily life, such as what you ate for lunch, or what television programmes you've watched, you run the risk of turning people off. Unless you are an in-demand celebrity, of course!

   Pay attention to the composition of your messages. Double check each message before publishing to avoid spelling mistakes and poor grammar. Resist the temptation to condense your messages with abbreviations. This may be acceptable for phone text messages to friends but not so in the on-line universe where everyone can access what you are saying. Imagine that your most important client, your most valuable cold prospect is reading these messages. What will be their impression of you?

3. **If you write a business blog, ensure it's up to date**. If the last post is more than a month old, get something on there quickly. Make sure that your blog content is not an unashamed sales plug. We covered this in detail in the previous chapter.

4. **Don't reveal inappropriate news or information** about your business that could portray you in a negative light. One of the pitfalls associated with social networking is the temptation to offload problems and to share humour that can sometimes be a little dubious. These messages, although perhaps acceptable in a social setting with friends and family, are best avoided when we are hoping to build a positive and powerful reputation on-line. There have been a number of high profile examples of sportsmen and celebrities being caught out by inappropriate on-line musings and this only goes to show how easy it is to fall into this trap.

   Let me illustrate this with some recent messages that I read on a social networking site.

   - A person left a message in all innocence stating that they had endured an incredibly frustrating day with a challenging client. What happens if that client is also reading their messages?
   - Another person left a message to the effect that their business was going through a financial crisis. What impression are they unwittingly communicating about the stability of their business?

- One person jubilantly shared details of a new client that they had just signed up. Revealing details in this way can backfire, though. It is information that a competitor may want to make use of, and it may be that their new client does not welcome such a public broadcast.
- Another person often leaves messages in which he shares rather inappropriate jokes, complete with expletives. What does this poor judgement say about his character?

5. **If you allow members of your team to access on-line social networks,** establish firm, written guidelines before they are allowed to start posting and responding to messages. What are they allowed to write about? What is off-limits? What tone are they allowed to take? How much time can they spend on these networks? Should they be posting messages in their own name or under your business name? These are just a few of the questions you will need to consider. If you don't establish guidelines there's a real risk that members of your team may spend their every spare moment on-line, engaging in banter and posting messages that are pointless at best and potentially damaging to your brand. An increasing number of small businesses are now including social media policy within their staff handbook, and seeking legal advice before doing so.

Chapter Summary

1. Don't abandon traditional marketing techniques in favour of on-line marketing unless you have compelling business reasons to do so.

2. Before plunging into social media, make sure that your website is up to the job.

3. A successful website must combine the four elements of design, copy, readability and usability.

4. Your website copy must address your visitors' wants and needs.

5. Your website must have a clear structure that identifies the pages and how they relate to each other.

6. Make sure that any images or visuals on your website enhance your message and complement your brand.

7. Use moving images sparingly on your website. Can the visitor be in control of these?

8. The navigation system on your website should tell the visitor where they are, where they have been and where they can go.

9. Make sure that the text on your website is easy to read. This includes the headlines and the body copy.

10. Keep your website up to date - review it every few weeks.

11. Are your clients using social media? It's worth asking before you plunge in!

12. Social media should complement your current marketing with additional opportunities to communicate in an informal setting.

13. Dip your toes into Twitter, LinkedIn and Facebook, evaluating each one before deciding whether to commit.

14. If you do decide to sign up, make sure that your messages and news are interesting and relevant. Avoid any hard sell.

15. You can improve the ranking of your website in the search engines with some DIY search engine optimisation.

16. Protect your reputation and your brand on-line. Always be professional, friendly and helpful.

17. Make sure that any members of staff understand and comply with your social media policy.

CHAPTER 8

QUESTIONS & ANSWERS

I hope this book has provided you with the answers to many of your marketing questions, challenges and dilemmas, and has clarified how to achieve the maximum value from the opportunities that come your way. In this, the final chapter, I address the most common marketing questions that small business owners have asked me in the last few years, questions that have not been covered in the previous chapters.

1. We Are Exhibiting at a Local Business Exhibition. How Can We Generate as Many Leads as Possible?

Local exhibitions can be an excellent source for new business if you are targeting a local audience, as it is local business people that make up the bulk of visitors to local exhibitions. Unfortunately though, not all small businesses that exhibit at local exhibitions take full advantage of showcasing their wares to this captive audience. They are largely unprepared, and in being so they unwittingly sell themselves short. Turning up just before the doors open to the public leaves little time to create an attractive and inspiring stand. If an exhibitor has not prepared the messages they plan on delivering to their audience, they can find themselves tongue-tied and struggling to strike up a meaningful conversation with visitors to their stand. And without allocating time at the end of the exhibition to follow up any leads that have been gathered, it is all too easy for the day-to-day task of running the business to take over, and for those potentially profitable leads to be neglected. To enjoy a successful exhibition, it is vital to make a wholehearted and enthusiastic commitment to the entire process.

This commitment starts when you make the decision to exhibit and should only finish when the last interested visitor has been followed up. Here's how you can make your exhibition a resounding success:

- **Find out if there are opportunities for you to speak** at the exhibition. Many exhibitions include a seminar programme and you will usually see exhibitors' names amongst the speakers. But you need to be quick in contacting the organisers in order to beat the other exhibitors keen to raise their profile. The advantage of speaking at an exhibition is that it enables you to stand out amongst your fellow exhibitors and consequently helps draw visitors to your stand. Also, the details of your seminar and a brief profile of who you are and what you offer will usually be included in any pre-exhibition material. In short, speaking at an exhibition provides a golden PR opportunity, one that is well worth brushing up your public speaking skills for. Plan out some relevant and interesting topics. What will attract visitors to your seminar? Cancelling a seminar due to insufficient attendees is something that every organiser wants to avoid. Don't oversell your offering. The fact you are standing in front of the audience is promotion enough.

- **Make a list of key people that you would like to visit you** at the exhibition and send them a personal invitation. Include those exhibition details that will tempt your invitees to attend, such as the seminar line up, subsidised refreshments, networking opportunities and any business clinics on offer. You may want to invite lapsed clients, cold prospects, warm prospects and your existing client base. Follow-up the invitation with an imaginative mailshot a few working days before the event to improve the likelihood of a good turnout at your stand. One business enclosed in the envelope the packaging from a neat travel alarm clock. The letter explained that to receive the clock itself, they would need to drop by the exhibition stand and say 'hello'. And guess which stand managed to attract the most visitors? If you are going to take the time and trouble to exhibit, these small touches could ensure a good turnout from the people you've invited on the day.

- **Make a list of everything that you will need** to bring to the exhibition, including items to make your stand look professional, original and eye-catching. You don't want your stand to be all but invisible while you watch the attractive stands of your competitors pulling in the visitors. This is your shop window. Helium balloons, pop-up banners, a striking display of flowers, good-quality fabric in your corporate colours, literature displays - these all help to give your stand the 'wow' factor. Can you bring along any props – items that illustrate what you do and that will help strike up conversations with visitors? Bring along any professional certificates or awards too and, if appropriate, samples of your work or portfolio. Try to ensure that your stand reflects your brand down to the smallest detail and that it looks professional and recognisable to your visitors. Practice the layout of your stand at home or in your office, trying different ideas before deciding upon a look that you are happy with. Make sure that it has height, colour and impact. Shoeboxes and biscuit tins covered with a good quality piece of cloth in your corporate colours are brilliant for creating height on your stand. Take a photograph of your stand so that you can replicate it accurately at the exhibition venue.

- **Decide upon the most appropriate literature to promote your business.** (Chapters 3 & 4 may help you here.) Visitors will need to be inspired and entertained if they are to stay for more than a few seconds. Displaying some eye-catching literature is a good way to initiate conversations with visitors to your stand, and these conversations are likely to be remembered whenever those visitors read about your business at home. You may want to include examples of recent press coverage, a voucher and your latest newsletter. How about a few client case studies? Consider running a competition or quiz on your stand. This will arouse the interest of visitors and chatting to them about your quiz is a great way to break the ice. In all likelihood, you will be rushed off your feet on the day, so assemble your literature beforehand.

- **Free gifts always go down well at exhibitions** but can also be counter-productive by encouraging the 'grab and go' brigade. Consider putting your free gifts in a goody bag and using these bags to attract prospects to your stand. Here's what Tracey Evans from Ashley Law Crawley Independent Financial Advisers has to say about goody bags after she exhibited at a local business exhibition.

  'We took on board Dee's advice and offered a goody bag at a local business exhibition. Our goody bags consisted of a pocket calculator, a ruler, a nice pen, one of those fuzzy little sticker bugs and some gold chocolate coins, all packaged in a clear cellophane bag. Instead of a standard gift tag, we used my business card and threaded some white ribbon through it to seal the bags. Because the bags looked so attractive, people were queuing up at our stand wanting to find out how they could get hold of one. Rather than just hand them out, we gave them as a gift to those visitors that took part in our quiz. It proved to be a great conversation

starter for our services. We also had lots of positive feedback from visitors about the goody bags. One accountant asked for an extra bag for his daughter. So they definitely worked, and as a result we have arranged several meetings. They cost us just £6 each.'

- **If the organisers are running a pre-exhibition event** for the exhibitors, either as a social get-together or to run an exhibition skills workshop, do not pass up the opportunity to attend. Whether you are an old hand at exhibiting or new to the experience, attending will provide an opportunity to meet your fellow exhibitors and to learn something new or brush up on your existing skills. Your fellow exhibitors could be potential new clients too, and networking in a convivial setting provides the chance to identify mutually beneficial opportunities. Can you make a special offer to the exhibitors? This works especially well if your business offers products or services that are in particular demand from businesses when they are exhibiting. A designer, printer or copywriter could offer to produce the exhibitors' literature. A signage company could supply pop-up banners and signage for the stands. A business that supplies promotional gifts could offer branded gifts or clothing for the exhibitors. Should you choose to make an offer of this sort, not only will every exhibitor see an example of your work but so will every visitor to the exhibition.

- **No one likes to think that their people skills are in need of improvement** but at every exhibition you will see exhibitors getting it so wrong in their eagerness to appeal to people visiting their stand. Excessive talking, failing to listen, not showing any interest in what is being said to them are all common mistakes. Nicky Kriel, a Life Coach and Neuro-Linguistic Programming (NLP) Practitioner who coaches people in the art of actively listening says,

'Never underestimate the power of really listening to every visitor that comes to your stand. Give them your full attention. Most people only listen for a gap in the conversation so that they can speak. They appear to be listening, but are really thinking about what they are going to say next. When you listen to someone as though they are the only person in the room, you make them feel valued as a person and you build a connection. The best listeners are generally considered to be the best conversationalists.'

Other exhibitors find it difficult to start a conversation, but don't help themselves if they have their nose buried in a newspaper or book, and make frequent trips to the cafe or loo. If you want to build relationships and make your visitors feel warm and friendly towards you, then polish those people skills. A book I heartily recommend that will help in this area is 'How to Win Friends and Influence People', by Dale Carnegie.

- **Don't underestimate the value of enthusiasm**. You need to radiate it consistently, even when your feet are aching and visitors are thin on the ground. The busy stands are usually those manned by people that are passionate about what they offer, that are enthusiastic about helping visitors and that genuinely enjoy building rapport. Make sure that you are enthusiastic and passionate when talking about the benefits that your business delivers and that you maintain this enthusiasm when you are doing the listening. Remind yourself why you are exhibiting. You probably only need to find a few new clients to make the event a success. Keep on smiling all the way through!

- **After the exhibition has ended, make sure that you have earmarked sufficient time to follow-up** each lead without delay. You may want to segment your leads into categories of importance, tackling the VIP leads with a phone call and less valuable prospects with a nice letter or e-mail. Each one, however, should be followed up in order to get a return on your investment. I met one business owner who had spent thousands of pounds on exhibiting, yet lamented to me that several weeks down the line he still hadn't followed up on the 150 leads from the event because he had been too busy! He was running the risk of missing this tremendous opportunity through not having prioritised follow-up time after the exhibition. Your follow-ups are more likely to be successful if they are personal and refer to the conversation that you had with the person at the exhibition. This jogs their memory and demonstrates that you really did listen to what they were saying and have taken on board their comments. An impersonal, standard letter is more easily dismissed by the recipient.

  And finally, when the dust has settled on the exhibition, do your sums to check whether it all paid for itself.

2. Does Advertising in Local Publications Work for Small Businesses?

It is easy to fall into the trap of adopting a rather hit and miss approach to advertising in local publications. But whether you are considering promoting your business in a local publication or even a national newspaper, it pays to invest in a little thinking time beforehand. Why do you want to advertise? What are your objectives?

Don't make the decision to advertise simply because you have a little spare cash or you are concerned about a recent lack of sales. If you do decide to advertise, then you are taking on the challenge of creating a benefit driven advert that will attract some of the readers sufficiently for them to get in touch with you. Steer clear of creating your advert at home in a Word document. These types of adverts always look cheap and tacky when reproduced in a magazine. However, I often appraise adverts that are beautifully designed with clear benefits and offers to stimulate responses yet despite this, responses have been thin on the ground. This is often simply because the readers don't have a deep underlying need for what the business is offering. In a more targeted publication it could well have delivered responses by the barrel load. Your business has to be the right fit for the publication and its readers. These are all important considerations that you should be thinking about before you decide to advertise.

So, when asked if local advertising works, my answer is 'Yes. But ...'

- **The publication must have sufficient readers** in the market to buy the products or services being advertised. Alternatively, the readers must be key influencers in the decision-making and purchasing process. Ask the editorial team for a profile of their readers before you commit. Look at your target audience. Are there strong similarities between their readers and your potential customers?

- **The distribution of the publication must be thorough and targeted**. There's a world of difference between a hand-delivered publication that reaches the desks or the doormats of readers and one that's left for people to grab as they walk by. Again, ask the editorial team for their distribution channels, the number of publications that are distributed and over what period of time. You don't want to include a time-limited offer that expires before the publication has been sent out.

- **The content of the publication has to be relevant and engaging**. If it's crammed with wall-to-wall advertising without a glimmer of informative and punchy editorial, the likelihood is that it will be skimmed through quickly before landing in the bin. It will have a reputation for being a thin read with little value. Review a copy of the publication you are considering advertising in, making a note of the editorial pages and the quality of the adverts. If it looks shabby and unprofessional, you have to question whether you want your business to be associated with it. We are judged by the company we keep.

- **The size of the advert must be big enough** for you to communicate those compelling messages that will motivate people to respond. An advert the size of a large postage stamp may be adequate for a fish and chip shop, especially if they use the space for a voucher, but if you have a more complicated product or service, it will be difficult for you to communicate sufficient information in the space available.

- **The cost of advertising has to be reasonable**. Calculate the total cost of advertising including design and copywriting fees. Then work out exactly how much business, new introducers or new clients you will need to get from advertising to cover those costs and tip you into profit. If the figures look impossible, you're better off saving your money.

And other things to bear in mind include:

- **Be prepared to negotiate.** Most publications will offer you their standard rate card and if you don't negotiate that will be the price you pay. Have a go at negotiating, even starting with a price that seems very low, allowing you some room to manoeuvre. But never pay more than you believe is reasonable or affordable. If the publication won't offer a discount, ask if they can offer some additional editorial or an increase in the size of your advert. This can work particularly well when the publication is nearing its deadline date and the sales person needs to fill the remaining empty space in the publication quickly.

- **Don't dismiss the idea of advertising in free local magazines and newspapers**. For many businesses, especially trades people and retailers, local advertising can be a gateway to an army of new customers on their doorstep. You can usually get a feel for whether your business will be successful advertising in a particular publication by flicking through it and noting how many of your competitors are in there. The costs of advertising in a free publication are usually very reasonable which of course lessens the risk. Fewer new customers are required to cover your costs and move you into profit.

Let's turn our attention now to the content of your advert. The following tips are inspired by the advertising legend, David Ogilvy, who famously said:

> *'I do not regard advertising as entertainment or an art form, but as a medium of information. When I write an advertisement*

I don't want you to tell me that you find it 'creative.' I want you to find it so interesting that you buy the product.'

1. **Make your product or service the hero of your advert**. In a small space, it's vital that the reader knows exactly what is being advertised, how they will benefit and why they need to act now. Three or four concise benefits are better than reams of waffle.

2. **As discussed throughout this book, don't talk about unique selling points** if in fact they are not unique. Readers will see through this. If you can say what's good about your product or service and do so clearly, this is more than good enough.

3. **Keep it simple**. Use every day language that readers will be familiar with unless you are communicating with people that appreciate complex and technical language.

4. **The headlines that work best are usually those that promise the reader a benefit.** Detail your new, improved offering including the words 'you' or 'your'. Using your headline as a quote will increase its positive impact too. 'The best Christmas ham you've ever tasted... or your money back.', 'Lose your fear of public speaking in just three sessions.'

5. **Use genuine testimonial from your happy customers**. One line can be enough in a small space.

6. **When advertising in a local publication,** responses can be improved simply by including the name of the city or

town in your headline. People are interested in what's happening where they live. 'Three genuine document shredding offers for Brighton businesses.'

7. **Caption any illustrations**. 'Sue before she lost weight.' 'Look at Sue now after completing our risk-free weight reduction programme!' People are often drawn to your advert by the captions accompanying the illustrations. You want your advert to catch their eye before they turn the page.

8. **If you are communicating more than one benefit it will help to highlight this**. 'Five reasons why 99% of our customers recommend our services.'

9. **Avoid essays.** What will your product or service do for the reader? Be specific. Look again at your positioning statement.

10. **Make an offer,** limited to a number of readers. Add a close date to encourage early responses. 'Free delivery on your organic vegetable box if you're one of the first 25 readers to respond by June 29th.', 'Bring this voucher to claim your half-price fish & chips.'

11. **Ask the publication to design your advert,** even if you have to pay for it. The look of your advert and the information it conveys is instrumental in generating responses. Don't design your own advert (unless of course you are a designer!)

12. **Once you have placed your advert, make sure that you measure its effectiveness.** I have met several small business owners that have been quick to say that local advertising has not worked for them when in fact they haven't really known if it has. Without tracking where new business has come from it is not possible to gauge whether your advert has been successful or not. Don't decide whether to continue advertising in a publication or not based on a gut feeling. Be in possession of the facts.

3. How Can I Encourage Our Existing Customers to Recommend Us?

There are many ways in which you can encourage your existing customers to recommend you. Which way you choose will depend on what you sell, the relationship you have with your customers and how easy it is for a customer to recommend you. For example, a customer would find it easy to recommend a supplier of office products if its products are competitively priced and delivery is reliable. Introducing a formal customer referral scheme with incentives would usually reap dividends in this case because customers don't need to go to too much trouble to recommend the business. Such a scheme would not be so appropriate for a provider of professional services, such as an accountant or solicitor. It could actually backfire and convey an unprofessional image if an accountancy firm suggested to their clients that they would receive a gift as a thank you for a recommendation. Bear this in mind as you study the tips that follow. Some will be appropriate for your business, others not so.

- **Plan several referral campaigns** that run throughout the year. Separate each campaign by a few months so that they don't lose their impact. People can become immune to your overtures if an offer appears to be never-ending. You may want to create some literature solely for the purpose of promoting your referral scheme. However, you can also add these details to your surveys, quizzes, sales letters and other marketing literature. One business that I work with has gained several new customers through recommendation simply by asking existing customers in their annual survey: 'If you are happy with our service, would you be happy to recommend us? If so, please tick 'Yes' and we will contact you.'

- **Don't ask your customers to recommend you to everyone they know.** Give them some clear direction. Ask them to recommend you to a family member, a work colleague, their best friend, three people from their address book, two people at their networking group, their accountant, bookkeeper or solicitor and so on. Have a think about the type of recommendations that you would really like and how realistic it is for you to ask for one.

- **What can you offer your customers as an incentive to recommend you?** Your answer should take into consideration what your customers buy from you now, the relationship you have with them and how much they spend with you. You may want to segment your customers into groups and make appropriate and targeted offers to each group based on these factors. You don't have to offer everybody the same incentive. The more personal and relevant you can be the better.

- **Stuck for incentive ideas?** How about free postage and packing on their next three orders; a goody bag; a little of what they usually buy for free or at a discount; let your customer choose their free gift up to a certain value; a free session; a voucher to redeem at a local restaurant; Marks & Spencer or Amazon vouchers, or vouchers for your business; a food hamper sourced with local food; a pampering kit supporting local or fair-trade suppliers.

The incentives that you offer must be appropriate to your brand, and be positively received by your customers. You don't want your referral scheme to backfire because you are asking for too much for too little. For this reason you may want to consider piloting your first referral scheme with a small handful of customers and seeking their feedback before rolling out to your whole customer base.

- **If you are struggling for inspiration, take a look at what your competitors are doing** and pay closer attention to the sales literature that you receive from the businesses that you use. One business, CNC, provides high-level outsourced IT support to small and medium-sized businesses. They have built up a loyal client base over many years. When they launched their first customer referral campaign for IT service contracts, they offered an iPad as an incentive for any recommendation that resulted in a new contract. It is a thoughtful, popular and high-value gift that, as you can imagine, was very well received by customers. One recommendation from an existing customer could be worth thousands of pounds of long-term business to CNC so the cost of the gift was acceptable given the potential value of the new client. The gift was also appropriate for their brand and their services. By contrast, Mantra Magazines offered a £20 Marks & Spencer's voucher to businesses currently advertising with them as a reward for any new advertisers that came on board as a result of their recommendation.

- **It's not always appropriate to introduce a formal incentive scheme** such as the type we have discussed so far. Your customers may not be allowed to take gifts for recommendations. This applies to many organisations in the public sector, for example. In these situations you are better placed to rely upon the goodwill of your existing customers, but you can still accelerate the recommendation process. For example, Advent IT provides bespoke software and data collection solutions to medical research teams in hospitals, colleges and schools. It would be inappropriate for Advent IT to offer clients a gift to recommend their service to other medical research teams. Not only would this damage their brand, which over many years has become trusted and respected in the medical sector, but incentives are prohibited. Instead, Ian Brownbill, the Managing Director, meets regularly with clients to discuss the progress of their project and to ascertain if there are other research teams that would benefit from Advent IT services and expertise. In these circumstances it pays to be specific about what you are looking for. You make it easier for your clients to recommend you as a consequence.

- **Don't request recommendations at too early a stage** in your relationship with a customer. Asking a brand-new customer to recommend you before they have built sufficient trust and confidence in your business is best avoided. They will still be at the stage of evaluating you and will therefore be reluctant to recommend you too early. By the same token, asking lapsed customers should be avoided. Instead, work on re-building these relationships rather than asking for referrals. Resist the temptation, therefore, to mail all your customers in one fell swoop with your referral campaign.

Consider starting with the customers that you know are fans of your business. Don't assume that they are already recommending you. It may not have occurred to them to do so and they may be unaware that you are seeking recommendations.

- **If you know your customers well, you are in a prime position** to decide who should be included in your formal and planned referral schemes, those that should be excluded, and whether your VIP customers warrant a more personal approach altogether.

- **After launching your customer recommendation campaigns, maintain a keen eye on the results,** measuring the success or otherwise of each campaign. What have you spent and how much new business have you gained as a direct consequence? Don't forget to thank each customer that recommends you with a personal message or a phone call in addition to their promised incentive. This small but important gesture will often have more impact than any tangible gift.

Of course, the best way to get your customers to recommend you is to consistently exceed their expectations. Over time this alone should lead to numerous positive recommendations, making any formal referral schemes that you introduce just the icing on the cake!

4. We Are Thinking About Organising a Seminar to Promote Our Business. What's the Best Way of Going About This?

Seminars are an effective way of showcasing your business to a captive and receptive audience. In order to help generate business when I first started up The Marketing Gym Ltd, I ran three seminars over six months. This resulted in many new clients and warm recommendations. For many businesses, particularly those that provide services to other businesses, a seminar enables them to share their expertise with a hand-picked audience. In doing so they can inspire people to want to do business with them, while at the same time further establish their status as an expert. A well-organised and content-rich seminar can also lead to a generous amount of PR for a business in local newspapers or magazines. With a little planning, it is possible to arrange a seminar on a shoestring budget. Here are my tips for doing so:

1. **Start with the basics - your venue.** Whether paying to attend a seminar or not, the attendees will expect a decent and convenient venue. Try to secure one with plenty of free on-site parking plus good rail and road links. Don't book a venue on the strength of the images on their website. Visit in person. Ideally, you are looking for a spacious, light and airy venue with plenty of room for people to network beforehand and afterwards. The acoustics in the room must be good too. A room with a vaulted high ceiling may look spectacular but it can wreak havoc with the sound. If you need a microphone and audiovisual equipment, make sure it's included in the price for the room. You should also confirm the maximum number of people that the room can comfortably hold. Do you prefer

the seats to be in rows or will it be more appropriate for your guests to be seated in small groups around tables? The seating pattern can influence the running of your seminar. Always negotiate on the price for the room hire and refreshments and check out the cancellation policy. If the worst comes to the worst and you have to cancel or postpone the event, it pays to know the extent of your financial liability. What's the earliest time that you can gain entry to the room? Allow yourself at least one hour before the start of the seminar to organise the room. You do not want to be still arranging the room when your guests are turning up. The same goes for the finish time too. Having to turf your guests out at the precise moment the seminar has ended because the room has to be vacated is not a good note to end on. Don't underestimate the impact that a lovely venue has in attracting people to your seminar and ensuring that they have an enjoyable experience.

2. **When is the best time and day to hold your seminar?** There are no hard and fast rules as to whether your seminar should be held on a morning, afternoon or evening, on a weekday or at the weekend. What you decide should come down to your target audience and their preferences. Why not ask some of them? Don't be guided solely by your own preferences. You are not selling the seminar to yourself.

3. **Although a free seminar could pay for itself in new clients, you may want to consider making a charge for your event.** It's not necessarily the case that more people will attend a free seminar than one they need to pay for. If your content is dazzling, your speakers have a good

reputation and there are not already similar seminars being offered by your competitors, you may want to make a small charge for each attendee to help cover your costs. Alternatively, if you decide not to charge for the event, why not consider a sponsor to help pay some of your costs in exchange for some promotion at your seminar? I have attended numerous free seminars at which a sponsor was sitting by a small table displaying their exhibition banner and their promotional literature. They were also promoted in the invitations. This arrangement can work particularly well if your sponsor's products or services complement what you offer.

4. **Who do you want to invite to your seminar?** Cold prospects, warm prospects, lapsed clients, potential introducers, influencers? Start your list in plenty of time as there's every chance that you will keep adding to it and making changes. If you are aiming to gain new business from your seminar, then it's a good idea to invite some of your existing clients too. Potential clients will then be able to speak with people who will be happy to vouch for your services. You may want to consider organising more than one event in order to segment your audience further and so deliver more highly targeted content. One of my clients, an independent financial advisor, is adept at this. She organises two free seminars every year. One seminar is aimed at chartered accountants - potential introducers for her services, and the other at small business owners that commission her services directly. Consequently she is able to tailor each seminar specifically to the needs of each audience.

5. **Don't skimp on the time spent planning your seminar.** Content is most definitely king, so treat it as such. Once you know your audience, you need to work on content that is not only topical, relevant and interesting but that is also inspiring and empowering. Your seminar may be free but the audience are giving up their time to attend and are unlikely to be pleased if you use the seminar as a ruse to promote your business. You may want to consider inviting another speaker to share the seminar with you, again on the basis that they are going to add value to each attendee's experience. This also takes the pressure off you to run the entire event yourself. A second speaker should also have their own pool of contacts and will therefore provide a new source of potential clients. I have seen this work very well at several events. For example, a search engine optimisation company running a free seminar on 'How to increase the visitors to your website in 10 easy steps' invited a copywriter specialising in writing information rich content for websites. The copywriter shared useful tips with the audience about how they could improve the copy on their website so that it would better appeal to their website visitors. If you are unsure about the content for your seminar, ask your clients and other contacts what topics they would be interested in learning about. You may find that there are one or two topics that would be of interest to a large number of people.

6. **When you have decided on the content of your seminar, you need to focus on how best to deliver it**. The most inspiring and helpful information can be difficult to absorb if delivered by the same person with no audience

interaction or breaks. If we take a two-hour seminar as an example, ensure that each speaker talks for no longer than 30 minutes, with time added for questions and answers. Also arrange for a couple of short networking breaks. Involve the audience from the start with an icebreaker exercise, such as getting each person to introduce the person sitting next to them to the other attendees. Split the audience into small groups and ask each group to discuss a topic relating to the subject of the seminar. Ask a nominated speaker from each group to share the key points of the discussions. This will keep the energy flowing in the room and the audience focused on your message.

7. **Once you have found your venue, planned your content**, practised your delivery and finalised your guest list, it's then the hardest task of all - getting people to turn up! Allow six to eight weeks between setting the date for your seminar and marketing it. Sending invitations by e-mail and sitting back with your fingers crossed may not be enough to fill your places. You usually need to promote it to every person on your list at least three times before they will start to take notice. When people have confirmed their attendance, maintain their enthusiasm with further communications, updating them with snippets of content. Encourage early responders by offering VIP seats at the front of the room and badges that show their VIP status. Make sure that the people that have not responded are aware that places are being snapped up, and remind them of what they will be missing if they don't attend. You may consider sending a lumpy mailshot as a first communication. Chapter 3 includes a letter written to

promote a 'Women Leading The Way' Conference. It succeeded in filling the remaining places at an event after previous e-mail communication had failed. It provides a template that you can adapt for your seminar.

When you are promoting your seminar, focus on the additional benefits that each person will gain from attending, such as the networking, refreshments and the lovely venue. Include your speaker biographies. Remind each confirmed attendee a few days before the seminar takes place. Send out a final communication to the people that have not yet responded, letting them know that there are a few places left if they want to attend. If numbers are low at this stage, consider adding an extra benefit. This may be in the shape of a high-value handout, e-book or White Paper, even a lovely goody bag courtesy of your sponsor.

8. **Your focus at the event should be on ensuring that everyone enjoys themselves, feels welcomed, appreciated and inspired by the content and delivery.** Steer clear of the temptation to spend too much time promoting your business. You don't need to do so. Sharing your wisdom and experience freely and demonstrating that you understand the needs of your audience is by far the best way to motivate people to want to do business with you. Enclose your sales literature in your goody bags and invite your guests to book an informal meeting with you if they are interested in finding out more about what you have to offer. Few, if any, of your guests will be resistant to receiving a follow-up call. They may not be in a position to do business with you immediately but if you have delivered a fantastic seminar, you will have sown seeds that could be harvested further down the line.

9. **Finally, after your seminar has been and gone,** don't forget to measure the impact on your bottom line. It is easy to get carried away with the feel good factor of delivering to a full audience, and you rightly deserve a pat on the back for your efforts. However, it pays to measure how much new or repeat business you have gained as a direct result of holding the seminar and, where this business has originated from. How does this compare with the cost of staging the seminar? You may have found a winning way of promoting your services but you won't know until you have done your sums.

5. How Can I Motivate My Commission Only Sales Team?

When the economy shrinks, the number of commission only contracts increases. But motivating a sales team paid solely on results can be a challenge. As I am writing this chapter, I am working with three commission only sales teams from three very different sectors - motor products, on-line credit management and local publishing. The value of a sale in each sector varies widely, from £75 for a small advert to £1,000 for an on-line credit management system. Consequently the commission earned from a sale varies also. However, I have learned that many of the principles behind motivating a commission only sales team remain the same, whatever the size or nature of the sale.

The bigger the sale, the harder it can be to close the deal. The potential buyer will usually take more time in the evaluation process before buying a more costly product or service than one that requires a modest outlay. They will want to be in possession of all of the facts and to be satisfied that their budget can afford the cost and that little, if any, risk is involved. So if your product or service requires a considerable outlay, then you will need to invest more time in training your sales team than if you are selling lower priced products. The potential buyer makes the decision to buy lower priced products or services quite quickly and so requires less persuasion.

Because of the nature of their relationship, it is unusual to find a commission only sales team with a high degree of loyalty to the business they work for. By employing them on a commission only basis, a business is in effect showing little commitment to them. Similarly, it would be unrealistic for that company to expect high levels of commitment from the sales team in return. If the product or service is marketable and the financial rewards are generous, the sales team will be loyal. But only whilst they are selling and earning good money! If the individuals within a sales team make enough money to reach their personal and financial goals and receive the right support from the business, they may stay for many years. But their decision to stay is likely to be based on their personal remuneration and on achieving their personal goals rather than any overwhelming loyalty to the company and its goals. The commission only sales person is understandably focused on earning as much money as possible, in as short a time frame as possible, and for as little effort as possible. On the whole they naturally prefer a shorter sales cycle. The decision to do business is made quite quickly and it is relatively straightforward to find the right person or group to pitch to. If they have to wait months for a sale, and therefore their commission payment, the likelihood is that they will lose interest and shift their attention elsewhere. In the main, commission only sales people prefer selling products or services for which the sales process is quite straightforward, they are supported with an ongoing lead generation programme, the pricing strategy facilitates an immediate or near immediate decision and the commission they receive is a fair reflection of the combined sum of their efforts to clinch the deal. There will of course always be exceptions to this rule - some commission only sales people will be happy to play the long game in order to scoop the highest rewards - but they tend to be in the minority.

If you employ a commission only sales team but wonder how best to motivate them, take a look at these proven tips.

- **Sales teams cannot sell effectively if they are lacking in knowledge** about the products or services they are expected to sell, the marketplace they are expected to sell into and the competitors they may encounter. Throwing a technical manual at them with an instruction to read it and 'get out there selling' can only take them so far. Time must be invested in training and motivating commission only sales teams in the same way that it is invested in salary paid employees. A comprehensive training programme is fundamental. Be prepared to pay their expenses, at least, to attend training, or better still, consider paying them for their time. Whilst many commission only sales people can see the value in a well structured training programme and therefore don't mind giving up some of their time without remuneration, they are likely to resent having to pay for travel, overnight stays and refreshments. You won't benefit if only half of your team pitches up. Don't skimp on the training under any circumstances. Build in time to find out the impact of your training on each individual. What have they really taken on board? Is it enough to enable them to sell effectively? Don't assume that because you have spent several hours extolling the benefits and virtues of what you offer that this has done the trick. How can you make the training interactive? Is it appropriate to include role-play, question and answer sessions, even multiple-choice quizzes to add variety to your training? This will also enable you to measure the impact upon each member of your sales team and to identify those individuals that need a little extra help. You may not achieve the desired results in just one session. It's usually a good idea to establish the date for the second training session at the first one, whilst your team is keen and motivated to learn.

- **Acknowledge and reward the top performers** at your training events. A framed certificate and a bottle of champagne given to the person demonstrating the highest levels of competence to market your products or services or for having the most positive attitude will help foster a friendly rivalry amongst the sales team. Sales people are naturally very competitive and like to be publicly acknowledged for their efforts.

- **Back up your face-to-face training with simple and clear notes** that cover all the points. Divide the notes into training categories - technical information, benefits, target audience, barriers and how to overcome them, and so on. Keep these notes up to date.

- **Demonstrate passion and enthusiasm** when speaking about your products or services. It will also help, if you are going to be delivering the training yourself, to have a good sales record or to have worked with sales people before. It will help you to empathise with your sales team and they will benefit from learning about your route to success. This can also be useful should an underperforming member of your team blame your products or service for being unsaleable! If you are not delivering the training yourself, it is still worth bearing in mind that on the whole, commission only sales teams prefer to be trained by a trainer with experience in the type of selling they will be expected to do. Therefore, check that any trainer you recruit has excellent selling credentials.

- **Establish a generous uncapped commission structure.** It always surprises me when a managing director bemoans the fact that they are paying their sales team too much. If you are paying big commission cheques every month it is a cause for celebration! It means that your team are doing what they are supposed to do. Don't begrudge those payments. You may need to benchmark your commission structure with what your team would be paid elsewhere to ensure that it's fair and competitive. Consider introducing some additional bonuses, maybe something for your top performers, a special achievement bonus when a particularly challenging project has been successfully completed, or a loyalty bonus. If you try to get away with paying as little as possible, you will not attract the best sales people and will engender feelings of resentment.

- **Consider introducing a lead generation programme** to support your sales team. Do you want them on the telephone trying to get appointments or are you better served if they are in front of a potential client? Only you can answer this question and it will vary depending on the product or service that you are selling. Selling advertising space in the main takes place over the telephone whereas for other professions most of the selling is face-to-face and the telephone is used only to open up the channel.

- **Although money is the key driver in retaining your commission only sales force,** you should make a point of getting to know each individual within your sales team. Find out what motivates them, their strengths and weaknesses. Do not give the impression that you have abandoned them and are only interested in their sales figures. Allocate time to listen to their concerns as you would for your salary paid staff.

- **Steer clear from overburdening your sales team with administrative tasks**. Completing reams of paperwork and chasing payments amounts to an unproductive use of their time. A commission only sales person is keen to spend as much of their time as possible in the field selling and earning money. For the same reason the paperwork they need to complete at the point of sale should be professionally designed and as easy to complete as possible.

- **Your sales team are your front line brand ambassadors.** They are the people at the sharp end, listening to objections and encountering barriers to a sale. Listen to their suggestions to improve what you offer and don't be afraid to make changes swiftly.

- **Organise sales meetings.** You may prefer to get your sales team together every couple of months or just a couple of times a year. Use these meetings to deliver additional training, to praise the top performers and the most improved performers and to re-energise the entire team.

- **Keep in touch in between meetings** with regular bulletins, phone calls and newsletters. When you learn something of relevance about a competitor, your target audience or your marketplace in general, let your sales team know. Don't assume they will be spending hours engaging in competitor research. It's your job to keep them up to speed and armed with facts, figures and benefits that will help them to sell.

- **Always be on the lookout to increase your sales team.** As mentioned earlier, you can't rely on the unrelenting loyalty from a commission only sales team. If your business needs four sales people, aim for six.

- **Pay any commission promptly.** Probably the most important point!

For further advice on this subject, I asked a successful self-employed business woman to explain how she motivates her own commission only sales teams.

Helen Reeves – Nutrimetics (*www.helen-reeves.co.uk*)

Part of the Tupperware Brands Corporation which is in the top $10 billion turnover companies, Nutrimetics is a global skin care and cosmetics business that started trading 50 years ago. Helen Reeves has built a very successful business under the umbrella of Nutrimetics. A growing part of her success has been her ability to nurture and motivate a team of like-minded self-employed consultants. Helen's tips, in her own words, for motivating and building a commission only sales team are:

- Start with your own goals and ambitions and the timescale in which you want to achieve them.

- Discovering what makes each person tick in your team is crucial. This can range from money, recognition and flexibility to friendship, working with a team, self development; the joys of running a business; the tangible rewards on offer for attainment of specific goals such as jewellery, free products, household equipment, free travel, even a company car.

- I help my consultants to set their short, medium and long term goals. When a consultant happily tells me their goals and puts an expected time limit on achieving them I know that they're confident, self motivated and on their way to success. I am a realist and never shrink from helping my team members to adjust their goals.

- Patience and being there for each person is important even if it means taking many phone calls out of hours and regularly responding to e-mails and requests for help. I am also on hand when a member of my team needs help presenting the Nutrimetics' product range to a gathering of customers or they have been invited to present Nutrimetics at networking events and seminars.

- Communicating regularly to my team is important because motivation levels fluctuate. I set communication dates and times on a regular basis and use e-mail, phone, text, Skype and of course face-to-face meetings.

- I am a huge advocate of regularly brainstorming, creating and sharing ideas to build 'colleagueship'.

- Celebrating every success with your team helps build loyalty and engenders a feel good factor. The small successes are just as worthy of celebration as the big ones.

6. How Can I Get Press Coverage for My Business?

It's a challenge for even the most resilient and tenacious business owner to get coverage in the national media. It's not impossible, but it's unlikely that you are going to find journalists clamouring for your story if you are relying on a press release alone to work its magic. Most journalists have reliable and trusted sources, such as PR agencies, feeding stories to their exact brief. It can be easier and less intimidating to start by targeting coverage for your business in local and trade publications. Alongside this you can begin the process of building relationships with journalists from the national publications by locating them on-line or finding them in the listings in printed publications. I cover how to do this in a little more detail later in the chapter. Journalists and editors are time-pressed and hungry for facts that align with their publication's subject matter. Because they are contacted by countless small businesses every day, they are likely to treat you as just another business owner trying to pitch your story to them, and treat you accordingly. You need to grab their attention by providing stories, angles and features that will genuinely inspire them and their readers. Even then you will sometimes have to accept that you won't always get a result in spite of your best efforts. A journalist does not want to listen to what amounts to the contents of your advertisement and they don't have the patience for a long winded sales pitch. Taking this all on board, however, with a little persistence, tenacity and attention to detail, you should be able to get press coverage for your business at both a local and national level. Here's how:

1. **Hone your craft before trying to focus on the national media.** Focus on the media in your local area. This includes the free community magazines that come through your door, the free and paid for local newspapers

and the glossy paid-for local magazines. Find out if they have an on-line presence too. It may be easier for you to get coverage for your business in their on-line publication. There may even be opportunities for you to write a blog or to submit regular articles, provided the subject matter is congruent with the publication and its readership. You will also need to demonstrate that you can submit a high standard of writing to their brief.

2. **If you are not comfortable writing articles and press releases,** then it's well worth scoping out your newsworthy stories and features but handing the job of writing the articles to a professional copywriter, experienced in submitting press releases to the media. A great story containing spelling mistakes and poor punctuation won't get you anywhere. Journalists and editors expect pin sharp copy, written in a style that suits their publication. Use a copywriter, and at least you'll end up with some excellent material for the news page of your website. But hopefully you may just land a prominent feature in a local publication or trade magazine with a readership largely made up of your target audiences.

3. **Use the Internet and printed publications to locate the names of the editors and journalists** for the publications you would like to be featured in. Then pick up the phone and call them, making sure that you have practised your pitch sufficiently to sound neither inexperienced nor lacking confidence. Ask what sort of content they are looking for, while having something in mind yourself. If you have not studied the publication before picking up the phone, you will be at a severe disadvantage. To impress with your

knowledge of their publication and your enthusiasm for their features, you will need to have read it from cover to cover. Explain that you are using a professional to write your press material if this is the case. If not, you will need to convince the journalist that you can write to a very high standard. They don't have time to re-write your article. So have a few pieces of your work (short and concise) available to e-mail at the end of the conversation to allow them to assess your writing ability. Ask for their editorial deadlines and whether there are any special forthcoming features that you can contribute to. You may call at just the right time. They may have an imminent deadline and have been let down by a contributor. The deadline could be only a few hours away, so having an article already prepared is always a good idea.

4. **Don't buy into the saying that 'all PR is good PR'.** The last thing that you want is coverage of your business that portrays you negatively. Think about the messages that you want to communicate and steer clear of any invitations by journalists to contribute your opinions to features that could cast you in a less than favourable light. Do you want to be associated with bad news or controversial stories? This could build the wrong impression of your business.

5. **Ensure that the news page on your website is stocked with current articles**, ready to attract the attention of a journalist looking for a story in your sector. Signpost your website visitors to your blog to reinforce the impression that you are a credible, professional business with an interesting story to tell.

6. **Search on Twitter and other social networks for the journalists and editors** with whom you are keen to build a relationship. Start following them. They will sometimes put out an SOS on Twitter for a particular story or quote. Don't sabotage what could be a good relationship by being tempted to send cheeky or cheesy Twitter messages. You may only get one opportunity to make a positive impression. Be prepared to follow a journalist for several weeks or months, only sending messages in response to their own postings when you have something relevant and of value to offer.

7. **You can often begin a good relationship with a journalist by responding** in an articulate, considered and genuine way to their on-line posts. Let the journalist know why you enjoyed reading their news, the impact it had on you. To provide an example, for a long time I have been a regular reader of the Financial Mail Women's Forum website, *www.fmwf.com*, finding the articles and features published on the site to be educational, interesting and stimulating. Every so often I would contact a journalist to comment upon a particular article that they had written, giving my opinions upon issues that they had raised and providing feedback whenever it was requested. As a result of this I was invited to write an article for the site myself, and I am now writing a fortnightly marketing column for the site.

8. **When you visit an exhibition, locate the press area** and introduce yourself to the attending journalists. Journalists tend to be relaxed in the exhibition environment and happy to chat while looking for a story that links to the

event. Share with them a well thought out, topical and interesting story or insight, one that ties in with the theme of the exhibition, and it may be your story that they write about after the event. By studying the exhibition organiser's website for any press contact details beforehand, you will be well prepared.

9. **If a journalist publishes their e-mail address within their article or column,** you can be confident that they are open to receiving e-mails. Julie Maxted, the founding licensor of the national pet minding and house sitting business, The Pets Homes and Gardens Company, took advantage of this opportunity with spectacular results. After reading a feature in the Daily Mirror about pet licensing opportunities, Julie e-mailed the journalist via the e-mail address in his article. Within 50 minutes of receiving her e-mail, the journalist contacted Julie, interested in discussing her story. Julie was well prepared. She had included her mobile phone number in the e-mail so that she could be contacted anytime and anywhere, and she had studied the franchising article in the Daily Mirror and had several interesting stories to discuss with the journalist. Consequently she was not caught on the hop when he rang. Two days after the conversation, The Pets Homes and Gardens Company was the main feature in the business section of the Daily Mirror. Invest some time writing your introductory e-mail, ensuring it is error-free and that it delivers in a few lines the reasons why readers will benefit from reading your story. A journalist is not interested in what you want to achieve from appearing in their publication. They want you to make their lives easier with a well-written, relevant and interesting piece. They

want to know that their readers will be inspired by your story too. Make sure that like Julie, you study the tone and the content of a journalist's article before sending your e-mail.

10. **Always thank a journalist for featuring your story**. If they are local, why not call in with some nice cakes? Small touches such as this can really make you stand out. If they are not local, send a charming e-mail thanking them.

11. **Above all, make sure that you actually invest time and energy** in your pursuit of getting your business featured in publications. Snatching the odd minute here and there won't yield results. Put the task of generating PR on your marketing agenda and chip away at it consistently.

I conclude with some very sound advice from two experienced and renowned women in the national media:

Helen Loveless, Enterprise Editor for Mail on Sunday

'How do I like to be approached by a business person looking to secure coverage? Well, definitely not on deadline day, as so many people do. The chance of me paying proper attention when I have subs breathing down my neck for that overdue story on business taxation is small, to say the least. While I may not know what I am missing, that doesn't help those with a wonderful business proposition either. I like to be approached with honesty and clarity. A concise summary of the business, or the idea, with the suggestion that we can speak once I have had time to think it through, always works far better than bombarding me with hyperbole and expecting me to make a decision on the spot. I almost certainly won't. But equally do be prepared to play a long game. Often I am very interested in a story or business proposition but it isn't right for that point in time. However, it may be perfect for in a month's time, or to tie in with a particular forthcoming event, so if I say please call me in a month, it is not an avoidance tactic. For me, what works well is if there is a news angle, something to make any coverage topical and up-to-the minute. A fresh angle also works well. Finally, don't promise me that this is exclusive to me if you are also contacting every other business section with the same story. It's a sure-fire way to lose my interest.'

Tabitha Cole, Freelance Journalist and Producer

'Make a journalist's life easy and research the publication before you call, finding out all of the information that is available in the public domain. Try an editorial secretary or a features assistant. It's not always a journalist that you need to speak to. Check which journalist covers which area on your target publication so that you can pitch to the right person. Do they publish advance features or 'Special Report' lists? Find out what their lead times are – some titles work months in advance. Never, ever pitch on press day. Understand the difference between news, features or comment. Be prepared to do things and to help at times when it's inconvenient - for example, at Easter and Christmas. Be on time, be accurate, don't puff up your firm and have multiple visuals and case studies available. Send the product if you can. Turn the tables round. If I was selling to you, what would you want? Journalists are just the same and equally, if not more, dismissive. If you can understand their editorial environment they're more likely to feature you.'

7. The Networking Group That I Joined is No Longer Producing Any Business for Me. What Can I Do?

Business networking is an enjoyable activity, an opportunity to meet fellow business professionals over a nice breakfast, lunch or evening drinks, to discuss business and to pass leads to one another. But although business networking can be a good investment of a business owner's time, it can just as easily prove to be unprofitable. Look closely at any business networking group and you'll find some members bemoaning their lack of referrals from their fellow members while others are benefitting from a strong pipeline of leads. If you have joined a promising networking group only to find that your leads have very quickly run dry, don't immediately look for an alternative group. It may be that changing *how* you network could release the potential of this particular group.

Here is my 'networking not working?' troubleshooting checklist.

- **Appraise your stand up presentation**. At many networking groups, you are given the opportunity to introduce your business each week to your fellow members. You are usually given a minute or so in which to do this. For some members, this brief window of time provides a great opportunity. They stand up, brimming with confidence, and speak with passion about their business. They are never at a loss for what to say and they generally captivate the members by being unpredictable in their delivery. They vary their message each week. These are usually the members that gain the most from the networking group. By contrast, others can be a little boring to listen to, repeating the same presentation every week. You can spot other members switching off as soon as they stand up. Do you know which category you fall into? Ask the successful members if they will give you some honest feedback on your presentation. Do they find it easy to understand what you sell? How straightforward do you make it for them to recommend you to their customers or even to use you themselves? Is your presentation inspiring, easy to listen to and motivating? What about your body language? Can they hear you or do they strain to catch what you are trying to say? If you don't ask these questions, there is a chance that people will simply accept any weaknesses in your presentation rather than risk embarrassing or offending you. If you deliver your presentation behind a quivering sheet of paper or you cling to your chair for support, you're unlikely to persuade people that you are the person they can recommend with confidence.

- **Let's assume that the feedback you receive suggests that your presentation has room for improvement**. What can you do to improve it? Start with the basics - your voice and body language. You have to be able to project your voice to a room full of people, so maybe you need to turn up the volume. Practice in front of the mirror at home or in the car. Try to inject some passion into your voice, some enthusiasm. Emphasise keywords. 'We have over 100 *absolutely delighted* customers.' Pause periodically to suppress the natural tendency to umm and err. Make sure that your body language supports your powerful and inspiring voice. Start off with your arms naturally by your side but then use your arms and hands to emphasise what you are saying. Look around the room, smile and nod your head, move your feet slightly so that you don't look rigid. You will be amazed at the difference this will make to your presentation. Again, practice in front of a mirror. If you need to use notes, pop a few key bullet points on a cue card. A cue card can be incorporated into a good presentation, whereas a full sheet of paper is more difficult to do so.

- **Focus on the content of your 60-second presentation.** Saying the same thing week in, week out, will only send people to sleep. Map out at least four presentations so that you are not struggling for content the night before. What can you say that will inspire people? Why not tell them a brief story about a delighted client? Or how you overcame a huge challenge for a client? Rather than letting the members know the full A-Z of your business and the benefits that you offer, focus on one or two key benefits at a time. What about some genuine offers to encourage members to use your services? Can you use some props or tools that will make you even more memorable? By way of example, when I'm sharing at a networking event, I may bring an alarm clock to emphasise how small businesses make very little time for their marketing, or I will simply hold up a copy of my book or my latest newsletter and focus on one aspect of it. Study the presentations of the successful members more closely to see if you can pick up any tips.

- **Try to make it as easy as possible for members to recommend you** to their wider pool of contacts. Be specific when telling the members of what constitutes your ideal client, even naming names if you are looking for introductions. This will make it easier for them to recommend you. Can you offer a risk-free introduction to your services, such as a free health check, MOT, or informal meeting? Your networking colleagues would probably find it easier to recommend prospects on this basis rather than produce fully-fledged clients. They are also more likely to feel comfortable about recommending you in this way to the people that they trust and value. And of course, whenever you work with a client introduced to you from your networking group, make sure to deliver in spades. You want that member to recommend you again and to let everyone at your networking group know what a great service you provided.

- **Believe that what you give out, you will get back in abundance.** How active are you at *really* trying to find warm prospects for the members in your networking group? Are you just sitting back and expecting the business to come to you without reciprocating? Evaluate the warm leads that you have passed to your fellow members. Are you reassured that you are doing your best, or could you do a little better? Realistically, you will not be able to find warm leads for every member, nor will you want to, but you do need to spend some of your time introducing those in which you have confidence to your own pool of contacts. You may need to step outside your comfort zone if you want to make warm introductions. It can be a tough call when you are busy but if you really want to build a pool of members that are loyal to you and are actively recommending you, you sometimes have to start the ball rolling by recommending them.

- **Be one of the first to arrive at your networking meetings** and try to stay a while after the event has ended. Some of the most promising and meaningful conversations occur at the start or end of the session, when people are more relaxed.

If after working through this checklist and putting the tips into practice you are still not getting results, it suggests that your networking group has lost its magic and it's time for you to move on to pastures new.

8. My New Product / Service Has Failed to Take Off. Why?

I have saved this question until last because it is without doubt the one question that I am most frequently asked by small businesses, and it requires the most detailed answer.

It can be incredibly frustrating. You invest time, money and passion into a new product or service and launch it full of hope, anticipating great success. However, sales turn out to be either poor or non-existent and you have no idea why.

It's tempting, in this situation, to resort to one of the following two courses of action:

1. Feeling dejected, deflated and lacking in confidence, you assume that there is insufficient demand for what you are offering and so you withdraw it, lamenting the amount of effort it took to bring it to market. This can be the wrong decision. There could be an awful lot of selling potential that you have not yet tapped into.

2. You step up your marketing activities. However, rather than stepping back and exploring whether the initial target audience were in fact the correct people to communicate with, or if alternative activities could be potentially more effective, you simply repeat the same process in the hope that this time it will work. If you have

relied on business networking to promote your offering, you start to attend more networking events. If you've been feverishly blogging and twittering to spread the word, you increase your blogs and start bombarding Twitter with your sales messages. If you have been targeting cold prospects with direct mail you may widen your prospecting net further but continue to attempt to catch more of the same audience. This can be a flawed strategy. Firstly, you're assuming that the tactic you have chosen is the most appropriate marketing activity. Secondly, you are making the assumption that you simply need to reach a greater share of the same audience in order to pull in the required sales. And thirdly, without even realising it, you are failing to consider whether you need to make any changes to your offering.

In order to determine the correct reaction to the poor initial sales, you need to spend time researching just why there has been little demand for an offering that you were confident would be a real winner.

Deciding to withdraw your product or service or to increase the same marketing activities may actually be the right thing to do, but the decision needs to be based on facts rather than gut instinct. There could be a number of reasons behind your initial lack of success and a knee-jerk reaction could prove to be misguided. But how do you discover the real reasons for poor sales?

Introducing The Marketing Troubleshooting Checklist

Many years ago I developed a marketing troubleshooting template - a systematic process that I work through with a business owner to identify exactly why their offering has failed to deliver. We are then able to embark on a corrective course of action with confidence, or perhaps mothball the offering if we discover that the time wasn't right to take it to market.

The troubleshooting checklist can be used in the following ways:

- **Before the launch**. Before you actually launch a new product or service, work through the checklist being scrupulously honest with your answers and undertaking the work necessary for the launch to be successful. Planning and preparation will give you the confidence that there really is a demand for what you're offering.
- **After the launch.** To determine why your product or service failed to generate sufficient demand. Rather than intensifying your existing marketing efforts in the hope that more of the same will lead to more sales, you can re-launch with absolute confidence or mothball the product or service knowing that your in-depth appraisal of the situation has led you to make a sound commercial decision.
- **To prevent complacency from creeping in**. Times may be good but it won't do any harm to work through this checklist, putting your products or services under the microscope. It will help you to positively refocus your efforts and potentially receive an even better return from your marketing activities. It can be all too easy when times are good to rest on your laurels whilst competitors

with a more proactive streak are reviewing their offering and their marketing. Put your products and services under the spotlight. Reappraise your marketing activities. You may find areas in which you can make improvements to both for a modest outlay.

If you want your business to benefit from this checklist, make sure that you set time aside to work through it. A few hours is a good starting point. This will allow you time to work through each question, take notes and hopefully arrive at accurate conclusions. Don't be tempted to start the checklist in the middle or end and work backwards. It has been designed to be worked through step-by-step from the beginning through to the end. Some sections you will breeze through whilst others will be more challenging. The checklist is likely to reveal that you are strong in some areas and are accomplishing as much as you can, whereas in other areas corrective action may be required.

Don't be disheartened if after this checklist you arrive at the conclusion that there is little point in continuing to market your offering. This does occasionally happen and it is better to discover this at the end of a diligent process, rather than continuing to market something for which there is little demand or requires more commitment than you can offer. On completion of the checklist, however, it is more usual for the business owner to realise that that there is plenty of demand for their product or service, but that their marketing strategy is responsible for the lack of sales

The Marketing Troubleshooting Checklist

In many cases, the reasons behind a lack of demand for a product or service will be found in one or more of the following categories:

1. The product or service.
2. Your competitors.
3. Your marketplace.
4. Your target audiences.
5. Your marketing toolkit.
6. Your marketing and sales methods.
7. Your marketing budget.
8. Your team.

1. The Product or Service

- **What inspired you to launch the product or service?** Did you know from your experience that there was a demand, a gap in the market that wasn't being served? Was it based on instinct or something more concrete?

- **Have you carried out any research?** Have you spoken to potential customers about what influences them when buying, the price they would be willing to pay, how they currently buy and what would make them buy from you? Do you understand their dominant needs? How does this research influence your product or service?

- **Do you have a clear price strategy?** Have you decided to charge less than, the same as or more than your competitors? Is this for a limited period or ongoing? Can you justify your pricing strategy so that customers do not think you are offering either an inferior or overpriced service? What has determined the selling price for your product or service?

- **Are there any elements of your product or service that are genuinely unique?** How do you know this? Does your research demonstrate this uniqueness? Do you know if customers value this uniqueness and are willing to pay for it?

- **Have you sought accreditations or endorsements** from influential people or trade bodies for your product or service to make it even more appealing? This is something that will help to break down resistance from your targeted customers.

- **Have you tested your product or service on friends, relatives or colleagues?** Have you run any trials with potential customers and smoothed out any glitches, taking on board their constructive feedback? Can their positive feedback be used as genuine case study or testimonial material?

2. **Your Competitors**

- **Have you undertaken any competitor research?** If not, what are your reasons for not doing so?

- **Who are your competitors?** Why do you believe they are your competitors? Are your competitors based in the same geographic area as you, targeting the same customer base? Do prospects mention your competitors when you talk with them?

- **Being ruthlessly honest, why do you think competitors are more successful than you?** Have they been trading for much longer than you and are therefore better established? Are they more active with their marketing? Do they have a more effective sales team? Do they offer better payment terms than you? Do they seem to be held in higher esteem? Do they hold better endorsements or qualifications? Is their product or service more in tune with what customers need? Have they built strong relationships with introducers/ strategic partners? Do they command more allegiance from re-sellers and strategic partners through better remuneration and sales support?

- **Have you considered how you can successfully compete** without having to make dramatic changes to what you are offering?

- **What can you learn from your competitors** to improve your product or service and so make it as appealing or more so than their offerings?

- **Are you in an intensely competitive marketplace?** Have you underestimated the amount of time it will take to generate sales and build up a presence?

3. **Your Marketplace**

- **Do you know all the potential marketplaces** for your product or service? Are you targeting the right marketplace? Have you any previous experience in this marketplace?

- **Have you researched the marketplaces** into which you are launching your product or service? Do you know the influential associations and membership organisations that could promote your product or service? Do you know the magazines, journals and newspapers that are read in this marketplace, and the on-line social networks in which hot prospects gather?

- **What is now happening in the marketplaces** in which you are promoting your product or service that could lead to a lack of sales? Are people spending less or switching to lower-cost alternatives in a bid to save money? Is your offering becoming obsolete?

- **What opportunities exist in those marketplaces** that you are yet to target?

4. **Your Target Audiences**

- **Have you identified the groups** of people that have the greatest need for what you are offering? Are you targeting these groups specifically with your marketing?

- **Are you relying too much upon your networking** activities to find the right people to buy from you?

- **Have you defined your positioning statement?** Are you absolutely clear about the benefits you are offering and the needs you are satisfying for each specific sector?

- **Have you carried out any research** into how people arrive at the decision to buy your product or services and whether more than one person is involved in the decision-making process?

- **Have you underestimated the amount of time** it takes for people to make the decision to do business with you?

- **Have you determined which audience to target** initially and why?

- **How many people are you actually targeting?** You may discover that you are in fact targeting fewer people than you think.

5. Your Marketing Toolkit

- **How professional and attractive is your marketing toolkit?** How does it compare with competitors?

- **Do you have a compelling sales message** based on your positioning statement and your knowledge of your target audiences?

- **Are you using case studies,** positive testimonial and PR to further enhance the appeal of your communications?

- **Are you relying on on-line communications** purely because they are cheaper than printed ones?

6. Your Marketing and Sales Methods

- **Have you decided upon the most effective communication channels** for the audiences you are looking to target? Is there evidence to support your decision?

- **Have you used The Continuum of Behaviour** (see Chapter 1) to plan a blended marketing communication programme for your target audience rather than isolated marketing activities?

- **Have you tested your approaches** and evaluated the results, making any changes in the light of the initial responses?

- **Have you considered any special offers** or incentives to encourage people to trial or buy your offering?

7. Your Marketing Budget

- **Have you allocated a budget?** Is it based on a calculation of all of your costs?

- **Are you curtailing any essential marketing activity** due to the restrictions of your budget?

- **Do you fear that the restrictions of your budget** will impact upon your ability to bring your offering to market successfully? If so, how?

- **Are you investing your budget in activities** that will deliver the results you require? Is there a risk that you are being too optimistic by not taking the strategic approach of matching the activities with the audience?

8. Your Team

- **Have you allocated sufficient time** and resource into planning and launching this offering?

- **Have you trained your team** adequately?

- **Have you used your team wisely,** working in collaboration to achieve results?

- **Do you believe that you have the most appropriate people** working on delivering this new offering? Have you got the right mix of experience and skill?

As mentioned earlier, this checklist is useful in prompting you to re-visit those areas that can have an impact upon the success or otherwise of a product or service launch. If the checklist is used prior to the launch it will hopefully help prevent any unnecessary and costly mistakes from being made beforehand. If completed after an unsuccessful launch, it should help provide the answers to why things have gone wrong.

You have reached the end of this book...

I hope that you have enjoyed reading The Ultimate Small Business Marketing Book and more importantly that you have found it useful and can see how it will help you to grow your business. I like to visualise the book as being covered in post-it notes, with scribbles in the margins and sections highlighted with a marker pen.

Now it is time to apply what you have learnt within these pages to your business. Don't worry that everything must be perfect before you begin. To quote a rather clichéd, but apt phrase, 'An imperfect plan today is better than a perfect plan tomorrow.'

I really do enjoy receiving feedback from my readers. It was lovely when it happened with my first book and I would be equally pleased to receive any comments or feedback that you may have on this book too. If you would like to contact me, you can do so through my website *www.themarketinggym.org*

I am also a keen marketing blogger and so if you would like to read a fortnightly dose of marketing insights, please visit The Blick Blog, again through my website, *www.themarketinggym.org*. Comments are always welcome there too.

Kind regards,
Dee

Acknowledgements

As a young girl, I can remember being asked on many occasions what I wanted to do when I grew up. ‘A geography teacher and an author’ was my stock response. Given that I was told to drop geography at the tender age of 15 because I found working my way around the world map to be a challenge to say the least, I am pleased to have been able to fulfil my other ambition. I was the geeky kid that always asked for extra English homework. I couldn't compose enough stories to satiate my hunger for writing so it seemed inevitable that I would choose marketing as a career - the opportunity to develop and write stories, and get paid for them. Then about 22 years into my marketing career, I decided that enough was enough. It was time to stop talking about writing a book and to roll up my sleeves and get on with it. I enjoyed it so much that a couple of years later I decided to write another book, a sequel to the first.

As any author will testify, writing a book can be a fulfilling but isolating process. You lock yourself away for hours on end, months at a time, eventually emerging into the sunlight with a manuscript that you’re happy to put your name to. Of course, your editor begs to differ and so you retreat back into your office, rewriting, rephrasing, and adding the final touches until you have a book that really is worth publishing in both yours and your editor’s eyes. I have never written a play, but I would imagine that the process of writing a book is not that dissimilar. Whilst the author is a pretty important part of the team, they are just one element in a process that requires the input of many for its successful execution. And so there are some truly talented, generous and supportive people that I would like to say ‘thank you’ to. Without their involvement I would have been lost, and The Ultimate Small Business Marketing Book would not have seen the light of day.

I will always be thankful to Lawrence Howard, the Managing Director of Hands Free Computing. Lawrence actually saved my marketing business from plunging into a dark hole when Repetitive Strain Injury affected my arms and shoulders to the extent that I could no longer type, and my handwriting arm would go on strike for intermittent periods of time. Lawrence introduced me to the magical powers of Dragon Speech Recognition Software and his very patient and kind trainers showed me how to use it. This book has been entirely dictated using speech recognition software. Thank you Lawrence; neither book would have been possible without your timely intervention.

My publisher, Chris Day, has been a joy to work with - always friendly, approachable and positively brimming with great advice. Thank you too to the incredibly talented and knowledgeable experts that have been willing to share their advice freely in this book, with no incentive other than the desire to help. They are; Paul Hopwood, Lesley Morrissey, Karen Skidmore, Sam Garrity, Dawn Brewer and Sue Atkins. I have to thank the many readers of my first book that contacted me enquiring when the sequel was arriving. Without your encouragement this book would probably still be in the 'mulling it over' stage now.

My favourite photographer, Andrew Bennett, was responsible for my author picture and for making me look like me, but at my very best. If you love the jacket of this book as much as I do, that's down to the super-talented Melanie Tilley. My two good friends Chris Baister and Claire Palmer were always on hand to give me advice and support, and listened patiently as I rattled on about the latest stage in my writing endeavours.

Finally, I have to pay tribute to my incredible family. My husband Malcolm has been a constant support. No one but your husband can offer the searingly honest feedback that compels you to return to the drawing board and rewrite a passage that you have previously thought was pretty damned good! My two sons Steven and Mark, although naturally not obsessively preoccupied with their Mother's writing endeavours, have now and again shown a flicker of interest in what was going on, and my brother Andrew has been fantastic - always there to offer wise words and a seemingly never ending enthusiasm for my work. My sister-in-law Caroline is one in a million too, as are my in-laws Rosalyn and Alan.

But the final heartfelt thanks have to go to my Mum, Ann Haley. When I rewind back to being that young girl again, it is my Mum's voice that I hear, a constant voice of encouragement and reassurance, telling me that I did have the ability to go to university and that one day I would achieve my dreams of writing a book.

Also by Dee Blick

Powerful Marketing on a Shoestring Budget for Small Businesses

Over 250 proven, simple and effective marketing tips, tools and strategies to transform your small business.

Chapters

1. The Practical Small Business Marketing Plan
2. The Secrets of Successful Networkers
3. How to Turn a Cold Call in to a Warm Lead
4. Powerful Targeted Direct Mail
5. Make Your Advertising Pay
6. Exhibition Skills to Bring Home the Business
7. Hold the Front Page! How to Win with PR
8. E-marketing gems for non-technical people (By Gareth Sear)

"This book should be required reading for anyone looking to grow their business. It ranks alongside Michael Gerber's *E-Myth* as essential guidance to all SMEs. What makes this book stand out is not the fact that it is choc-full of useful tips for building sales, but the way the messages are easy to read, a style which can be readily applied to businesses to get significant, long-term results without having a degree or in-house marketer." **Federation of Small Businesses**

At the time of going to press, Powerful Marketing on a Shoestring Budget for Small Businesses had been in the top 5 bestselling small business marketing books on *www.amazon.co.uk* for over 12 months, with 33 five-star reader reviews.

Details

- **Title:** Powerful Marketing on a Shoestring Budget for Small Businesses
- **Paperback:** 276 pages
- £13.99
- **Publisher:** AuthorHouse (8 Dec 2008)
- **Language:** English
- **ISBN-10:** 1438937539
- **ISBN-13:** 978-1-4389-3753-3
- **Product Dimensions:** 22.8 x 15 x 2 cm